There is too little 'action research' in the field of restorative and criminal justice. This collection of essays is therefore a welcome addition to scholarship on conflicts in 'intercultural' settings. While there has been some empirical work on Northern Ireland, the chapters on Austria, Hungary and Serbia provide readers who are very familiar with Anglo-American research with something new.

Carolyn Hoyle, *Professor and Director of the Centre for Criminology, University of Oxford, UK*

The volume presents a variety of approaches for dealing constructively with conflicts and a treasure of expertise collected in different geographic areas, starting from Scandinavia, up to Central and South-East Europe. It is based on a fruitful and multidisciplinary cooperation between scholars and practitioners from Norway, Belgium, Austria, Hungary, Serbia and Northern Ireland. Some of them have a solid track record in restorative justice in the field of criminology, others are experts in mediation, conflict transformation and conflict resolution in local communities or intercultural settings, and others are eager to cope with the legacies of violence in post-war societies. All case studies have one finding in common: in certain settings, involving stakeholders and making them take responsibility for problem-solving will offer more convincing and sustainable paths to justice and security, rather than institutionalized forms that rely on the force of law or violence. Moreover, the book gives insights in a highly innovative approach: it demonstrates that action research is a very appropriate way to address these sensitive issues, as it involves the people on the ground and allows for trust-building and mutual learning between those who work in and on conflicts, and those who are stakeholders and those who observe and analyze (or facilitate) the process.

Dr Martina Fischer, *Peace Researcher and Political Scientist, Berlin, Germany*

Action Research in Criminal Justice

To understand how people experience justice and security is a challenging task in times of unrest, marked by growing perceptions of insecurity, discrimination and uncertainty. The European project ALTERNATIVE aimed to understand justice and security experiences related to conflicts in intercultural settings, when citizens are given the means to actively contribute to these processes.

This book relates how the project was set up as an action research through the concrete description of four action sites: social housing estates in Vienna, Austria; a small community in Hungary with a Roma population; three border towns in Serbia; and three communities in Northern Ireland. These four sites have been compared through an innovative methodology, which leads to a deeper understanding of the impact of participatory and restorative justice oriented processes, and – in a more general way – of what action research may entail in the criminological field. Bringing together researchers and case studies from around Europe, this book examines the scientific potential of action research as a methodology in criminal justice settings.

This book is one of two volumes resulting from the work by a group of researchers in six European countries having cooperated intensively during four years in ALTERNATIVE, an action research project funded under the EU Seventh Framework Programme.

Inge Vanfraechem is affiliated researcher at the KU Leuven Institute of Criminology, where she has worked for many years as senior researcher and co-promoter on national and European projects with regards to restorative justice. She also runs her own business in consultancy and research (Libra).

Ivo Aertsen is Full Professor of Criminology at the University of Leuven and leads the Leuven Institute of Criminology Research Line on 'Restorative Justice and Victimology'. His main fields of research and teaching are victimology, penology and restorative justice. He is Editor-in-Chief of *Restorative Justice: An International Journal*. He was the academic coordinator of the European FP7 project ALTERNATIVE.

Routledge Frontiers of Criminal Justice

www.routledge.com/Routledge-Frontiers-of-Criminal-Justice/book-series/RFCJ

40 The Penal Voluntary Sector
Philippa Tomczak

41 Transforming Summary Justice
Modernisation in the Lower Criminal Courts
Jennifer Ward

42 Stop and Search and Police Legitimacy
Ben Bradford

43 Young Offenders and Open Custody
Tove Pettersson

44 Restorative Responses to Sexual Violence
Legal, Social and Therapeutic Dimensions
Edited by Estelle Zinsstag and Marie Keenan

45 Policing Hate Crime
Understanding Communities and Prejudice
Gail Mason, JaneMaree Maher, Jude McCulloch, Sharon Pickering, Rebecca Wickes and Carolyn McKay

46 The Special Constabulary
Historical Context, International Comparisons and Contemporary Themes
Edited by Karen Bullock and Andrew Millie

47 Action Research in Criminal Justice
Restorative Justice Approaches in Intercultural Settings
Edited by Inge Vanfraechem and Ivo Aertsen

48 Restoring Justice and Security in Intercultural Europe
Edited by Brunilda Pali and Ivo Aertsen

49 Monitoring Penal Policy in Europe
Edited by Gaëtan Cliquennois and Hugues de Suremain

50 Big Data, Crime and Social Control
Edited by Aleš Završnik

Action Research in Criminal Justice

Restorative Justice Approaches in Intercultural Settings

Edited by Inge Vanfraechem and Ivo Aertsen

Routledge
Taylor & Francis Group
LONDON AND NEW YORK

First published 2018 by Routledge

2 Park Square, Milton Park, Abingdon, Oxfordshire OX14 4RN
52 Vanderbilt Avenue, New York, NY 10017

Routledge is an imprint of the Taylor & Francis Group, an informa business

First issued in paperback 2019

British Library Cataloguing in Publication Data
A catalogue record for this book is available from the British Library

Library of Congress Cataloging in Publication Data
Names: Vanfraechem, Inge, editor. | Aertsen, Ivo, editor.
Title: Action research in criminal justice : restorative justice approaches in intercultural settings / edited by Inge Vanfraechem and Ivo Aertsen.
Description: Abingdon, Oxon ; New York, NY : Routledge, 2018. |
Series: Routledge frontiers of criminal justice ; 47 | Includes bibliographical references and index.
Identifiers: LCCN 2017017397| ISBN 9781138120914 (hardback) |
ISBN 9781315651453 (ebook)
Subjects: LCSH: Restorative justice. | Action research. | Criminal justice, Administration of.
Classification: LCC HV8688 .A28 2018 | DDC 364.6/8–dc23
LC record available at https://lccn.loc.gov/2017017397

ISBN: 978-1-138-12091-4 (hbk)
ISBN: 978-0-367-22751-7 (pbk)

Typeset in Times New Roman
by Wearset Ltd, Boldon, Tyne and Wear

Inge Vanfraechem would like to dedicate this book to Jan and Lea Vanfraechem, as well as to Koen, Mirthe, Stinne and Maurice Danhieux.

Ivo Aertsen from his side takes the opportunity to celebrate the Leuven living and working environment.

Contents

Figures

Tables

Contributors

Ivo Aertsen is Full Professor of criminology at the University of Leuven (Belgium). He holds degrees of psychology, law and criminology from the same university. At the Leuven Institute of Criminology (LINC) he is leading the Research Line on 'Restorative Justice and Victimology'. His main fields of research and teaching are victimology, penology and restorative justice. He has been chair of the European Forum for Restorative Justice (EFRJ) from 2000 to 2004, and has coordinated COST Action A21 on Restorative Justice research in Europe from 2002 to 2006. He has been expert for the UN, the Council of Europe, the OSCE and the European Union. Furthermore, he was appointed as expert to the Belgian Parliamentary Commission on sexual abuse in the church (2010–2011), followed by membership of the Permanent Arbitration Chamber on sexual abuse (2012–2016). He is Editor-in-Chief of *Restorative Justice: An International Journal*. In ALTERNATIVE he acted as the European academic coordinator.

Gabriella Benedek is a researcher and social development professional. She is active in the field of restorative justice since 2005. Besides her involvement with issues of justice, security, and social exclusion, she has been actively working with local and small communities, and community foundations in various capacities. Her professional approach is characterized by solidarity, community and participation as target values, as well as respect for change and the acceptance of its unpredictability. She lives and works in Budapest with her family. She is a project manager at the Foresee Research Group, and works in the core team of the national support programme for community foundations. She is supervisory board member of the Hungarian Association for Community Development and member of the board of the Roots and Wings Foundation. She also chaired the board of the Ferencváros Community Foundation in her local community for six years until 2016. At an international level she is associated with the European Community Development Network (EuCDN) and the European Forum for Restorative Justice. In ALTERNATIVE, she was leader of Work Package 5 – 'Practicing encounters'.

Hugh Campbell is a Senior Lecturer in the School of Sociology and Applied Social Studies at Ulster University. From 2003 he has led the Restorative

Practice developments in the University. This has meant: co-authoring the Northern Ireland Youth Conference Service Practice Manual; the establishment of Post Graduate Diploma and Master's programmes in Restorative Practices and an undergraduate Certificate; management and delivery of the above programmes; and engagement with the practice field in Northern Ireland. Prior to 2003 he was the Course Director for the BSc Hons in Community Youth Work at the University. He also has a long background in sports coaching in rugby, soccer, Gaelic football and athletics.

Tim Chapman is Visiting Lecturer at Ulster University in Northern Ireland, UK, teaching on the Master's in Restorative Practices. He has contributed to the development of restorative conferencing in both the voluntary and statutory sectors in Northern Ireland. He spent 25 years working in the Probation Service in Northern Ireland. He played an active part in developing effective practice in the UK particularly through the publication of *Evidence Based Practice*, written jointly with Michael Hough and published by the Home Office. His 'Time to Grow' model for the supervision of young people has influenced youth justice practices especially in Scotland. He has published widely on restorative justice and effective practice and has conducted significant research into restorative justice in Northern Ireland including the ALTERNATIVE project. In 2015 he wrote with Maija Gellin and Monique Anderson 'A European Model of Restorative Justice with Children and Young People'. He is chair of the Board of the European Forum for Restorative Justice. In ALTERNATIVE, he was leader of Work Package 7 – 'Activating community through a multi-agency approach'.

Sanja Ćopić is Senior Research Fellow at the Institute of Criminological and Sociological Research in Belgrade and a researcher and president of the Executive Board of the Victimology Society of Serbia. She has participated in numerous research and action-oriented projects on victims of crime, domestic violence, human trafficking, discrimination, reconciliation, victim support and restorative justice, and has published extensively on these topics. The main focus of her recent work has been on the use of restorative justice in criminal matters and victim's position in Restorative Justice programmes, and applying restorative approaches in intercultural settings. She is Deputy Editor of *Temida* – an academic journal on victimization, human rights and gender, published by the Victimology Society of Serbia. In the past years she was also engaged with research conducted by the Victimology Society of Serbia and other European research institutions within the EU-funded FP7 research project ALTERNATIVE, where she acted as leader of Work Package 6 – 'Fostering victim-oriented dialogue'.

Éva Győrfi holds, among other positions, those of a lawyer, expert in communication, and mediator. She is also active as a childwelfare and children's rights specialist, and as a trainer in the field of restorative practices. She has been working as a facilitator and counsellor in the Foresee Research Group in

Budapest, Hungary, where she was involved in the action research part for the ALTERNATIVE project. She is also directing a group of professionals for development of school social work and child well-being at KONTIKI Educational Centre.

Ida Hydle is Norwegian Research Professor at NOVA, the Welfare Research Institute, University College of Applied Sciences in Oslo and Akershus, and Adjunct Professor at the University of Tromsø, Department of Social Work and Child Protection. She holds PhD degrees in medicine and social anthropology. She has experience from practical work as a medical doctor within social medicine and rehabilitation, geriatrics and mental health work as well as teaching and training at all academic levels, research planning and implementation within social medicine, mental health work, medical and legal anthropology, visual cultural studies and peace studies, restorative justice and restorative practice studies. In ALTERNATIVE, she took the lead for Work Package 2 – 'Conflict transformation analysis'.

Katrin Kremmel is a PhD candidate at the Social and Cultural Anthropology Department of the University of Vienna, where she works on asylum practices, statehood and citizenship in a rural Austrian town. Prior to her PhD studies, she worked as a researcher at the Institute for the Sociology of Law and Criminology (IRKS) in Vienna, where she pursued her research interests in migration and legal sociology within the ALTERNATIVE project, where she was the leader of Work Package 4 – 'Activating civil society'.

Philip McCready is a lecturer and researcher in the School of Criminology, Politics and Social Policy at Ulster University in Northern Ireland. He was awarded a PhD by Ulster University for his thesis on the capacity of community-based restorative justice to activate civil society within a working-class Loyalist area in South Belfast. He has a degree in Law and an MSSc in Criminal Justice from Queen's University Belfast. His current research as part of a European Commission Horizon 2020 project Gaming For Peace (GAP), led by Trinity College Dublin, aims to generate an online-based training curriculum for personnel involved in conflict prevention and peace-building missions. His lecturing and research interests include theories of crime and deviance, young people in conflict with law and justice, restorative justice and the role of restorative practices in response to legacy issues of hegemonic and patriarchal control by state and paramilitaries in post-conflict societies.

Vesna Nikolić-Ristanović is Full Professor of criminology, victimology, juvenile delinquency and child abuse at Belgrade University/Faculty for Special Education and Rehabilitation, director of the Victimology Society of Serbia, active member of the European Academy of Sciences and Arts, and former president of the European Society of Criminology. Her research work is focused on war victimization, violence against women, truth and reconciliation, restorative justice, yoga, victim support and trafficking in people. She is the initiator and coordinator of the 'Association Joint Action for Truth and

Reconciliation' in Serbia. In the past years she was also engaged with research conducted by the Victimology Society of Serbia and other European research institutions within the EU-funded FP7 research project ALTERNATIVE. She is a founder and Editor-in-Chief of *Temida*, the journal on victimization, human rights and gender. She is an author and co-author of a large number of books, book chapters and articles published in Serbia and abroad.

Christa Pelikan is a researcher at the Institute for the Sociology of Law and Criminology in Vienna. She has been working in the field of criminal law, especially juvenile justice and in the field of family law. Starting in 1985, she has been doing accompanying research on the large Austrian pilot project on 'Victim-offender-mediation in juvenile justice' and later on a pilot project 'Victim-offender-mediation in general criminal law'. She has chaired the 'Committee of experts on mediation in penal matters' within the European Committee on Crime Problems (CDPC) and has been a member of the Criminological Scientific Council to the CDPC of the Council of Europe. She is a founding member of the European Forum for Restorative Justice and has been the chair of its 'Communication Committee', participating in various GROTIUS, AGIS, and COST projects at EU-level. She was involved in research within the project ALTERNATIVE.

Nikola Petrović is Assistant Professor at the Department of Psychology, Faculty of Philosophy, University of Belgrade and a research fellow in the Victimology Society of Serbia. He is also the Secretary General of the Association for Cognitive and Behavioral Therapies of Serbia and a member of the Ethics Board of the Association of Psychologists of Serbia. His research was primarily focused on psychotherapeutic practice and ethics, victimization and juvenile delinquency, but he also participated in action-oriented projects on topics such as domestic violence and reconciliation. He is a rational emotive behavioural psychotherapist and works in the field of individual and couples therapy. In the past years he was also engaged with research conducted by the Victimology Society of Serbia and other European research institutions within the EU-funded FP7 research project ALTERNATIVE.

Mario Ragazzi is a consultant on international development cooperation; he has worked for the Catholic Church, international non-governmental organizations and the European Union in post/during-conflict countries like El Salvador, Colombia, Pakistan and Afghanistan for a dozen years. His research interests lie with issues of state formation, institution-building and security in development.

Bejan Šaćiri is a PhD student at the Department of Psychology, Faculty of Philosophy, University of Belgrade, and a researcher in the Victimology Society of Serbia. He is involved in supporting victims in the victim support service 'VDS info and victim support', which works within the Victimology Society of Serbia. His research work has been mainly focused on discrimination, peace building, reconciliation and restorative justice, professional ethics in psychology, domestic violence, and the position of female prisoners. He is a transactional psychotherapist in training and actively works in the field of individual and marital counselling. In the past years he was also engaged with research conducted by the Victimology Society of Serbia and other European research institutions within the EU-funded FP7 research project ALTERNATIVE.

Dóra Szegő is a sociologist and PhD student at Corvinus University Budapest and a researcher at the Foresee Research Group. Her research, policy and project management work focuses on restorative justice, prison rehabilitation, ethnic minorities and other vulnerable groups in society. In 2013 she became a trained mediator at the University of New Mexico. Since 2012 she has been working in the European ALTERNATIVE project and in action research programmes led by the European Forum for Restorative Justice, as well as in a European project implementing peacemaking circles in the judicial system of three European countries. She has been working in experimental prison rehabilitation programmes with restorative approaches, including family group conferences, circles and restorative conferences.

Inge Vanfraechem is affiliated researcher at the Leuven Institute of Criminology (KU Leuven), where she has worked for many years as senior researcher and co-promoter on national and European projects with regard to restorative justice and intercultural settings, Restorative Justice (RJ) and crime prevention, RJ and victims, conferencing, and RJ and community relations/schools. Her research interests lie with victimology, restorative justice and youth justice. She is editor of *Restorative Justice: An International Journal* and an active member of the ESC Working Group on Victimology. Some of her recent publications are *Restorative Justice and Victims* (Routledge 2015, co-edited with Bolivar and Aertsen), *Justice for Victims* (Routledge 2014, co-edited with Pemberton and Ndahinda) and *Conferencing and Restorative Justice* (Oxford University Press 2012, co-edited with Zinsstag). She also runs her own business in consultancy and research (Libra). In ALTERNATIVE she acted as the European project manager.

Derick Wilson has been involved in the Corrymeela Reconciliation Community since 1965. He is Reader Emeritus in Education at Ulster University, specializing in Community Relations and Restorative Practices. He chaired the Youth Council for Northern Ireland (1987–1989); was a founder of Mill Strand Integrated School (1987–1992); a member of the Broadcasting Council for Northern Ireland; a founding Trustee of the Spirit of Enniskillen Awards; a Commissioner with the Equality Commission for Northern Ireland (2003–2008) and a member of the Victims and Survivors Forum. His doctorate was on facilitating contentious issues in mixed tradition groups. He was awarded: the MBE for Community Relations in 1994; a Distinguished Community Fellowship by the University in 2003; and a Lifetime Award for Services to Community Relations from the Northern Ireland Community Relations Council in 2007.

Acknowledgements

This book – together with a second book publication and a series of research papers – is the result of lengthy and collective efforts spent in the ALTERNATIVE project during more than four years. We are grateful to the EU, which funded the project through its Seventh Framework Programme for research and innovation, and to Carla Rocha Gomes from the Research Executive Agency, who accompanied us as project adviser. In addition to these, many people and organisations are to be thanked.

We would like to thank first of all everyone who believed in the project, everyone who supported it, but also people who questioned or challenged some of our premises and actions, as without them we would not have been able to move forward in the true spirit of participatory action research.

First of all, our deepest gratitude goes to the core teams of the ALTERNATIVE project based in our partner organisations in six European countries, who worked together as one big committed, engaged and creative team. The research participants were, more specifically: from the Leuven Institute of Criminology (LINC), KU Leuven – Ivo Aertsen, Inge Vanfraechem, Brunilda Pali and Mario Ragazzi; from the European Forum for Restorative Justice (EFRJ) – Edit Törzs, Katrien Lauwaert, Emilie van Limbergen and Emanuela Biffi; from Ulster University – Tim Chapman, Derick Wilson, Hugh Campbell and Philip McCready; from the Institute for the Sociology of Law and Criminology in Vienna (IRKS) – Christa Pelikan, Katrin Kremmel and Evelyn Klein; from the Norwegian Social Research Institute (NOVA) – Ida Hydle, Espen Marius Foss and Marie Louise Seeberg; from the Victimology Society of Serbia (VDS) – Vesna Nikolić-Ristanović, Sanja Ćopić, Nikola Petrović, Bejan Šaćiri and Jelena Srna; and from the Foresee Research Group – Borbala Fellegi, Gabriella Benedek, Gábor Héra, László Balla, Gyula Galyas, Éva Győrfi, Erika Magyar, Szilvia Süki-Szíjjártó, Dóra Szegő, Balázs Berkovits and Eszter Balogh.

Second, we would like to extend our gratitude to the local actors that were central to the work of all the project partners. Sometimes they felt supported by us, but at other times they made themselves willingly vulnerable to our research, and without that openness and trust there would have been no project. This gratitude is extended more specifically to the following persons and organisations.

On behalf of our coordinating team in Belgium, we would like to thank, for efficient administrative, budgetary and legal support, KU Leuven Research and Development, in particular Tine Heylen, Karolien Mariën and Laurent Vandevelde; for support with films, the KU Leuven Institute for Media and Learning, in particular Christoph Cammans, Erwin Heylen, Anke Pesch and Stef Stes; for the exchange of ideas with our colleagues from Brussels, Odisee University College, namely Erik Claes, Iman Lechkar and Nele Gulinck; Monique Anderson and Kris Vanspauwen for support by the European Forum for Restorative Justice Secretariat; and Nadia Fadil, Lode Walgrave and Stephan Parmentier for support for the doctoral project of Brunilda Pali. Additionally, the members of the project's Advisory Board are to be thanked for their advice and valuable input during the project: Marieke Arnou, Martina Fischer, Joachim Kersten, Tove H. Malloy, Raul Carstocea, Ilina Taneva and Bas van Stokkom.

On behalf of our team in Norway, we would like to thank employees, volunteers and participants in the Norwegian Mediation Service and Red Cross Street Mediation for willingly sharing their experiences, which have given us valuable insights as comparative ground in the project.

On behalf of our team in Austria, we deeply thank the women of the Women's Café, who so warmly welcomed us into their group, and all residents, who supported our work with their patience, openness and participation. Further, we thank the team of the community centre Bassena, who embarked on reflective journeys with us and all *wohnpartner* staff members, who provided us with insightful depictions of their work and courageously dared to explore the potential of restorative justice for neighbourhood disputes in social housing estates.

On behalf of our team in Hungary, we would like to thank all the local residents, organisations and institutions and the City and Roma Minority Council of Kisváros for supporting our action research with their ongoing contribution, participation, openness and trust and by sharing their opinion, feedback and even critical reflections with us.

On behalf of the team of the Victimology Society of Serbia, we deeply thank our local partners in three multi-ethnic communities in Serbia – Prijepolje, Bačka Palanka and Medvedja – for their support, dedicated fieldwork and commitment to exploring the potential of restorative approaches in preventing and solving problems and conflicts in their communities. Further, we thank citizens of these three local communities who participated in the survey for their trust and sharing personal stories and victimisation experiences with us as researchers: this offered valuable knowledge that helped us to better understand the context and to implement the action research. Last, but not least, we are grateful to seminar participants for their active participation and showing readiness to network and further work on promoting restorative approaches in the intercultural field. Thanks to all of them, this research was a valuable journey in exploring the potential role restorative approaches have to play in a much wider context of people's everyday life and in various relationships.

On behalf of our team in Northern Ireland, we would like to acknowledge the contribution of Mark Black and Deborah Guy from the CARE project; Harry

Maguire and Jim McCarthy from CRJI; Sam White from the Resolve Project; David Kennedy from John Jay College, New York; John McCord from Ulster University; Old Library Trust Derry City; Restorative Justice for Oakland Youth; California Intervention Network Approach, Antioch, California; The Northlands Centre, Derry City; and The Creggan Healthy Living Centre, Derry City.

Finally, we thank all those who cannot be mentioned by name, the participants and speakers in regional workshops and at our final conference, but also – at the more personal level – our families, our colleagues, the strong network of caring hands that is behind anyone and anything.

Editors,
Inge Vanfraechem and Ivo Aertsen

Introduction

ALTERNATIVE understandings of justice and security through restorative justice approaches

Inge Vanfraechem

When we set out to introduce restorative justice (RJ) practices in intercultural settings, we were surprised to (re)discover the lack of literature with regard to implementing action research in the criminological field. It is this gap the book at hand aims to fill through the detailed description and explanation on a European action research project, within four sites (Austria, Hungary, Serbia and Northern Ireland).

This book is based upon the work carried out in a European FP7 project entitled 'Developing alternative understandings of security and justice through restorative justice approaches in intercultural settings within democratic societies' (ALTERNATIVE).[1] The four-year project (2012–2016) was coordinated by the Leuven Institute of Criminology (KU Leuven, Belgium) and partners in the project were: the European Forum for Restorative Justice (EFRJ, Belgium), Norwegian Social Research (NOVA), the Institute for the Sociology of Law and Criminology (IRKS, Austria), Foresee Research Group (Foresee, Hungary), Victimology Society of Serbia (VDS) and Ulster University (UU, Northern Ireland). The results of the research are available on the website (www.alternativeproject.eu) and Film online platform (http://alternativefilms.euforumrj.org). This book offers original contributions on the action research methodology and results, while theoretical findings are spelled out in Pali and Aertsen (2018).

The ALTERNATIVE project aimed to develop alternative understandings of justice and security through the implementation of restorative justice approaches in intercultural settings. As European societies are witnessing increased diversity, questions arise on how communities can cope with the challenges faced. In public opinion, media and political discourses, the increasing diversity has often been portrayed as a threat to security, because of growing tensions and according to some even higher crime rates. Although criminological research does not provide evidence for the latter, these images persist and configure social insecurity to a large extent.

The ALTERNATIVE project challenged the link between security discourses and diversity as well as the shielding mechanisms through which communities are separated. The starting base was found in the framework of restorative justice, which views crime in a relational and social context, looking at the harm created by a conflict and searching for means to address this harm.

Restorative justice

Restorative justice emerged within the context of criminal justice from the 1970s onwards (Aertsen *et al.*, 2004). Various definitions exist, referring on the one hand to the importance of the process through which the parties in the offence communicate, as in Marshall's definition (1999, p. 5): 'Restorative justice is a process whereby parties with a stake in a specific offence collectively resolve how to deal with the aftermath of the offence and its implications for the future.' Other definitions, on the other hand, focus more on the outcome of repairing the harm, as in Walgrave (2008, p. 21): 'Restorative justice as an option for doing justice after the occurrence of an offence that is primarily oriented towards repairing the individual, relational and social harm caused by that offence.'

ALTERNATIVE wanted to examine the possibilities of introducing restorative justice approaches for conflicts in intercultural settings, thus broadening the scope of restorative justice as it had been mostly focused upon criminal acts rather than social conflicts and had not been implemented (to our knowledge) within intercultural settings. At the start of the project, a research paper focused on both principles of and practices in restorative justice (Törzs, 2012). The main practices seen as core to restorative justice are mediation, conferencing and circles. The mediation process offers victims and offenders an opportunity to meet in a safe, structured setting and to engage in a mediated discussion of the crime and its consequences. With the assistance of a trained facilitator, the parties are able to share their stories and views on what has happened, as well as the crime's physical, emotional and financial impacts (Liebmann, 2000; Umbreit, 2002). In a conference, support people for both parties as well as professional actors such as a police officer or lawyer may be involved (Zinsstag and Vanfraechem, 2012). Peacemaking or healing circles furthermore include other professional actors and representatives of the community/society and focus, besides on the harm and needs arising from it, more on societal implications and values (Pranis, 2005; Weitekamp, 2016).

From the start, ALTERNATIVE was looking towards exploring the circles' approach to dealing with conflicts on a community level. Broader models of social mediation and other practices based on non-violent communication could offer concrete examples of how to address conflicts in broader settings besides crime and the criminal justice system, to which restorative justice practices were mostly confined (Törzs, 2012). The survey undertaken in ALTERNATIVE showed that 24 out of 33 respondents apply restorative justice in intercultural settings, although none of their organizations are specifically aiming at those conflicts: they deal with conflicts in general but the background of participants may bring intercultural elements to the fore. Training on the topic, including mediators with a migrant background or bringing in translators in a mediation process are the methods most used to address interculturality. Summarizing, Törzs (2013, p. 24)

> affirm[s] that although RJ is not yet widely used in case of intercultural conflicts in Europe and specific RJ practice methods for intercultural conflict settings only exist sporadically, the topic is addressed at the level of

professional trainings and a general awareness to the topic of interculturality is present in the respondent RJ organisations.

Since the response rate to the survey was rather low, Törzs (2013) concluded that the topic of interculturality remains under the radar within the restorative justice field (see also Pali, 2014).

Conflicts in intercultural settings

In a restricted or 'negative' way, conflict has been defined as competition over resources. Avruch (s.d., p. 1) for example defines conflict as 'competition by groups or individuals over incompatible goals, scarce resources, or the sources of power needed to acquire them'. This competition is determined by the individual's perception, as well as culture, which Avruch defines as 'the socially inherited, shared and learned ways of living possessed by individuals in virtue of their membership in social groups'. According to the author, '[c]ross-cultural conflict' refers to 'conflict occurring between individuals or social groups that are separated by cultural boundaries' (p. 5).

Conflict in a more positive framework can be viewed as an opportunity to communicate and create understanding (Christie, 1977; Kremmel and Pelikan, 2013). Conflict can be seen as 'a potential for social change' (Christie, 1977): the victim gets a chance to have his/her say and relate his/her personal story while the offender can explain why he/she did what he/she did, which does not lead to exoneration. The neighbourhood and state can be involved and norm-clarification becomes possible (see Walgrave, 2008).

Terms like 'ethnicity', 'culture' and 'religion' are often used to refer to socio-cultural differences in the population. However, in conflict situations the use of these terms may sometimes not only result in confusion, but also in maintenance and escalation of conflicts. In ALTERNATIVE we have therefore deliberately chosen to use as a central term 'conflicts in intercultural settings' rather than 'intercultural conflicts' (see Foss *et al.*, 2012). The four settings studied in ALTERNATIVE (Austria, Hungary, Serbia and Northern Ireland) are defined or described as intercultural from the outset, but the conflicts may comprise as their central aspects e.g. gender, age, class or income. The framing of the conflict as comprising an intercultural element will then depend on various factors, including public opinion and politics (Ragazzi, 2015).

ALTERNATIVE as action research

Within the project, we opted for an action research approach because, on the one hand, this would offer us the flexibility to adapt the research to the realities on the ground and, on the other hand, we wanted to have an open view on the matters we were studying: rather than defining beforehand what type of restorative justice practices we would apply for what kind of conflicts, we wanted to enter the field with an open mindset.

Action research was implemented in four different settings (see infra) but the whole project as such was also set up as an action research (see Chapter 1, this volume). Three work packages developed a theoretical framework against which the four action research work packages were set: one work package on 'alternative espistemologies' dealing with (restorative) justice and security (Pali, 2015), one on 'conflict and conflict transformation analysis' (Foss *et al.*, 2012; Hydle, 2014) and one on restorative justice models (Törzs, 2013, 2014).[2] The action research was set out in Vienna, Austria (Kremmel and Pelikan, 2013, 2014, 2015), a small town in Hungary (Berkovits and Balogh, 2013; Szegő, Benedek and Győrfi, 2015; Héra *et al.*, 2015), three border towns in Serbia (Nikolić-Ristanović and Ćopić, 2013; Nikolić-Ristanović *et al.*, 2014; Ćopić and Nikolić-Ristanović, 2015) and three communities in Northern Ireland (Chapman, Wilson and Campbell, 2012; Campbell, Chapman and Wilson, 2013; Chapman *et al.*, 2013; Chapman, Campbell and Wilson, 2014; Chapman *et al.*, 2015). The action research results were fed back, according to a specifically developed methodology, into the theoretical frameworks, with a comparative work package (Ragazzi, 2015) integrating the empirical results (see Chapter 8, this volume). Dissemination activities were spread throughout the project and included a newsletter, workshops and seminars, international seminars and conferences, newsflashes, policy briefs, a Facebook page and Twitter account, an online film platform and a manual, a summer school and various publications.[3]

To get as broad a view as possible, we looked at conflicts at the micro-level (between individuals), at meso-level (between local communities) and at macro-level (on society level). The settings were chosen accordingly: micro-conflicts between neighbours with a migrant background in social housing in Vienna (Austria), meso-conflicts at the level of a small town with Roma (Kisváros, Hungary), and macro-conflicts between citizens of different ethnicity (border towns in Serbia) and between people of different religion (Catholics and Protestants) or with immigrants and drug users (Northern Ireland). (See Figure I.1.)

Through this holistic perception of conflicts related to intercultural issues, we hoped to arrive at findings that could be translated throughout Europe, always taking the local situation into account. The research shows that the 'societal ecology' (Bolivar, Pelikan and Lemonne, 2015; APAV, 2016) is crucial: findings can never 'just' be transposed from one context to another since the socio-economic, historical and societal context needs to be understood in order to enable implementing practices. Therefore, during the first year, the action researchers studied the local context to evaluate how restorative justice approaches could be implemented. While the idea was to then start implementing these practices, in all four settings it became clear that further work was needed to provide the conditions for implementing restorative justice: community work and trust building as well as training citizens in conflict resolution and non-violent communication proved to be necessary.

As the book will show, action research methods varied in the different sites. Nevertheless, the results were discussed both in local team meetings, within the

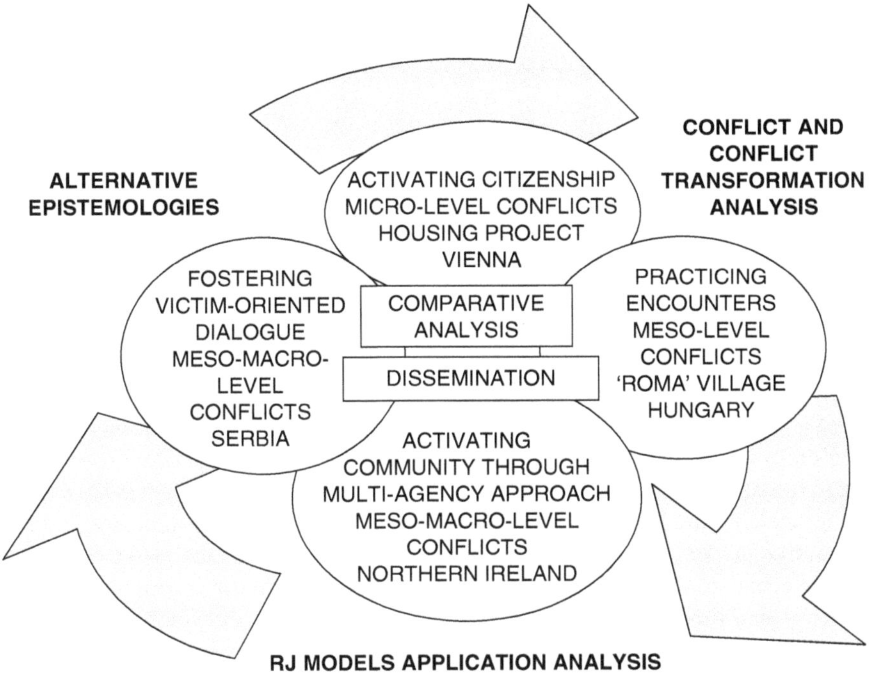

Figure I.1 Overview of ALTERNATIVE as an action research.

project's European steering committee meetings that took place twice a year and through more detailed discussions of the local partners with the research team in Leuven (see also Chapter 8, this volume).

Contents of the book

In Chapter 1, Aertsen sketches the wider scene of action research in criminology and criminal justice settings to frame the action research carried out in ALTERNATIVE. The chapter shows that, although action research has been in existance for a couple of decades, its implementation within the criminological field remains limited. Therefore, the chapters thereafter offer a detailed description of the action research implemented in the four intercultural settings in which theory and action mutually influence one another.

Hydle and Szegő first focus on the specificity of using filming as a supporting action research method. Hydle presents theoretical insights from social sciences on visual representation and visual culture in Chapter 2, while Szegő in Chapter 3 explains the various uses of filming as a participatory approach in the four settings. The Hungarian example is spelled out in more detail to give a concrete example of the potential and challenges of using filming as an action research tool.

The following four chapters are based upon a common structure in order to describe the action research as it was carried out in the four sites: the main theoretical concepts dealt with, the methods used and some of the findings. These chapters point to the commonalities and differences in the concrete action researches being situated in quite different social, cultural and political environments. This all formed important challenges for the comparative research as is shown in Chapter 8.

In Chapter 4, Kremmel and Pelikan focus on the challenge of getting involved and remaining distant when implementing action research in social housing in Vienna, Austria. The action research there from the beginning focused on the concept of active participation and tried out various methods to involve citizens in their neighbourhood, such as workshops on non-violent communication, circles and filming.

Szegő, Benedek and Győrfi explain in Chapter 5 how, in a small town in Hungary, challenges were related to turning resistance into cooperation: through their analysis of the field, the researchers found that the town dealt with conflicts through a so-called 'culture of silence' in which different groups talk about but not to one another. Through community-building efforts, the ground was laid for restorative justice practices such as mediation and circles to take place.

In Serbia, the post-war context still makes it difficult to openly discuss conflicts and therefore the researchers took the option to develop a survey on victimization and to feed the survey results into participatory seminars in which citizens of different ethnic groups were brought together to discuss a fictive case through a circle. As Nikolić-Ristanović and colleagues explain in Chapter 6, these seminars led to the creation of restorative teams and a manual, which can be used for further developing a restorative justice model in the region.

Chapman and colleagues in their research (Chapter 7) focused more on group dynamics and identities through studying and supporting community-based restorative justice. Rather than implementing restorative practices, the research team entered into dialogue with partners in the field and supported processes of change in three areas: Derry/Londonderry, focusing on drug issues; South Belfast, supporting the organization CARE to become a community-based restorative justice project; and West Belfast, capturing the organization Community Restorative Justice Ireland's (CRJI) narrative of their relationship with the state.

Despite these very different settings and action research methods, Ragazzi in Chapter 8 shows how an innovative comparative methodology was developed in order to grasp the differences and similarities in the four settings. While this is not done through a standardized survey, a qualitative comparative method was used and developed to gather descriptive findings and come to a conceptual realignment within the ALTERNATIVE project as a whole. This enabled the project to come to findings with regard to the challenges of justice and security in intercultural settings.

In the conclusion, Aertsen and Vanfraechem look back at Chapter 1 and reflect upon what can be learnt from this project with regard to action research in the criminological field as well as with regard to the further development of restorative justice.

Notes

1 This project has received funding from the European Union's Seventh Framework Programme for research, technological development and demonstration under grant agreement no. 285368. The opinions expressed throughout the book are the authors'.
2 The results of the theoretical work can be found in Pali and Aertsen (2018).
3 See www.alternativeproject.eu/publications/public-deliverables [accessed 29 March 2017].

References

Aertsen, I., Mackay, R., Pelikan, C., Willemsens, J. and Wright, M., 2004. *Rebuilding community connections – mediation and restorative justice in Europe*. Strasbourg: Council of Europe.

Apoio à Vitima (APAV) ed., 2016. *Implementing victim-oriented reform of the criminal justice systems in Europe*. Lisbon: APAV.

Avruch, K., s.d. *Cross-cultural conflict*. Available at: www.eolss.net/ebooks/Sample%20 Chapters/C14/E1-40-01-01.pdf [accessed 30 October 2012].

Berkovits, B. and Balogh, E., 2013. *Theoretical report on the main concepts in the community: securitisation and minorities*. Budapest: Foresee. Available at: www.alternativeproject.eu/assets/upload/Deliverable_5.1_Theoretical_report_on_the_main_concepts_in_the_communities.pdf [accessed 29 March 2017].

Bolivar, D., Pelikan, C. and Lemonne, A., 2015. Victims and restorative justice: towards a comparison. In: I. Vanfraechem, B. Bolivar and I. Aertsen, eds. *Victims and restorative justice*. London: Routledge, pp. 172–200.

Campbell, H., Chapman, T. and Wilson, D., 2013. *Report on the contribution of restorative justice to peace building*. Public deliverable 7.2 of the ALTERNATIVE project. Available at: www.alternativeproject.eu/assets/upload/Deliverable_7.2_Report_on_the_contribution_of_RJ_to_peace_building.pdf [accessed 29 March 2017].

Chapman, T., Campbell, H., McCord, J. and McCready, P., 2013. *Baseline report of conflicts in three conflict areas*. Belfast: University of Ulster. Public deliverable 7.4 of the ALTERNATIVE project. Available at: www.alternativeproject.eu/assets/upload/Deliverable_7.4_Baseline_report_of_conflicts_in_three_conflict_areas.pdf [accessed 29 March 2017].

Chapman, T., Campbell, H. and Wilson, D., 2014. *Appropriate restorative justice interventions tailored to each site designed in the form of a practice manual*. Belfast: University of Ulster. Public deliverable 7.5 of the ALTERNATIVE project. Available at: www.alternativeproject.eu/assets/upload/Deliverable_7_5_Appropriate_restorative_justice_interventions_manual.pdf [accessed 29 March 2017].

Chapman, T., Campbell, H., Wilson, D. and McCready, P., 2015. *Comprehensive final report on RJ interventions in interethnic conflict and multi-agency approach*. Public deliverable 7.6 of the ALTERNATIVE project. Belfast: Ulster University. Available at: www.alternativeproject.eu/wp-content/uploads/2014/12/Deliverable-7.6-Comprehensive-final-report.pdf [accessed 29 March 2017].

Chapman, T., Wilson, D. and Campbell, H., 2012. *Literature review on local conflicts in Northern Ireland*. Belfast: University of Ulster. Public deliverable 7.1 of the ALTERNATIVE project. Available at: www.alternativeproject.eu/assets/upload/Deliverable_7.1_

Literature_review_on_local_conflicts_in_Northern_Ireland_1.pdf [accessed 29 March 2017].

Christie, N., 1977. Conflicts as property. *The British Journal of Criminology*, 17(1), pp. 1–15.

Ćopić, S. and Nikolić-Ristanović, V., 2015. *Manual on best practice on applying restorative justice in intercultural settings*. Public deliverable 6.4 of the ALTERNATIVE project. Belgrade: VDS. Available at: www.alternativeproject.eu/wp-content/uploads/2014/12/Deliverable-6.4-Manual-on-best-practices.pdf [accessed 29 March 2017].

Foss, E.M., Hassan, S.C., Hydle, I., Seeberg, M.L. and Uhrig, B., 2012. *Report on conflicts in intercultural settings*. Deliverable 2.1 of the ALTERNATIVE project. Available at: www.alternativeproject.eu/assets/upload/Deliverable_2.1_Report_on_conlicts_in_intercultural_settings.pdf [accessed 8 June 2016].

Héra, G., Benedek, G., Szegő, D. and Győrfi, E., 2015. *Comprehensive final report*. Public deliverable 5.5 of the ALTERNATIVE project. Budapest: Foresee. Available at: www.alternativeproject.eu/wp-content/uploads/2014/12/Deliverable-5.5-Comprehensive-final-report.pdf [accessed 29 March 2017].

Hydle, I., 2014. *Final research report on conflict and RJ*. Public deliverable 2.4 of the ALTERNATIVE project. Available at: www.alternativeproject.eu/assets/upload/Deliverable%202.4%20Final%20research%20report%20on%20conflict%20and%20RJ%20(1).pdf [accessed 29 March 2017].

Kremmel, K. and Pelikan, C., 2013. *Theoretical research report on activating civil society*. Public deliverable 4.1 of the ALTERNATIVE project. Vienna: IRKS. Available at: www.alternativeproject.eu/assets/upload/Deliverable_4.1_Theoretical_report_on_activating_civil_society.pdf [accessed 8 June 2016].

Kremmel, K. and Pelikan, C., 2014. *Research report on the sociological/legal description of and conflict resolution in small-scale conflicts*. Public deliverable 4.2 of the ALTERNATIVE project. Vienna: IRKS. Available at: www.alternativeproject.eu/assets/upload/Deliverable_4.2_Research_report_on_the_sociological-legal_description.pdf [accessed 29 March 2017].

Kremmel, K. and Pelikan, C., 2015. *Follow-up materials for supporting RJ activities in intercultural settings*. Public deliverable 4.5 of the ALTERNATIVE project. Available at: www.alternativeproject.eu/wp-content/uploads/2014/12/Deliverable-4.5-Follow-up-materials.pdf [accessed 29 March 2017].

Liebmann, M. ed., 2000. *Mediation in context*. London: Jessica Kingsley Publishers.

Marshall, T., 1999. *Restorative justice. An overview*. London: Home Office, Research Development and Statistics Directorate. Available at: www.homeoffice.gov.uk/rds/pdfs/occ_resjus.pdf [accessed 20 March 2006].

Nikolić-Ristanović, V. and Ćopić, S., 2013. *Research report on dealing with conflicts by NGOs and the state*. Belgrado: VDS. Public deliverable 6.1 of the ALTERNATIVE project. Available at: www.alternativeproject.eu/assets/upload/Deliverable_6.1_Research_report_on_dealing_with_conflicts_by_NGOs_and_the_state.pdf [accessed 29 March 2017].

Nikolić-Ristanović, V., Ćopić, S., Petrović, N. and Šaćiri, B., 2014. *Research report on interethnic conflicts and citizens' perceptions of security*. Belgrado: VDS. Public deliverable 6.2 of the ALTERNATIVE project. Available at: www.alternativeproject.eu/assets/upload/Deliverable_6.2_Research_report_on_interethnic_conflicts_and_citizens_security_perceptions_.pdf [accessed 29 March 2017].

Pali, B., 2014. *Case analysis report on intercultural conflicts*. Non-public deliverable 1.2 of the ALTERNATIVE project. Leuven: KU Leuven.

Pali, B., 2015. *Final research report on restorative justice and security*. Deliverable 1.3 of the ALTERNATIVE project. Leuven: KU Leuven. Available at: www.alternative-project.eu/wp-content/uploads/2014/12/Deliverable-1.3-Final-research-report-on-restorative-justice-and-security.pdf [accessed 29 March 2017].

Pali, B. and Aertsen, I., 2018. *Restoring Justice and Security in Intercultural Europe*. London: Routledge.

Pranis, K., 2005. *The little book of circle processes: a new/old approach to peacemaking*. Intercourse: Good Books.

Ragazzi, M., 2015. *Report on comparative analysis in the action research sites*. Public deliverable 8.5 of the ALTERNATIVE project. Leuven: KU Leuven. Available at: www.alternativeproject.eu/wp-content/uploads/2014/12/Deliverable-8.5-Report-on-comparative-analysis.pdf [accessed 8 June 2016].

Szegő, D., Benedek, G. and Győrfi, E., 2015. *Evaluation and follow-up report*. Public deliverable 5.4 of the ALTERNATIVE project. Budapest: Foresee. Available at: www.alternativeproject.eu/wp-content/uploads/2014/12/Deliverable-5.4-Evaluation-and-follow-up-report_revised_201512_01.pdf [accessed 29 March 2017].

Törzs, E., 2012. *Report on restorative justice models*. Public deliverable 3.1 of the ALTERNATIVE project. Leuven: EFRJ. Available at: www.alternativeproject.eu/assets/upload/Deliverable_3.1_Report_on_RJ_models.pdf [accessed 8 June 2016].

Törzs, E., 2013. *Survey analysis on RJ practices in intercultural settings*. Non-public deliverable 3.2 of the ALTERNATIVE project. Leuven: EFRJ.

Törzs, E., 2014. *Analysis of relevant EU policies*. Public deliverable 3.3 of the ALTERNATIVE project. Leuven: EFRJ. Available at: www.alternativeproject.eu/assets/upload/Deliverable_3.3_EU_policies.pdf [accessed 29 March 2017].

Umbreit, M.S., 2002. *The handbook of victim offender mediation*. San Francisco: Jossey-Bass.

Walgrave, L., 2008. *Restorative justice, self-interest and responsible citizenship*. Cullompton: Willan Publishing.

Weitekamp, E., 2016. *Developing peacemaking circles in a European context*. Final report. Tübingen: Eberhard Karls University.

Zinsstag, E. and Vanfraechem, I. eds., 2012. *Conferencing and restorative justice: International practices and perspectives*. Oxford: Oxford University Press.

1 Action research in intercultural settings and restorative justice

Setting the scene

Ivo Aertsen

Introduction

> If you want to know how things really are, just try to change them.
> (Lewin, 1958, cited in Huizer, 1993, p. 60)

The quote above from the man who is historically considered to be the founder of social psychology is well known, but less well integrated in the self-image of what social scientists can do in their daily work. Indeed, the predominant idea of social research is to understand individual and social realities by looking at them from the outside. Social research requires distance, neutrality and objectivity when approaching the objects of study. Giving up this external position, mingling subject and object, is threatening and feels highly uncomfortable. Good research then would be no longer possible. Action research seems to question these assumptions fundamentally. How can this challenge be understood, and how does action research appear in studies on crime and social control?

In this opening chapter, we first introduce action research by situating it within the development of social sciences from the middle of the twentieth century. Then we have a look at the role of action research within the field of criminology and criminal justice, referring to examples from various countries. The action research approach in intercultural settings and the concept of action research as developed within the European FP7-project ALTERNATIVE, is explained in the third part of this chapter. We will come back to the role of action research at the end of the book, after discussing in the next chapters action research as it was used in the respective work packages of ALTERNATIVE.

Action research in social sciences

The growth of a movement

Action research as a social research approach developed from the 1940s onwards, first in the USA, then in the UK and other European countries. Initially, from a social-psychological approach the focus was on problem-solving processes in small groups. Social-political movements discovered action research in the 1960s and 1970s, among others in Germany. A recurrent, main objective of the researchers was to narrow the gap between theory and practice. In that period, authors such as Moser (1975) criticized existing forms of empirical-analytical research. They introduced action research as a fundamentally new approach in social sciences, a new paradigm focusing on the development of social theory where the observer's and participant's positions were essentially interlinked. At the core of their argument was the replacement of a 'monologue' concept of truth by a 'dialogical' one. In various European countries, action research got through in the wake of university democratizing movements in the 1970s and early 1980s. Against this background, action research was not to be reduced to a new form of applied research, but was given a strong normative, societal function thanks to the researchers' commitment. Through action research, a connection was made between research, learning, education and awareness-building while bridging between the individual and societal level.

Action research is closely linked to the theoretical perspective of symbolic interactionism in social sciences. The line of thinking started from a critical attitude twoards a formalistic approach of social realities where insufficient room was given to the subjective life world of people and their capacities to give meaning, to communicate and to act in a social environment. In the 1970s, action research was also supported by Marxist-inspired epistemologies, where the scope of study broadened to the social-structural and historical context of the phenomenon, and of which Paolo Freire with his 'pedagogy of the oppressed' (1972) is the most prominent example.

Throughout the years, action research has developed in diverse fields: in health care, school work, youth care, community development, adult education, social work, industry, trade unions, and foreign aid in developing countries. The diversity of this field of application might explain the variety in action research models and varying emphases. However, action research never witnessed a breakthrough in the field of criminology or criminal justice.

A revival of action research took place in the 1990s. According to some, the spirit of the age made this possible (Reason and Bradbury, 2001, pp. 1–14). According to new understandings of science, the existence of an external world independent from our interpretation and construction is no longer accepted. In a post-modern era, the researcher becomes a partner in the construction of his object of study. Acquiring 'objective' knowledge is no longer possible, since the researcher is always part of the concerned field. The development of knowledge cannot be neutral or without interest, since doing research always happens in a context of power structures which also determine our ways of thinking. Hence, the new challenge is to counteract epistemological hegemonies. In this perspective, it becomes attractive to address minority positions and various forms of deviant behaviour, in order to disclose 'new' interpretation schemes of social phenomena. Here, criminology appears with a renewed interest in action research, as it is also reflected in new theoretical movements such as the 'constitutive criminology' of Henry and Milovanovic (1996).

Defining action research

What is action research more precisely? Qualitative research methods always require a certain level of psychological and/or social 'understanding' and a form of empathy. To a certain extent, the researcher is always 'involved' in the setting. However, when this involvement results in an active intervention of the researcher in the function of direct problem solving or improvement of practice, we might speak of 'action research'. Hence, action research is distinct from other types of qualitative research by the direct involvement of the researcher in a process of action. Action research aims at developing and implementing a process of planned change in practice and at the same time acquiring knowledge on both the process of change and the results thereof (Aertsen and Peters, 1995, pp. 224–226). Action research can be defined as a form of action starting from a problem in order to change the situation in close cooperation with those involved in the field, but also often with the underlying goal of developing or contributing to theory (Bouverne-De Bie, 1989, p. 147). A more classic definition reads as follows:

> Action research ... aims to contribute both to the practical concerns of people in an immediate problematic situation and to further the goals of social science simultaneously. Thus, there is a dual commitment in action research to study a system and concurrently to collaborate with members of the system in changing it in what is together regarded as a desirable direction. Accomplishing this twin goal requires the active collaboration of researcher and client, and thus it stresses the importance of co-learning as a primary aspect of the research process.
>
> (Gilmore, Krantz and Ramirez, 1986, p. 161)

Action research means linking action to research through providing ongoing exchange in a cyclical process. The element of 'action' implies intervention and change, according to predetermined goals. Strategy and envisaged process are discussed beforehand, together with the practitioners. The element of 'research' concerns the development of knowledge and includes parts of process and outcome evaluation. Researchers and researched persons are equal partners in the discussion, although specific capacities or skills can be mobilized rather on one or the other side. Those researched are the experts in their own experience and perceptions, while the researchers are more skilled in collecting, analysing and presenting data. In sum, contrary to what is the case in traditional empirical-analytical research, in action research the field of study is not merely object but also the subject actively contributing to the research.

But as mentioned, action research is not only an instrument for practice improvement or policy development, it also contributes to theory in a given domain (see Dick, Stringer and Huxham, 2009). Therefore, the classic function between fundamental or theoretical research on the one hand and applied or empirical research on the other hand, must be nuanced. In action research, theory development occurs in an inductive way and is interpretative, rather than explanatory or predictive.

Among the many existing definitions of action research the following are worth adding in the context of our project:

> Action research is a form of *collective* self-reflective enquiry undertaken by participants in social situations in order to improve the rationality and justice of their own social or educational practices, as well as their understanding of these practices and the situations in which these practices are carried out.
>
> (Carr and Kemmis, 1986, p. 162)

> Action research is an orientation to knowledge creation that arises in a context of practice and requires researchers to work *with* practitioners. Unlike conventional social science, its purpose is not primarily or solely to understand social arrangements, but also to effect desired change as a path to generating knowledge and empowering stakeholders. We may therefore say that action research represents *a transformative orientation to knowledge creation in that action researchers seek to take knowledge production beyond the gate-keeping of professional knowledge makers*.
>
> (Bradbury Huang, 2010, p. 93; original emphasis)

> Action research happens when people research their own practice in order to improve it and to come to a better understanding of their practice situations. It is action because they act within the systems that they are trying to improve and understand. It is research because it is systematic, critical inquiry made public.
>
> (Feldman, Bennett and Vernaza-Hernández, 2015, p. 89)

Types of action research

Notwithstanding the presence of a shared conceptual framework as mentioned above, there remains a lot of confusion about action research. Sometimes all types of 'field research' are considered to be action research, independently of the final goal of the initiative. Sometimes, action research is associated with 'practice-oriented research': various types of research that should contribute to the solution of practical problems. In this sense, also the term 'accompanying research' is used (Pelikan, 2009). In some instances, carrying out a 'pilot project' or an 'experimental project' is seen as action research. For some, different types of 'consultancy' work and all kinds of mutual exchange between researchers and practitioners is action research. And finally, sometimes action research is discussed in very general terms as every type of research that serves both the theoretical interests of the researchers and the pragmatic needs of policy makers.

Different functions might be allocated to action research. Action research can be used as a strategy for innovation and change (social engineering), as a research method, or as an alternative paradigm or discourse. Moreover, action research can adopt a normative or a more pragmatic orientation: in the first case the objectives of the action are co-decided by the researcher, while this is not the case in the pragmatic variant. Action research in the domain of restorative justice has often a normative-exemplary function, where a perspective of generalization of the new type of action prevails (Aertsen, 2002).

A frequently used term is 'participatory action research'. In this type of research, the emphasis is on the potential for those involved in practice – often within organizations – to fully participate in the research and to optimally use its results in order to improve the situation. Here, the members of the group participate actively throughout the whole research process, from defining the research questions, drafting the research design, implementing the research activities, collecting and interpreting the data and reporting the results. In this type of far-reaching action research, the role of the researcher is rather one of 'facilitator' or 'coach', who provides and supports learning processes within the organization (Whyte, 1991). In the same sphere 'community-based action research' has to be considered, where practitioners as direct stakeholders investigate the problems systematically, search explanations and finally elaborate problem-solving strategies (Stringer, 1999).

Reason and Bradbury (2001, pp. xxv–xxvi) attempt to bring an order in the diversity of action research practices by distinguishing three types depending on the scope of the research: 'first-person action research', starting from the personal environment of the researcher; 'second-person action research', focusing on the interpersonal level of research activities or the group level; and 'third-person action research', where the results of pilot studies are transferred to a larger societal context.

Phases in action research

In action research, the process is not determined into detail in advance. The process evolves in function of the options that are taken continuously by the partners after evaluative moments. Therefore, action research typically is characterized by a cyclical process. It is a spiral movement in which the same phases return repeatedly (Stringer, 2007, p. 8):

1 Look: the problem, assumptions and starting positions are discussed and defined, with the active involvement of the stakeholders;
2 Think: meanings are clarified in mutual consultation, the problem is further interpreted and analysed;
3 Act: planning of the action, implementation, adaptation and evaluation.

Hence, in participatory action research, 'self-reflexive cycles' occur (Kemmis and Wilkinson, 1998): (1) planning the process of change; (2) implementing the action and observing the process and its results; (3) reflecting about this process and its consequences; and (4) planning again the further process of change.

Two additional phases might be important in the 'empirical cycle' of action research, and they have proved to be relevant for the fieldwork in ALTERNATIVE

(Van Dijkum, van Dobben de Bruyn and Kats, 1981, pp. 38–47): both a preliminary and a concluding phase have to be added. The preliminary phase entails mutual orientation between researchers and practitioners: the respective positions, interests and possibilities are discussed; full attention is given to building up the relationship; a first exploration of the problem is undertaken; decisions are made whether to cooperate or not; and finally concrete arrangements are made. A concluding phase can be necessary when the solutions are evaluated positively, since then a phase of 'stabilizing' and 'transfer' is needed, this is: a cycle of transfer of learning and influencing.

Methodological principles in action research

Some of the most important methodological principles can be summarized as follows (Frognier, 1980):

- In action research, the research topic is decided upon through a process of consultation or negotiation between the direct stakeholders, the researchers and the commissioner (funder) of the project.
- A de-localization of the researcher takes place: the researcher is neither an external expert nor a group member; he is a kind of 'associated' or 'affiliated' participant; it concerns no longer research about, but research with.
- The action research is a learning process. The learning process cannot be reduced to a series of evaluations at given moments. It requires an ongoing alternation of analysis and action. It is a collective learning process focusing on the creation of new, common opportunities.

In action research, the researcher takes a role that is quite different from traditional research. The researcher is very much involved in the field and will co-direct the course of the action. He does not only collect and analyse information. He also looks after the general process development and will take initiative if necessary. He supports and stimulates the project partners by offering information and documentation, by exchanging ideas and suggestions. The researcher participates in local partnerships and if necessary coordinates the action in the field. In sum, for the 'researcher' there can be a function of consultant, trainer and investigator. Or, as others argue, there are the functions of initiator, actor and multiplicand.

Thus, action research must clearly be distinguished from participatory observation. In the latter, the researcher usually does not intervene in an active way with a view on changing the situation. Action research also differs from evaluative research, where the researcher from an external point of view and equipped with previously determined research instruments is studying a practice. According to some, the researcher in action research should not combine involvement and guidance of action on the one hand and evaluation on the other hand.

Some further methodological conditions are crucial as well. This is the case for ongoing registration (recording) and reporting, a task usually to be done by both practitioners and researcher. But it is often the researcher who will elaborate and offer the instruments (diaries or logbooks, templates, check lists ...) for registration and reporting. This permanent way of collecting information allows for systematizing the experiences. In this way, knowledge is acquired on the general development of the process and on the influencing factors. These insights can be used immediately for the adjustment of the action, or will be useful for the later transfer and generalization of the model or new method.

Action research in criminology and criminal justice

Understanding the limited use of action research

The rather limited use of action research in the field of criminal justice and criminology has been referred to above. One might wonder what the reasons are for the restricted role of this research approach. Criminology as a research field deals with the study of the phenomenon of crime and related factors, on the one hand, and the response side to crime, on the other hand. Therefore, the distinction is made between explanatory theories and normative theories, while a permanent concern is whether and how both types of theoretical understandings relate to each other. Action research might, on a first view, have to do more with normative attempts to deal with crime and its consequences in practice. Some of the reasons of the limited use of action research in this field might relate to the relatively small group of researchers and research institutes as compared to the fields of psychology, educational sciences, sociology and health sciences. But even within the domain of criminological sciences, which represent a growing field of applied research mainly in Western and Asian societies and Latin American countries, chapters on action research can hardly be found in methodological handbooks and the methodology is seldom taught to students. An important hinder to set up action research in the field of criminal justice (including the sectors of police, courts, probation and prisons) could relate to the relatively closed nature and hierarchical structures of the involved institutions in many countries. Concerns of keeping (a feeling of) control on police and judicial files and practices go hand in hand with extreme caution or even resistance to be open minded and to show vulnerability through open relationships. The closed nature of criminal justice institutions – often both physically and psychologically – leads to reluctance to engage with open methods that have reflections and transformation at their core. Practices in closed systems are usually outcome driven and task oriented, including a tendency to deny feelings and a desire to engage in ritual task performance (Walsh *et al.*, 2014). The professional and organizational culture of criminal justice agencies – predominantly autocratic rather than democratic – does not always allow for active participation in interagency partnerships, and sometimes researchers are seen as intrusive or interfering with the autonomy and decision-making power by judicial authorities. The result of this is that researcher-practitioner partnerships in the domain of police and criminal justice are often characterized as 'a dialogue of the deaf' or a 'hit and run' business where researchers are enabled to collect and publish sensitive data without giving any feedback or return to those who have provided the information. As a consequence, law enforcement agencies become hesitant 'to embrace ideas regarding crime control and prevention from academics, as they see these approaches as disconnected from the daily challenges of police work'; researchers from their side become frustrated by the low impact of their findings, insights and recommendations on the field (Tillyer *et al.*, 2014, p. 404). Tillyer and colleagues (2014) having applied action research (seen as a 'co-generative process') with a police department in a large American city in order to develop new crime analysis tools, distinguish three spheres of influence to be considered in specific configurations depending on the case, in order to achieve success: (1) researcher-based factors (e.g. crime analysis skills), (2) practitioner-based factors (e.g. the agency's philosophy towards crime control and unit-specific factors such as process or outcome orientation, and the support of middle managers), and (3) processional interaction factors (the identification of common goals between researchers and practitioners, effective collection of valid data, and the dissemination of results in mutually beneficial ways).

It is also my experience and that of other researchers in Belgium (see infra), that action research, more than other types of research, require a high level of mutual understanding and a process of trust building between researchers and practitioners' institutions, which can often not be sufficiently offered in the framework of a one-off research project. Developing a more permanent relationship with criminal justice agencies and their representatives might provide a more fertile soil. In some cases it is even a condition for setting up action research in a fully reciprocal relationship as explained in the previous section.

The potential of action research in criminal justice

Despite institutional and inter-agency barriers, there are important arguments in favour of intensive cooperation between researchers and criminal justice agencies. The 'closed' world of criminal justice systems, the often alienating character of its procedures vis-à-vis the life world of citizens, the (budgetary) pressures on criminal justice agencies to focus and prioritize on core tasks, and the gap in justice expectations and experiences between the public and the system might all be good reasons to develop community-oriented approaches with the help of civil society and research institutions. Conceiving and applying innovative practices in an interdisciplinary manner might help to better understand how in criminal justice settings social and personal realities can be understood in an authentic way without 'subsuming' personal experiences under legal or administrative categories and one-sided, monologue rationales. By not only exploring experiences and needs in a process of dialogue with the direct stakeholders but also by trying out new types of intervention, action research can offer a space for doing and learning. In particular where new partnerships are needed to tackle complex problems – as believed nowadays in many crime reduction strategies – action research seems to be a valuable research tool, starting with developing new models of collecting and handling inter-organizational information on local needs, contexts and interventions (Wastell *et al.*, 2004).

A methodology emerging from action research, and which is also applied in criminal justice settings, is 'action learning'. Noga and colleagues (2016, p. 136) report about an action learning project as 'an approach to engaging multi-agency staff operating under opposing occupational goals and cultures, in the development of shared practice-oriented service improvement outcomes'. In an attempt to provide police services in England and Wales better tools to assess individual mental health needs among persons under custody and to develop pathways for adequate referral processes to mental health and social care services, the researchers discovered how at the local level collaborative practices and joint decision-making processes within a complex network of professionals have to be developed in order to effectively reach the complex treatment needs of many mentally ill persons in contact with the police. The creation of a new screening tool on its own and offering training to the police were insufficient; what became clear, was the need for individuals and organizations to go through a process where they can learn about the topic from each other. This common learning process was observed by the researchers as showing a number of critical themes, including engagement and motivation processes, relinquishing control by the group leaders, overcoming a defeatist mindset, group dynamics when attempts were made to also include service users (offenders) in the group's discussions, and strengthening the partnership also on several non-foreseen topics.

An 'action learning group' was also established to initiate the development and piloting of an assessment tool and care planning process to support the health and social care of older prisoners in a prison in England (Walsh *et al.*, 2014). Action learning was used as 'a method of simultaneously developing practice and collecting data in action research projects' (p. 139) throughout its consecutive phases in order for each cycle to inform the next. The action learning group consisted of health care staff, prison staff and older prisoners. Data were collected through reflective notes from the action learning group facilitator, reflective diary writing from group members, emails, research-project steering-group meeting notes and interviews with action learning group members. These data allowed for analysis of the themes related to the process of developing the assessment tool, involving the perspective of the prisoners continuously.

'Service learning' is an educational concept that is applied in criminology and criminal justice curricula of various universities at present. The teaching model integrates academic learning with learning through service and is defined as a 'reciprocal learning with intentional reflection: students apply classroom learning to their service experience, and simultaneously bring the service experience back in the classroom where they further connect their real-life experiences to the course content' (Hirschinger-Blank and Markowitz, 2006, p. 70). In service learning more than in usual internships a variety of perspectives is integrated, including for example those of prisoners and justice professionals in common classes in prison together with the (university) students. These experiences contribute to de-constructing stereotypical images of each other, while also offering room to students to contribute to social change (Nurse and Krain, 2006).

Examples of action research in the criminal justice field

Some examples of 'participatory action research' (PAR) in criminal justice settings have been published recently. Some of these projects relate to prison settings and are able to demonstrate very well the potential of action research, probably also thanks to the clear and visible division between the insider and the outsider perspective that is offered by the prison walls. Crabtree, Wall and Ohm (2016) report on the set-up of an occupational therapy education programme in an American prison, where through a participatory action research methodology a university researcher collaborated with three inmates to evaluate the programme. Such reflective exercises may deal with topics such as how to understand 'power differentials' between the external expert and the insiders. In the given project, the common reflection was made on the basis of field notes, meeting minutes and memories kept by both the outside researcher and the inside co-researchers. Participants critically reflected on the different phases of the programme evaluation, each one from their perspective: how the research questions were identified against background experiences of 'occupation deprivation' in prison, how the research methodology was decided upon, how to gather and analyse data and how to disseminate the results.

> Some concepts change your life because they feel like a vessel that holds your experience, capturing thoughts and emotions that before were falling around you like rain. Occupation deprivation was such a concept for each of us insiders, a concept that finally captured and helped make sense of the desert wasteland of the prison experience.
>
> (Crabtree, Wall and Ohm, 2016, p. 248)

The common evaluation resulted in an understanding of 'occupational justice' and how to further this in a prison context.

In an Australian participatory action research Sherwood and Kendall (2013) undertake a 'community collaborative' project in order to develop an understanding of the social and emotional well-being and resilience of Aboriginal mothers in prison, 'identifying culturally safe models of health care required to meet their needs in custody and for transition back into the community' (p. 86). Therefore, an indigenous informed conceptual framework was adopted on the basis of indigenous health paradigms and utilizing a 'decolonizing' methodological approach. 'The experts were the women themselves, along with their families, communities and service-providers' (p. 86). The decolonizing methodology allows for creating 'knowledge spaces' that facilitate healing and self-determination. The involved indigenous communities contribute to collaborative discussion, storytelling and deep listening, and participatory planning and decision making, incorporating the ethical praxis and protocols of their community.

The project activities contain a consultation phase and an operational phase. In the former phase, important joint steps are: building trusting relationships, conceptualization of the research, development and approval of actions to be undertaken, and data collection and management. The implementation of actions happens on the basis of iterative consultation and adaptation, e.g. understanding the trauma experienced by Aboriginal women in contact with the criminal justice system led to re-formulation of related questions in the survey.

As a last example, we present a totally other field of application for participatory action research in the context of crime policies: organized crime, in particular the Italian Mafia. Saija and Gravagno (2009) – researchers in the Department of Architecture and Urban Planning at the University of Catania in Sicily – report on an action research working with a committee of residents and local vendors around a local market place where life was for many years organized according, and deeply linked to, both the Mafia's exploitation and their social support systems. From an urban planning perspective, the researchers identified conflicting approaches to historical markets: markets can be considered as stable physical urban features embedding local identity or they can be considered from an evolving nature of historic identity, 'to be fed, rather than a stable structure to be kept'. In the latter, markets become 'diverse' places by excellence, and 'are seen as tools for social integration and upward mobility'. It is under the influence of growing awareness, social movements and external factors (immigrant populations, shopping malls, EU policies, national prosecution policies …) that also local power structures evolve, not to erase the Mafia, but to modify its internal organization. Within this evolving context, a partnership between the university and the market area committee was set up, and a series of group actions undertaken according to different phases resulting in policy plans and recommendations. The researchers reflected on the role and the process of action research, for example on possibly difficult and disruptive moments of the project and hence the necessity to reframe the situation and the goals while maintaining a clear ethical focus to orient the actions. One of the beneficial changes from the side of the participants was that after some time they did not come just to discuss their complaints and priorities, but to discuss common rules and goals for the process, resulting in a number of decisions and further insights in a deliberative way. In their final considerations, the authors refer to the double goal of participatory action research: to achieve tangible and intangible changes and improvements to reality on the one hand, and to develop theoretical and methodological findings that contribute to collective knowledge on the other hand. They conclude that the lessons learnt from this action research have a wider relevance, taking into account the global character of the Mafia model of crime, and the fact that crime in many places cannot be dealt with by simple citizen-oriented surveillance but requires an understanding of the interwoven nature of historical, social, economic and political factors.

The experience of action research in Belgium

Before starting action research in the ALTERNATIVE project (see infra), at KU Leuven we had experience with various action research projects since the 1990s (Aertsen and Peters, 1995; Aertsen and Lauwaert, 2001; Aertsen, 2002; Vanfraechem, 2006; Van Doosselaere and Vanfraechem, 2010). A first project (1991–1993) took place in the field of victim assistance, where in close cooperation with five services for mental health new types of therapeutic intervention were implemented, besides practices to better assess psychological consequences of victimization and to elaborate referral procedures for victims mainly at the level of the police and by family doctors. A second action research project (1993–1996) was set up in a partnership between the university, the office of the public prosecutor, the probation service and a victim support programme. The research focused on the applicability of mediation in cases of severe crime committed by adult offenders. A twofold objective lay at the basis of this project: whether, and how, an appropriate model of mediation could be developed in practice, and how mediation for more serious crimes would relate to the criminal justice process. Mediation cases were documented in detail, discussed and analysed by a steering committee consisting of representatives of the partner organizations, and followed by regular adaptation of the model. The project expanded to other judicial districts in the country and finally resulted in a federal law on mediation (2005). A third action research project was on 'restorative detention' (1998–2000), and focused on the central question how prison life can be reconsidered and organized to offer room for victim-oriented action. The project was a partnership between two universities employing two researchers and six prisons engaging an action research practitioner in each institution. The project revealed the importance of first developing a number of 'preparatory actions' in prison in an administrative, organizational and informative way, before reparative actions more directly oriented to the victim could be tried out (Hodiaumont *et al.*, 2005). Also this project resulted in important policy implications, including a transfer of the experiences to all prisons in Belgium, a handbook on developing restorative justice in prisons and the appointment of a fulltime 'restorative justice advisor' in each prison. However, a policy decision was made in 2008 to transform the function of the latter into a more general management position within the prison. This new development evinced the vulnerability of the programme and the difficulty on how to evaluate long-lasting effects in such institutional contexts as prisons (Aertsen, 2012). A fourth action research programme developed from within KU Leuven Institute of Criminology was on developing a model of family group conferencing in cases of serious youth delinquency (2000–2003) (Vanfraechem and Walgrave, 2001). The project was implemented at the level of the youth courts in five judicial districts. A model of family group conferences was designed and tested, followed by evaluative research on the basis of personal observation, interviews and surveys. The model was fully incorporated in the new Juvenile Justice Act of 2006 (Put, Vanfraechem and Walgrave, 2012).

The Belgian examples as briefly presented above, might look like real success stories of action research in the criminal justice field. They indeed had a distinct policy and societal impact nationwide. However, each of the projects witnessed a specific relationship with 'the field' and revealed different ways and degrees of involvement from the side of the researchers. A critical success factor seemed to be – as referred to above – the pre-existence of a positive relationship between the university on the one hand and the field of practice and policy making on the other hand. A sustainable relationship had been built during the last decades, which was facilitated by the engagement of a group of criminologists previously trained at the university and adopting leading positions in society after a while. Action research proved to have the capacity to function as a strategic lever for change in the criminal justice field, from a clear bottom-up, inclusive approach. It was shown how researchers were taken out of their ivory tower, and how they were given the opportunity to translate both theoretical insights and previous empirical research findings into innovative practices and policy making.

However, we also faced important risks and downsides. The strong input from the side of the university made us wonder whether we as researchers were imposing our agenda and our priorities, and whether we were sufficiently respecting social, institutional and personal realities and paces of development. Who has, in action research, the ownership of the findings: can they be considered as research outcomes, or should they rather be attributed to merits and realizations of the involved practitioners? Another, frequently heard concern, refers to the supposed neutrality and distance of researchers vis-à-vis their object of study. In action research, the positions of researcher and researched become interwoven in a certain way, and this would imply special conditions in terms of independent evaluation of the undertaken actions. And finally, it goes without saying that action research – similar sometimes to other types of applied social research – entails a considerable amount of time investment and practical organizational work. This is not always considered or valorized as part of academic work.

The outline of action research in criminology and criminal justice as sketched on the previous pages might demonstrate its potential. Action research for sure does not offer a panacea for all kinds of issues. Penal reform might benefit from different types of cooperation between legal experts, researchers and those seeking justice. Action research specifically can offer a safe and structured environment to develop a better, complex understanding of personal and social realities in order to initiate pilot projects in different types of inter-agency cooperation and to finally evaluate its processes and outcomes. We also think that action research might have a special meaning for the interdisciplinary character of criminology: through action research, the dynamic interaction between theory and practice becomes concrete and visible, bridging between the conceptual and the pragmatic, between theoretical criminology and policy-oriented criminology. Criminology is then conceived as the study of the dialectic relation between phenomena of crime as they are legally defined on the one hand, and their meaning and role for citizens and society as they appear through participation on the other hand: action research observes participatory processes where people redefine their understanding of crime and justice through personal involvement. This brings us to the following section, how action research was done in the FP7-project ALTERNATIVE.

Action research to understand justice and security in intercultural settings

A focus on intercultural contexts

Applying participatory action research in intercultural settings, or in culturally complex societies, faces specific challenges. Ethical dilemmas arise because of differences between cultural groups related to religion, societal norms and values. Differences exist between participants and researchers in relation to personal meanings and beliefs. These differences 'are seemingly amplified and extended when the researcher-participant or participant-participant relationship occurs within a cross-sectional setting' (Balakrishnan and Claiborne, 2017, p. 187). Differences in moral issues and values within and between cultural groups, including intergenerational differences, lend themselves very well for exploration by participatory action research, since action research values the cultural, political and economic context of daily life situations. However, it may remain difficult for a researcher to be sufficiently sensitive to the variety of perspectives, values and abilities between community members and between representatives of different communities, and to respect different time frames to come to solutions. Power imbalances may hinder the establishment of egalitarian relationships, certainly in multi-ethnic settings. At that moment, the researcher must adopt the role of facilitator or mediator, and to stay impartial so that participants feel free to look at all perspectives (Balakrishnan and Claiborne, 2017, p. 199). Because of the creation of an interactive space for equal and active participation where personal meanings and weak voices can be heard, and the facilitative role of the researcher in this process, action research becomes an interesting tool for restorative justice practitioners and researchers, in particular when they try to understand different or evolving perceptions and experiences related to notions, practices or virtues such as justice and security.

For many years, culture was deemed not important in conflict resolution. Avruch (2012) explains how conflict resolution theorizing from within the disciplines of social psychology and international relations mainly built on concepts of rationality, be it at the individual level or the level of the state. Nowadays, 'understanding the concept of culture is a prerequisite for effective conflict analysis and resolution' (p. 9). Culture is no longer considered as homogeneous, stable, singular or an entity, but must be considered as situational, reflexive and responsive. There is a plural understanding of culture at the individual level (belonging to an ethnic, national, professional, social … group) and culture is no longer a uniform social label, nor simply a synonym for attitudes, norms and values. Moreover, culture as an evolving constituent of both human cognition and action 'is rarely by itself the cause of conflict. The mere existence of cultural differences is usually not the primary cause of conflict between groups. However, culture is always the lens through which differences are refracted and conflict pursued' (p. 12). Because of the framing function of culture in relation to conflicts, its tendency to narrowly define the issues under dispute, and the risks of this 'culturalization' to ignore other and more important issues on the basis of the conflict such as social class, education, gender or poverty, we have taken the option in the first phase of the ALTERNATIVE project to no longer speak of 'intercultural conflicts', but of 'conflicts in intercultural settings' (Foss *et al.*, 2012).

The settings that have been chosen to carry out action research in four countries (see infra) are characterized by cultural diversity and could be considered from an outsider perspective as simply 'multicultural' or 'intercultural'. This does, however, not necessarily imply that the conflicts as such are intercultural fixed entities. Moreover, the ALTERNATIVE team has preferred the term 'intercultural' above 'multicultural' in order to include a perspective of interaction, exchange and communication (Törsz, 2014; Vanfraechem, 2015). In one of the deliverables of the project the conceptual background of culture, multiculturalism and interculturalism has been further elaborated (Foss *et al.*, 2012). The distinction is made between two main types of definitions of culture, one that emphasizes historical continuity and another that emphasizes the possibility of communication, and also the distinction is made between culture as a thing (subject of reification) and culture as 'a process one shapes'. Furthermore, multiculturalism is seen as referring more to state policies of plural societies with respect to e.g. indigenous peoples or migrants, whereas

> the concept of interculturalism has been more strongly linked to the idea of 'intercultural dialogue' and communication, and thus contrasted to multiculturalism by the assumption that it stands for something more mutually enriching than mere peaceful coexistence. Interculturalism is also, in extension, assumed to be more synthesising, i.e. more committed to a stronger sense of the whole, to social cohesion and also to open and constructive criticism of illiberal cultural practices.
>
> (Foss *et al.*, 2012, p. 25)

Action research in ALTERNATIVE

The ALTERNATIVE project was designed on the basis of three theoretically oriented work packages and four practice-oriented work packages, the latter ones conceived as case studies to be implemented in Austria, Hungary, Serbia and Northern Ireland. Both types of work packages – theory and practice – had to support and to feed into each other mutually, and this during the whole period of the project (four years). Therefore, the project as a whole was set up as an action research. During the first year, a number of key theoretical concepts were identified, defined and translated into operational terms, and theoretical analyses related to concepts such as justice and security were made. These formed the background for the implementation of different forms of participatory action by the local researchers in cooperation with local residents in the four sites. The field experiences, as initially observed, reported and analysed by the local research teams, then fed back to the theoretical understandings according to an evaluation methodology constructed for the project and used in a coordinated way. Part of the observations was done through film-making, in particular a model of 'participatory film-making' (see Chapters 2 and 3, this volume). The goal of this was to use film not only as a data collection instrument to present social environments in a more original and complete way, but also as a tool to activate concerned citizens and to enable them to bring their own images and pictures of their lives, resulting in a new type of knowledge. While the action research could be situated at the level of the whole project with its various theoretical and practice-oriented work packages, elements of action research also shaped the work at the local level where room was given to ongoing reflection and adaptation of practice.

In ALTERNATIVE as a whole, the action research was less focusing on practical problem solving or achieving immediate results. The potential to contribute to new forms of self-critical and self-reflective knowledge to be developed by researchers and practitioners looking at their own work environments from a variety of angles came much more to the fore in the course of the project (Pali, 2016, pp. 9–30). The cyclical process of action research, as depicted above, expressed itself in the consecutive phases of problem identification and critical reflection about the problem definition; next a 'diagnosis' phase in the local sites where conditions were prepared to set up actions and interventions, and resulting in a reflective evaluation first at the local then at the central project level. In this sense, knowledge was co-constructed through an ongoing, collective and participatory process at different levels. Notions and experiences related to justice and security were approached from an epistemological point of view more than a pragmatic one, however, without losing sight of the necessity to connect local 'symptoms' to underlying structural causes where needed (Ledwith, 2007).

The four action research sites

With the overall objective of developing alternative security approaches for citizens and communities, the project gathered knowledge about the framing of societal conflicts and resources mobilized to the handling of such conflicts, with a special focus on restorative justice interactions. This was done – as already mentioned – through four local action research projects in rural and urban sites situated in Austria, Hungary, Serbia and Northern Ireland. In Austria, the research focused on everyday conflicts in social housing estates in Vienna, exploring the potential of active participation of citizens and of civil society organizations (NGOs), aiming at enhancing security and diminishing feelings of insecurity. In Hungary, the research dealt with conflicts in a small village, taking into account the position of minorities (such as Roma). In Serbia, interethnic conflicts taking place in three border villages were in the focus, with special attention to victims, to observe their roles in democratic processes for peace building and conflict resolution. In Northern Ireland three different urban settings were researched, with the focus on the relationship between the state system and local communities in the context of the past armed conflict and the restorative potential of promoting community development. The set-up of the action research in the four sites, the activities deployed and the main findings are further discussed in Chapters 4 to 7 of this book.

References

Aertsen, I., 2002. Actie-onderzoek. In: K. Beyens, J. Goethals, P. Ponsaers and G. Vervaeke, eds. *Criminologie in actie. Handboek criminologisch onderzoek.* Brussel: Politeia, pp. 445–462.

Aertsen, I., 2012. Restorative Prisons: Where are we heading? In: T. Barabás, B. Fellegi and S. Windt, eds. *Responsibility-taking, Relationship-building and Restoration in Prisons.* Budapest: P-T Muhely, pp. 263–276.

Aertsen, I. and Lauwaert, K., 2001. Criminologie als bemiddeling. In: L. Dupont and F. Hutsebaut, eds. *Herstelrecht tussen toekomst en verleden.* Liber Amicorum Tony Peters. Leuven: Universitaire Pers Leuven, pp. 33–55.

Aertsen, I. and Peters, T., 1995. Actie-onderzoek, een hefboom voor beleidsontwikkeling? *Panopticon*, pp. 220–238.

Avruch, K., 2012. *Context and pretext in conflict resolution. Culture, identity, power and practice.* Boulder: Paradigm Publishers.

Balakrishnan, V. and Claiborne, L., 2017. Participatory action research in culturally complex societies: opportunities and challenges. *Education Action Research*, 25(2), pp. 185–202.

Bouverne-De Bie, M., 1989. Actie-onderzoek als onderzoeksstrategie. Een situering binnen de 'kwalitatieve' onderzoeksbenaderingen. *Tijdschrift voor Sociale Wetenschappen*, pp. 139–155.

Bradbury Huang, H., 2010. What is good action research? *Action Research*, 8(1), pp. 93–109.

Carr, W. and Kemmis, S., 1986. *Becoming critical. Education, knowledge and action research.* Lewes: Falmer.

Crabtree, J.L., Wall, J.M. and Ohm, D., 2016. Critical reflections on participatory action research in a prison setting: toward occupational justice. *Occupation, Participation and Health*, 36(4), pp. 244–252.

Dick, B., Stringer, E. and Huxham, C., 2009. Theory in action research. *Action Research*, 7(5), pp. 5–12.

Feldman, A., Bennett, K. and Vernaza-Hernández, V., 2015. Responsible action research for the pursuit of justice. *Educational Action Research*, 23(1), pp. 85–103.

Foss, E.M., Hassan, S.C., Hydle, I., Seeberg, M.L. and Uhrig, B., 2012. *Report on conflicts in intercultural settings.* Public deliverable 2.1 of the ALTERNATIVE project. Oslo: NOVA. Available at: www.alternativeproject.eu/assets/upload/Deliverable_2.1_Report_on_conlicts_in_intercultural_settings.pdf [accessed 25 March 2017].

Freire, P., 1972. *Pedagogy of the oppressed.* Harmondsworth: Penguin.

Frognier, A.P., 1980. Actie-onderzoek en sociale verandering. In X., ed. *Acta van het colloquium: Methodologie en Praktijk van het Actie-Onderzoek.* Brussel: Diensten van de Eerste Minister – Programmatie van het Wetenschapsbeleid, pp. A9–31.

Gilmore, Th., Krantz, J. and Ramirez, R., 1986. Action based modes of inquiry and the host-researcher relationship. *Consultation*, 5(3), pp. 160–176.

Henry, S. and Milovanovic, D., 1996. *Constitutive criminology. Beyond postmodernism.* London: Sage.

Hirschinger-Blank, N. and Markowitz, M.W., 2006. An evaluation of a pilot service-learning course for criminal justice undergraduate students. *Journal of Criminal Justice Education*, 17, pp. 69–86.

Hodiaumont, F., Malempré, H., Aertsen, I., Daeninck, P., Van Camp, T. and Van Win, T., 2005. *Vade-mecum justice réparatrice en prison.* Gent: Academia Press.

Huizer, G., 1993. Participatory action research in rural development. In: D. Boog, H. Coenen, J. Foolen and L. Keune, eds. *De actualiteit van handelingsonderzoek.* Tilburg: Tilburg University Press, pp. 57–75.

Kemmis, S. and Wilkinson, M., 1998. Participatory action research and the study of practice. In: B. Atweh, S. Kemmis and P. Weeks, eds. *Action research in practice. Partnerships for social justice in education.* London: Routledge, pp. 21–36.

Ledwith, M., 2007. On being critical: uniting theory and practice through emancipatory action research. *Educational Action Research*, 15(4), pp. 597–611.

Moser, H., 1975. *Aktionsforschung als kritische Theorie der Sozialwissenschaften.* München: Kösel-Verlag.

Noga, H., Foreman, A., Walsh, E., Shaw, J. and Senior, J., 2016. Multi-agency action learning: challenging institutional barriers in policing and mental health services. *Action Research*, 14, pp. 132–150.

Nurse, A.M. and Krain, M., 2006. Mask making: incorporating service learning into criminology and deviance courses. *Teaching Sociology*, 34(3), pp. 278–285.

Pali, B., 2016. Doing restorative justice in intercultural contexts: an alternative discourse of justice and security. PhD Dissertation. Leuven: KU Leuven.

Pelikan, C., 2009. Research informing practice – practice informing research. IRKS Working Paper no. 9. Vienna: IRKS.

Put, J., Vanfraechem, I. and Walgrave, L., 2012. Restorative dimensions in Belgian youth justice. *Youth Justice*, 12(2), pp. 83–100.

Reason, P. and Bradbury, H., 2001. Inquiry and participation in search of a world worthy of human aspiration. In: P. Reason and H. Bradbury, eds. *Handbook of action research. Participative inquiry and practice.* London: Sage, pp. 1–14.

Saija, L. and Gravagno, F., 2009. Can participatory action research deal with the Mafia? A lesson from the field. *Planning Theory & Practice*, 10(4), pp. 499–518.

Sherwood, J. and Kendall, S., 2013. Reframing spaces by building relationships: community collaborative participatory action research with Aboriginal mothers in prison. *Contemporary Nurse*, 46(1), pp. 83–94.

Stringer, E.T., 1999. *Action research.* 2nd edn. London: Sage.

Stringer, E.T., 2007. *Action research.* 3rd edn. London: Sage.

Tillyer, R., Skubak Tillyer, M., McCluskey, J., Cancino, J., Todaro, J. and McKinnon, L., 2014. Researcher–practitioner partnerships and crime analysis: a case study in action research. *Police Practice and Research: An International Journal*, 15(5), pp. 404–418.

Törsz, E., 2014. Restorative justice approaches in intercultural conflict settings – findings of a survey and implications for practice. *Temida*, September, pp. 87–102.

Van Dijkum, C., van Dobben de Bruyn, I. and Kats, E., 1981. *Actie-onderzoek. Een discussie- en werkboek.* Amsterdam: Boom.

Van Doosselaere, D. and Vanfraechem, I., 2010. Research, practice and policy partnerships. Empirical research on restorative justice in Belgium. In: I. Vanfraechem, I.

Aertsen and J. Willemsens, eds. *Restorative justice realities. Empirical research in a European context*. The Hague: Eleven International Publishing, pp. 57–94.

Vanfraechem, I., 2006. *Herstelgericht groepsoverleg*. Brugge: die Keure.

Vanfraechem, I., 2015. Anders omgaan met interculturele conflicten. *Tijdschrift voor Herstelrecht*, 15(3), pp. 12–27.

Vanfraechem, I. and Walgrave, L., 2001. Een wetenschappelijk begeleid experiment met herstelgericht groepsoveleg. *Panopticon*, pp. 479–493.

Walsh, E., Forsyth, K., Senior, J., O'Hara, K. and Shaw, J., 2014. Undertaking action research in prison: developing the older prisoner health and social care assessment and plan. *Action Research*, 12(2), pp. 136–150.

Wastell, D., Kawalek, P., Langmead-Jones, P. and Ormerod, R., 2004. Information systems and partnership in multi-agency networks: an action research project in crime reduction. *Information and Organization*, 14, pp. 189–210.

Whyte, W.F. ed., 1991. *Participatory action research*. London: Sage.

2 Visualizing action research in the ALTERNATIVE context

Ida Hydle

Introduction

> It is an illusion that photos are made with the camera … they are made with the eye, heart and head.
>
> (Henri Cartier-Bresson)

In this chapter I will discuss some of the intentions and reasons behind the films from ALTERNATIVE, how film-making was conceptualized and some of the challenges in general that were faced during the project. The film-making was planned to act both as a part of the action research, e.g. a methodology for participatory research, and as a tool for disseminating preliminary as well as final results. Partly these tools were meant to go inseparably together. First, I will present participatory film-making as part of research in general in the social sciences. With this approach, the focus turns to the field of restorative justice and the ALTERNATIVE project. How was the concept of participatory film-making interpreted and applied according to the local realities of the different sites, and how could the action research project benefit from filming? What were the ethical questions implied and how did the research teams handle them? Some of the answers to these questions are to be found in Chapter 3 by Dóra Szegő. In this chapter, my ambition is to describe and analyse the complexity of growing practical skills and knowledge in the constructing of films linked to action research as visual and auditory storytelling. Based on the films from the four research sites in ALTERNATIVE and relevant examples from the Norwegian filming of restorative justice processes that were used as comparative examples, I will reflect upon our film-making development in practice, what the main challenges were and what solutions were found. I claim that filming in the social sciences is an inescapable part of present-day research and action reality, due to an ever-increasing digitalized and visualized societal worldview in general. Recent development in the neurosciences contributes to a deeper understanding of why this is so. This should lead to changes in researchers' education with the needed theoretical and methodological development, both for data collection, analyses and dissemination. The film-making experiences from ALTERNATIVE serve as empirical evidence of the needed, but complex learning process that stands before social scientists in general.

Theory approaches to visual representations

> Of all the means of expression, photography is the only one that fixes a precise moment in time.
>
> (Henri Cartier-Bresson)

Filming in the social sciences

Participatory video found its origins in social anthropology, social work, community development, psychotherapy, alternative education and arts (Jablonko, 1968; Freudenthal and Niemela, 1972; Rollwagen, 1988; Shaw and Robertson, 1997), and served different purposes for anthropological research, social engagement, community development and advocacy, social resource management and project evaluation (Nemes *et al.*, 2007). Academic interest for visual methods and participatory filming outside anthropology was raised later within various disciplines, including development studies and sociology, and applied as participatory research methods and approaches (White, 2003), with the main aim of giving expertise to the subjects of the research and to shorten the gap between researchers and the community.

Film used for research today may be seen as a recapturing of an anthropological approach to vision and look, in more than one sense of the terms. First the observation, i.e. the look, is one of the main tools in the collecting, ordering, analysis and presentation of data, often taken for granted, or black-boxed[1] (Latour, 1999), by researchers themselves (Grasseni, 2009). Vision is an instrument for information, for the development and dissemination of ideas, for thoughts and practices. Second, vision and look are in use as active tools in the expression and development of critical anthropological self-understanding when informants are turned into co-researchers and co-producers, when they themselves are behind the camera (Holtedahl, 2006; Waage, 2007; Foss, 2016) or when they are involved in directing and editing.

One of the famous phrases of the famous Norwegian press photographer, Tom Martinsen, was that ‘the pictures are there, you just have to take them’ [my translation]. For years Martinsen edited a Norwegian newspaper column called ‘Moment’ (*Øyeblikket* in Norwegian), showing central masterpieces from the history of photography. The name of the column he borrowed from the expression of the famous French photographer Henri Cartier-Bresson, ‘the precise moment’, which Cartier-Bresson defined as the simultaneous recognition in a fraction of a second, of the critical moment, as well as the precise organization of forms that gives the instance its right expression.

However, in spite of sharing a common interest for precision with photographers, researchers are well acquainted with the fact that all visual practices are linked to representations, like all human sensory activities, be it texts, sounds or pictures. A relevant, but sad example is the history of Kevin Carter who committed suicide some months after he had received the Pulitzer Price for the best photo ‘for a haunting Sudan famine picture’.[2] He sat for 20 minutes under a tree, smoking a cigarette, while he looked at a dying baby and a vulture. He waited for the vulture to spread its wings. He used the waiting time in composing an arrangement of the picture. The picture was not just there; it was being planned and shot in a specific and expected way. But this did not change the story. The story about the baby and the vulture was changed by our knowledge about the context, not about the famine in Sudan, but by the fact that the photographer, the 'looker' behind the camera, committed suicide afterwards.

Contrary to Carter's way of describing, the researchers' ambition is basically different. Anthropologists as researchers often describe situations in which they are present themselves. Thus they participate in something of which they are therefore partly co-producers. Researchers are never invisible or innocent as storytellers. We do not just observe those whose story we will tell, they also observe us and take in their impressions of us. We affect both how people speak when they suffer (as in the Carter example) and how they speak about their suffering. We become part of their suffering. In addition, our description turns from what we interpret from them to be our own story (Sachs, 2003).

As described in the story about Kevin Carter, visual representations are similar to speech or texts in terms of innocence and vulnerability. Recent anthropological knowledge about the senses contributes to new perspectives on vision, not as an isolated given, but within its interplay with the other senses. Moreover, it explores vision as a ductile, situated, contested and politically fraught means of situating oneself in a community of practice (Grasseni, 2007). This relates not only to pictures, but even more to film. In the critical scholar discussions on the issue of documentary filming, this may be seen as a recapturing of an approach to vision and look exceeding the sense in the terms as described above. Film is used as a strategy for the discovery of coherences in the world and their dissemination. Film as a disseminating tool of knowledge may on the one hand undress researchers' 'best knowledge' (Holtedahl, 2006). On the other hand, at some point a film may offer a different perspective on the reality that will reveal incoherence and ambiguities of phenomena that were previously conceived differently with other research methods.

Theory approaches to participatory filming in ALTERNATIVE

The empirical focus in ALTERNATIVE lies with the communication with and within very different groups of people in four different conflict settings in Europe (see Chapter 1, this volume), taking part in justice and security issues by learning about and practising restorative justice and restorative processes. My theoretical focus on communication across senses is e.g. based upon 'dialogism' as a theory of knowledge, embodied in the work of the Russian theorist of culture Mikhail Bakhtin (Bakhtin, 1981) and the Swedish linguist Per Linell (2009). Thus the discussion will also include how anthropological filming skills the vision – in a dialogical perspective. Dialogue is also the headline of restorative practices and therefore this theoretical approach is in accordance with our practice fields in more than one respect. Another theoretical reference is the actor network theory (Latour, 2005, 2012), where filming is understood as a network process between man and matter, between the person(s), i.e. the researchers and the informants, on the one hand, and the technical and material tool(s), i.e. the cameras and the display tools in this project, on the other hand.

Beyond words: the visual turn

Dialogue then, goes far beyond verbal dialogues or non-verbal (listening) acts. Vision may also be seen as a dialogical tool. 'Visuality' is part of human intra- and interaction, embedded in different environmental circumstances. In her book *Picturing Pity*, Gullestad (2007) analyses the published photographs taken by Norwegian evangelical missionaries during their missionary operations in Northern Cameroon from the early 1920s until today. She shows how local and detailed representations of the people, in this case through pictures, are embedded in a much wider context of international relations. The missionaries in their effort to justify their activities to their donors in Europe created and maintained a particular view upon the Africans. This visual rhetoric became established as a convention that also can be traced in other secular fields such as international development and relief organizations, mass media or foreign policy. Gullestad's turn as a social scientist from text to visual representation may be seen as a 'token for her time', marking not only the realization of culture as visual, but also capturing that culture has become visual: visual culture is everyday life.

I will continue here to reflect on the use of the senses vision and hearing, the bodily eye and ear and on the remarkable fact that we do not, neither in Norwegian nor in English, Hungarian, German, Dutch or Serbian have a term, a concept or a word for 'meeting sound' in the same way as we 'meet light', with the look or the gaze – when we watch, see, observe or view. Light is thus the absolutely necessary physical condition for human sight, look or gaze. The gaze or look is what we cannot see ourselves, but what others can see and meet, i.e. respond by a look or gaze back to the sender. The gaze or look is thus a dialogical term and tool in the sense that *I* am dependent upon *your* seeing for the registration of a gaze or a look. Is it accidental that the term vision both refers to a physical phenomenon and a mental – two separate phenomena, which are seemingly independent of each other? The complexity of human communication consists of physical, chemical, biological and mental factors at the same time.

The deaf anthropologist Hilde Haualand (2002) claims anthropology to be phonocentric, i.e. we take sound as a given. Do we also take light as a given? What about the living picture(s) and the ability and power of the look and the vision (film, television, worldwide web, smart phones) attracting and creating new forms of communication, new spaces, new times and new places? Film creates a space between the man and the world or between partners in a dialogue. It is also with this perspective on the space of human communication that we may explore restorative justice practices in general as well as in the ALTERNATIVE project.

Filming in the ALTERNATIVE project

> As far as I am concerned, taking photographs is a means of understanding which cannot be separated from other means of visual expression. It is a way of shouting, of freeing oneself, not of proving or asserting one's own originality. It is a way of life.
>
> (Henri Cartier-Bresson)

The ideas of participatory filming

As member of the group that worked out the idea of ALTERNATIVE, I suggested filming as part of the project from the very start. I was not a novice to this visual approach. First of all, I had collaborated since 2000 with visual anthropologists, in particular at the University of Tromsø, Visual Cultural Studies, and at the University of Bergamo. I had thus dug deep into important theoretical contributions of Christina Grasseni (2007, 2009), Sara Pink (2012), David MacDougall (2005), Tim Ingold (2002, 2010, 2011) which I will come back to in this chapter.

The idea behind the filming and in particular 'participatory filming' I had borrowed from my experiences as external examiner at the Visual Cultural Studies at the Arctic University of Tromsø. The curriculum in their masters' degree involves theories, methodology, training and practice in filming and editing based upon the filmed subjects' own participation in filming as well as in editing. Thus participation in filming means a comprehensive dialogue between researcher and researched, not only blurring the roles, but contributing to a mutual and emancipatory understanding of each other. The project 'Youth Gaze' as an example, demonstrates the utilization of 'film dialogue' as a creative strategy for developing scientific understandings of youth's identity and culture in Northern Norway. It is a research collaboration between Visual Cultural Studies, the Institute of Psychology and the outreach social services in Tromsø (Wang *et al.*, 2012).

Thus gradually we are a group of researchers who develop our research approaches upon different hypotheses, also in the conflict resolution fields, such as:

- Liminality[3] and conflict create social capital, i.e. human resources.[4]
- Dialogues in conflicts, in a Linellian perspective (Linell, 2009) and relationism can enhance understanding, creativity and conflict resolutions (Hasund and Hydle, 2004).
- If applying the use of visual means and skills by e.g. filming people in dialogues, this can compensate for lack of verbal/language skills.

Visualization of the handling of conflicts may overcome a range of different barriers that may be summarized as a kind of 'speech disadvantage'. Thus, the conduct of the different qualitative investigations also supplements each other. Such approaches may be supplemented by visualization in our experiences:

- Exploring the linguistic content in restorative justice processes with young people who have been involved in crime and offences (Hasund and Hydle, 2007);
- Broadening the analytical work with life histories of young offenders as they emerge in interviews and conversations (Gullestad 1996, 2004);
- Investigating the young offenders' own approaches to information and communication technology (ICT) as part of the rehabilitation process;
- Describing and analysing the local strategic implementation processes and consequences for local peace and security building and for the development of democratic deliberation (Hydle and Lønneberg, 2014).

What is to be commented in this chapter, as in Chapter 3, is how the ALTERNATIVE filming developed with only partial degrees of informants´ participation in the filming, let alone the researchers' participation – and the reasons and consequences thereof. What is left to the empirical parts of this kind of action research, i.e. such participatory filming endeavours, is the amazement of the power of the story itself, i.e. the 'rehearsal' and continued dissemination of the story long outside the researchers' and the other participants' own reach. Thus this would be e.g. an analysis of other peoples' reactions to what they saw and heard during the film displays – and the impact this may have for the continuing dissemination of the stories.

A summary of filming practices in ALTERNATIVE

The ALTERNATIVE action research project included several different intercultural settings, three in Serbia, two in Vienna, two in Northern Ireland and one in Hungary. Although we as researchers intended to keep to a common conceptual background, and also received the same training, our differences evolved during the project. Different approaches to action research as well as filming were elaborated. Local films were constructed in the field with different research, restoration, education and dissemination purposes and with different roles assigned to the local residents in the filming processes. A common final film was intended to be a collection from the local footage, to be used for training and dissemination. Making one final film including all the various local stories, reflecting the whole project, with synthetizing all the different approaches of the local film-maker teams was a great challenge. It showed the complexity and uniqueness of each research site. Thus we created a final film in which the researchers explained the research process and results. This final film is also a valuable visual and auditory document that might be used for second analyses and as data for research on social-scientific epistemology (on the enhanced use of human senses).

The film-making process took place throughout the four years of the project. One of the project partners, European Forum for Restorative Justice coordinated this process, together with the KU Leuven Instituut voor Media en Leren (LIMEL) that was asked to assist in teaching the researchers in filming and editing and worked in close cooperation with the project coordinator. Most of the partners were unacquainted with even thinking visualization, let alone holding or moving a camera or editing the footage. Thus this part of the work and the collaboration proved to be more demanding than I had realized when suggesting this methodology as part of the action research. The LIMEL colleagues had the same epistemological platform as I knew from Visual Cultural Studies. They trained our partners both on the technical aspects of film-making and about the film as 'visual language' and its characteristics.

We all as partners created a film as a start to present our own research organizations. These films were the first films on the ALTERNATIVE homepage. Then partners continued in various ways with filming in their action research sites parallel or as part of their research. Some partners edited several short films, which were used for dissemination before the end of the filming process. Other partners were interviewed by trained film people about the project. The films were shot at the various sites, and the final film was recorded in Leuven through interviewing all partners (April 2015).

The output of the filming process consists of a general/introductory film, four local movies, teasers, eight interviews, extra materials and an online platform where all the outputs are presented (http://alternativefilms.euforumrj.org). By providing the films together with a practitioners' manual that we developed during the project, the manual contextualizes the films and provides more textual information to the images. Simultaneously, the films illustrate the manual and provide a multimedia approach to possible trainings or workshops. We believe that this presentation of the films enables the use of these materials for training, workshops, and conferences as well as for raising awareness on the project. Each time new extra (video and other) material from the partners is uploaded, the platform is relaunched via social media and the monthly newsflash of the European Forum for Restorative Justice (EFRJ). The ALTERNATIVE Film Online Platform (http://alternativefilms.euforumrj.org/) has been launched and has gained attention from all over the world.[5] One short film was made by the Foresee Research Group from Hungary, which was first presented only to a closed audience. After no objection by filmed participants, it was openly shared with a larger audience through an EFRJ Newsflash as well as on the net (www.youtube.com/watch?v=uXKWrq0aksY).

But participatory filming?

> The most difficult thing for me is a portrait. You have to try and put your camera between the skin of a person and his shirt.
>
> (Henri Cartier-Bresson)

As Dóra Szegő describes in Chapter 3, the human resources and local conditions of the research sites resulted in different approaches to the use of visual representation as a research tool. Participation in filming was not systematically achieved as I had suggested and as was intended from the beginning. Through the project years, I realized the difficulties, as a non-intended part of the research process, in spite of the extraordinary goodwill and close cooperation between all partners. It is difficult for social scientists without practical film training, to catch the ideas and most of all, practical skills, in participatory filming, let alone filming participatory research or action research. The results of this are described in detail in the following chapter by Dóra Szegő. My contribution at this stage of hindsight is to use our experiences as data and reflect on some of the possible reasons for this development in the project. As analytical comparative background, I will first use the experiences from Norwegian participatory filming projects, in particular the filming in the teaching of peace students in restorative justice at the University of Tromsø and in Red Cross Street Mediation – a methodology of teaching restorative justice to vulnerable young people 'on the street' between the ages of 13 and 25. Thus both of these experiences refer to an extreme variety of people, academics and school students filming and editing real-life stories, i.e. documentaries, either from their own life or stories about others.

The visual cultural study approach has been used to film closely what goes on in various parts of street mediation in Oslo and Tromsø. The films give a different intake of ethnographic data compared to traditional fieldwork, i.e. filming forms an enlargement of the fieldwork, in addition to the value as disseminating tools of people's skills and achievements in creating secure environments. As described above, Visual Cultural Studies at the University of Tromsø has been an inspirational force in addition to practical data-sampling processes in our work. It is rooted in the recognition of the potential of the teaching of cross-cultural understanding that lies in playful explorations of the interpretive quest between actors from different life worlds. The camera serves as a tool for explorations and negotiations that not only give insights in differing concepts and perspectives, and different social worlds, but also recognizes the need for creating new concepts, perspectives, methodologies and practice. The use of film in the cross-cultural teaching context and in the relationship with local populations and audiences has proven highly valuable in the promotion of reciprocal learning and dialogue. The more than 150 films that have been produced at the university constitute an important archive on local conflicts and conflict-solving practices in most parts of the world, due to the country origin of both teachers and the master's students.

I also experienced in Tromsø how master's students used filming as an explorative as well as an evaluative tool in the restorative lecturing and training of the peace students, involving and sharpening the students as well as me in the importance of visualization of what goes on in a group like this.

In Oslo the youth who were trained as street mediators were given the camera to film the process, and invited to reflect and edit the final film of a study journey they joined to other young people in Copenhagen to exchange restorative justice experiences. This filming process made them both aware of their tasks and also proud of their learning and skills in mediation and peace building in the streets. The restorative justice process is seen as a dialogical and rehabilitative tool; an action research approach in which meetings and conferences in the Red Cross are seen as the action and the research is based upon the analysis of the dialogues between parties during the restorative processes and the concluding results at different societal levels.

The filming projects examine the conditions, which have led to the present-day situation as well as the possibilities of creating a sustainable self-image for the future, e.g. self-respect, a belief that you can master future difficulties in life, that you can lead a decent life, that you are a valuable person in your network, etc. One comes to grips with the young participants' own approaches to visualization as part of the process in a mediated communication between them and the outer world, Red Cross, family and community. Thus, the development of identity and subjectivity may link up with mediated communities or arenas and young peoples' alternative forms of expression with film.

Films from street mediation, both in Oslo and in Tromsø, have been used as teaching tools and demonstration of the use and results of restorative justice training and skills. However, there are at least two lessons to learn from ALTERNATIVE with the Norwegian filming experiences as background.

Teaching and learning to be visual

With these theoretical and practical complexities in mind as described above, I entered a course in digital storytelling in the Media section at my own University College of Oslo and Akershus. Digital storytelling is another methodology of visualization that we used in ALTERNATIVE. It clarifies nevertheless the complexities of and also 'cross-fertilizes' the understanding of human visualization. We were organized as a community of knowledge and of (growing) practice, as was also mentioned by Grasseni (2007) when she wrote about vision as a means of situating oneself in a community of practice. Wenger-Trayner *et al.* (2014) as well as Dysthe (2001)[6] demonstrate how the process of learning improves in meaning, applicability and effectiveness when the learners are organized in practice communities. From ALTERNATIVE I had also the experience in organizing research and education meetings according to these learning principles.[7]

I was invited together with the other media community members to imagine the best story, the best images and the best text read – with my own voice. I gradually got the feeling of handling a piece of *art*, inspired by the multivocality of both realizing and then disseminating some of my results in this way. Even if the digital storytelling follows a very short and rigid pattern of time, sequence and narrative and the IMovie-program forces you to obey its rules of conduct, there is a wide freedom in the selection of time, sequence and narrative images and sound qualities, voice and music. My previous focus on communication across senses, based upon dialogism gradually took form. During this selection process I discovered how these theoretical approaches work in practice: Bakhtin's terms 'dialogism' and 'polyglossia'[8] as a tool for an understanding of the layers upon layers of happenings and acts in a research project.

My other approach for understanding is of Latour in his actor-network theory (ANT), which explains how to understand that man and machine together construct a result (2005, 2012), e.g. a digital story or a film as is described above. Picturing or filming is thus understood as a network process between man and matter, between the person(s), i.e. the researchers and the informants and the technical and material tool(s) – i.e. the cameras, smartphones, computers etc. I realized how the construction of the digital story 'skills the vision', to use the expression from Grasseni's book, *Skilled Visions* (2007) – in a dialogical perspective. This particular dialogical perspective led me into the argument of the anthropologist Tim Ingold (2002, p. 245) that 'we see things before light, and hear sound before things'. Ingold hardly knew then how his anticipation of how we see and hear, later has been documented by neuro-research. The discovery of mirror-neurons, which enable the brain to react and 'mirror' outer visual stimuli even before the reaction reaches the cognitive parts of the brain, i.e. before we even acknowledge that we react, explains how we learn through mimicry and also why we are able to feel empathy with others before our conscience tells us.[9] Mirror-neurons may be seen and interpreted as dialogical tools, without which humans would not be able to develop the necessary communicational skills from infancy onwards. However, vision is also embedded in different environmental circumstances. In this way, Ingold's way widens the understanding of the use and thus also disseminating effectiveness of digital storytelling.

The practical learning experience

These theoretical bases enhanced my analytical context for understanding the participatory filming-construction in ALTERNATIVE as a more than complex learning experience. For example, to learn to write the screenplay in short and popular wordings is not at all comparable to a general demand for a researcher whose expertise is to thoroughly analyse and explain complexities and models at length. The challenges of conveying a complex context and content visualized throughout ALTERNATIVE's various action research sites were comprehensive. For example, one needed ingredient of this challenge is to imagine images, again a foreign feeling for social scientists. Even if we tried to work as a mutually advisory group, this filming demand came on the top of the general demands for written texts, articles, book chapters and reports.

Through the new learning experience with short digital stories I was struck by the *art* perspective of the work – in the sense of 'expression or application of human creative skill and imagination, typically in a visual form such as painting or sculpture, producing works to be appreciated primarily for their beauty or emotional power' (Oxford Advanced Learner's Dictionary, 2016).[10] The (difficult) invitation for a researcher is to use the senses in new ways to express a scientifically based message.

Through the skills and skilled vision of our teachers we were led through the complex process of practising film-construction in ALTERNATIVE. Even if some of us had someone else skilled in practically filming, one had to think of voice-over, either one's own or someone else's voice that would fit the content. Also one had to imagine and think practically upon particular pieces of music to play the background 'mood' of the whole issue. Music is neither innocent nor neutral. The brain processes music or musical sounds differently from other sounds. Music constructs another nature of meaning and thus conveys other emotional messages than texts or pictures (Clynes, 2013). But this is not in the repertoire of a social scientist.

Conclusion: visual culture is everyday life

Filming peace and security practices as documentaries is not unusual. In the ALTERNATIVE project, filming was built in as both a data-gathering and dissemination tool – and to a limited extent as participatory action, although the function of dialogue was clearly present, e.g. in Hungary, and to a lesser extent in Vienna (as described in Chapter 3). However, the space, place and time for making such documentaries are of utmost importance. Young people today use more and more visualization in their everyday life and learning. Visual tools and programmes play an increasing role in most peoples' lives. With documentaries, one may succeed in 'touching the hearts of many' because of e.g. empathy, a crucial part of restorative justice, that may clearly be visualized and that may transcend culture and mentality – one of the possible aims of ALTERNATIVE. I have, however, focused upon visualization as more than shooting a film on a relevant issue. The question that I have raised is shooting by whom and for what purpose. My emphasis is on the visual and (or instead of) lingual and auditory expressions and interpretations as research tools as is increasingly used within applied visual anthropology and participatory video filming.

The challenge is to involve people and work together with them, as is crucial in restorative justice and local security, to skill the vision in order to visualize the invisible. An interactive video process, as is carried out in a demonstration project,[11] includes the following steps, of which the third was recognizable in ALTERNATIVE, in the Hungarian village in particular:

1 the researcher introduces the issue and video/DVD/technology, plans and discusses an approach with the community;
2 the community articulates issues, performs role-plays, dramas and everyday life on video/DVD;
3 the DVD or video is played back with carefully facilitated discussions between the researcher and the community (Freudenthal, 2000).

Filming in and of Red Cross street mediation and the teaching exercises in peace building in both Oslo and Tromsø may be seen as both part of practice and of research methodology. Several groups of street mediators in Oslo have participated in filming; giving a glimpse into what happens during this education of juveniles, training to come to grips with new understandings of conflict handling. The filming has contributed to answering our questions concerning their visions and changes in visions of themselves and who they are, which is part of our hypotheses concerning alternative security work.

As I have mentioned earlier, neither images nor sounds are innocent. You will always add a personal touch, through all the selections that are made in the process of constructing a film. It is not possible to believe in objectivity or neutrality. Even if the images are 'taken by a camera', there is an eye behind and a new eye to interpret. Cartier-Bresson, wrote in his book *The mind's eye, writings on photography, and photographers* (1998, p. 13) that

> For me the camera is a sketch book, an instrument of intuition and spontaneity, the master of the instant which in visual terms, questions and decides simultaneously. In order to 'give a meaning' to the world one has to feel oneself involved in what one frames through the viewfinder. This attitude requires concentration, a discipline of mind, sensitivity, and a sense of geometry – it is by great economy of means that one arrives at simplicity of expression. One must always take photographs with the greatest respect for the subject and for oneself.

To involve oneself is to be seen as a personal process. This may in a somewhat old-fashioned epistemology be regarded as 'un-academic' or 'too emotional to be a good research and dissemination approach'. Many leading science theorists have left this point of view or so-called neutral science approach. Latour is one of them, dissolving the artificial distinction between objective and subjective. We are all subjects in relationships. Objectifying 'the other' is an act of power. We use our bodily senses, as well as the work of the hands, in the construction of a film. We find ourselves in the relationships between mind and body, art and science.

Notes

1 As Latour (1990, p. 304) phrases:

> The way scientific and technical work is made invisible by its own success. When a machine runs efficiently, when a matter of fact is settled, one need focus only on its inputs and outputs and not on its internal complexity. Thus, paradoxically, the more science and technology succeed, the more opaque and obscure they become.

2 Kevin Carter – Photojournalist: www.kevincarterfilm.com/ [accessed 29 June 2015].

3 Liminality means to be in an intermediate stage, phase or condition of uncertainty, ambiguity and/or disorientation, to be 'on the threshold', often used to describe the phase between two stages of a ritual, a ritual passage.

4 www.hioa.no/Om-HiOA/Senter-for-velferds-og-arbeidslivsforskning/NOVA/Publikasjonar/Rapporter/2010/Sosial-kapital-og-andre-kapitaler-hos-barn-og-unge-i-Norge [accessed 27 March 2017].

5 Until July 2016, there have been more than 3,485 sessions i.e. the period of time a user is actively engaged with our film platform. The total number of pages viewed in our film platform is 5,018. This includes repeated views of a single page. Pages refer to the film platform pages (e.g. the single partners' pages, but also 'the project', 'resources', extra material). 2,840 people have had at least one session within the date range 01/06/2015–11/07/2016. The number includes both new and returning users.

6 See also Lillejord and Dysthe (2008).

7 See www.alternativeproject.eu/assets/upload/Deliverable%202.4%20Final%20research%20report%20on%20conflict%20and%20RJ%20(1).pdf [accessed 27 March 2017].

8 The literary and culture theorist Michail Bakhtin develops in his work *The Dialogic Imagination* (1981) a theory of how the meaning of a text always is generated in a context, in Bakhtin's term heteroglossia. Language is of a hybrid nature, in terms of polyglossia and there is always a relation between different utterances, i.e. an intertextual relation. Texts are always built upon other texts, whether oral (auditory), written (visual) or visualized (e.g. pictures, films).

9 www.apa.org/monitor/oct05/mirror.aspx [accessed 29 June 2015].

10 www.oxforddictionaries.com/definition/learner/art [accessed 2 February 2016].

11 Association Française des Anthropologues: http://diss.kib.ki.se/2000/91-628-4183-1/ [accessed 24 March 2017].

References

Bakhtin, M., 1981. Translation Holquist, M. *The dialogic imagination: four essays*. Austin: University of Texas Press.

Cartier-Bresson, H., 1998. *The mind's eye. Writings on photography and photographers*. New York: Aperture.

Clynes, M. ed., 2013. *Music, mind, and brain: the neuropsychology of music*. Berlin: Springer Science & Business Media.

Dysthe, O. ed., 2001. *Dialog, samspel og læring*. Oslo: Abstrakt forlag.

Foss, E.M., 2016. Dialogens paradoks: Fremveksten av 'gjenopprettende prosesser' i Norge. PhD dissertation. Oslo: University of Oslo, Department of Social Anthropology.

Freudenthal, S., 2000. *Visualising the invisible: exploring interactive video in HIV prevention in rural Zambia*. Stockholm: Karolinska Institutet, Institutionen för folkhälsovetenskap/Department of Public Health Sciences.

Freudenthal, S. and Niemela, P., 1972. *A winters day with Emma and Vigert*. 30 minutes, black and white, sound (in Swedish). Belongs to Swedish Television, broadcast on Swedish Television, January 1973.

Grasseni, C. ed., 2007. *Skilled visions. Between apprenticeship and standards*. Oxford: Berghahn Books.

Grasseni, C., 2009. *Developing skill, developing vision: practices of locality at the foot of the Alps*. Oxford: Berghahn Books.

Gullestad, M., 1996. Modernity, self, and childhood in the analysis of life stories. In: M. Gullestad, ed. *Imagined childhoods: self and society in autobiographical accounts*. Oslo: Scandinavia University Press, pp. 1–39.

Gullestad, M. 2004. Blind slaves of our prejudice: debating 'culture' and 'race' in Norway. *Ethnos*, 69(2), pp. 177–203.

Gullestad, M., 2007. *Picturing pity. Pitfalls and pleasures in cross-cultural communication. Image and word in a North Cameroon mission*. Oxford: Berghahn Books.

Hasund, I.K. and Hydle, I., 2004. Evaluating a Norwegian RJ project: mediation as supplement to punishment in cases of serious violence. *Newsletter of the European Forum for Victim-Offender Mediation and Restorative Justice*, 5(2), pp. 1–3.

Hasund, I.K. and Hydle, I., 2007. *Ansikt til ansikt. Konfliktrådsmegling mellom gjerningsperson og offer i voldssaker*. Oslo: Cappelen akademisk forlag.

Haualand, H., 2002. *I endringens tegn*. Oslo: Tanum forlag.

Holtedahl, L., 2006. Klovn; klovnen som model for kulturformidling. *Rhetorica Scandinavica*, 40, pp. 78–92.

Hydle, I, and Lønneberg, M.G., 2014. Teaching peace and restorative practices at social sciences master level. Paper presentation at the 8th International Conference of the European Forum for Restorative Justice, June 2014.

Ingold, T., 2002. *The perception of the environment: essays on livelihood, dwelling and skill*. Abingdon: Psychology Press.

Ingold, T., 2010. Ways of mind-walking: reading, writing, painting. *Visual Studies*, 25(1), pp. 15–23.

Ingold, T., 2011. Worlds of sense and sensing the world: a response to Sarah Pink and David Howes. *Social Anthropology*, 19(3), pp. 313–317.

Jablonko, A., 1968. *Dance and daily activities among the Maring people of New Guinea: a cinematographic analysis of body movement style*. Doctoral Thesis, University of Maryland, with its companion film Maring in Motion. Additional footage.

Latour, B., 1999. *Pandora's hope: essays on the reality of science studies*. Cambridge, MA: Harvard University Press.

Latour, B., 2005. *Reassembling the social – an introduction to actor-network-theory*. Oxford: Oxford University Press.

Latour, B., 2012. *We have never been modern*. Cambridge, MA: Harvard University Press.

Lillejord, S. and Dysthe, O., 2008. Productive learning practice. A theoretical discussion based on two cases. *Journal of Education and Work*, 21(1), pp. 75–89.

Linell, P., 2009. *Rethinking language, mind, and world dialogically: interactional and contextual theories of human sense-making*. Scottsdale, AZ: Information Age Pub Inc.

MacDougall, D., 2005. *The corporeal image: film, ethnography, and the senses*. Princeton: Princeton University Press.

Nemes, G., High, C., Shafer, N. and Goldsmith, R., 2007. Using participatory video to evaluate community development. Paper for Working Group 3 XXII European Congress of Rural Sociology, Wageningen.

Oxford Advanced Learner's Dictionary 2016. Available at: www.oxforddictionaries.com/definition/learner/art [accessed 2 February 2016].

Pink, S. ed., 2012. *Advances in visual methodology*. New York: Sage.

Rollwagen, J.R. ed., 1988. *Anthropological film-making: anthropological perspectives on the production of film and video for general public audiences*. London: Psychology Press.

Sachs, L., 2003. *Lidandet har blivit en global handelsvara*. Stockholm: Svenska Dagbladet, Under strecket, 2 April.

Shaw, J. and Robertson, C., 1997. *Participatory video: a practical guide to using video creatively in group development work*. London: Routledge.

Waage, T., 2007. Om bilders potensial i samfunnsforskning. *Sosiologi i dag*, 36(1), pp. 105–116.

Wang, C., Wright, R., Hope, S. and Waage, T., 2012. Ungdomsblikk: Selvrefleksivt filmkurs som terapeutisk metode. *Tidsskrift for Norsk psykologforening*, 49(9), pp. 861–869.

Wenger-Trayner, E., Fenton-O'Creevy, M., Hutchinson, S., Kubiak, C. and Wenger-Trayner, B., 2014. *Learning in landscapes of practice: boundaries, identity, and knowledgeability in practice-based learning*. London: Routledge.

White, S. ed., 2003. *Participatory video: images that transform and empower*. London: Sage.

3 Participatory filming as part of action research in ALTERNATIVE

Experiences from four countries

Dóra Szegő

Introduction

In this chapter we introduce how film-making was conceptualized in the ALTERNATIVE project with the multiple aims of research, development and dissemination. First, participatory video as a development and research approach is discussed, as well as its interpretation within the framework of the ALTERNATIVE project. How was the concept of participatory film-making interpreted and applied according to the local realities of the different sites, and how could the action research project benefit from filming? What were the ethical questions implied and how did the research teams handle them? Based on the Hungarian example, the chapter will then present in detail how film-making happened in practice, what the main challenges were and what solutions were found. We present experiences gained and lessons learnt in a manner of use for other research projects when filming is planned as an action research tool.

Theoretical approaches to visual representations

The origins of participatory filming

Participatory filming found its origins in community development. The first, well-known experiment with a participatory video approach was the work of Don Snowden (2011), a Canadian who used filming as a community development approach in a fishing community of Newfoundland, in the 1960s. Through watching each other's films, the different villagers on the Fogo island realized similarities within their problems and started to act together for problem solution. The films reached policy makers and resulted in a substantial transformation on a governmental level. Snowden summarized his experiences in formulating basic principles of video for community development. The most important principle he laid out is the concept of exchange learning, where the interchange via the medium of video is used to facilitate communication within the community and between the community and policy-making actors.

Despite the endeavour to create guidelines, participatory filming does not have a consistent theoretical and methodological approach, as well as an institutional or academic background. The practitioners interpret the lack of standards with the flexible, contextual and culturally sensitive nature of the approach. Most initiatives operate on a micro-level and aim for local change. Due to their focus on action, in many cases they lack a systematic methodological background, documentation and analysis. They do not tend to build upon each other's experiences. Social anthropologists, social workers, community developers and alternative educators use participatory video in their own ways, according to their own contextual aims. The common ground that ties the different approaches together is the active participation of the addressed community that can take place in various ways, and the importance of the participatory process over the product.

Based on the literature of participatory video, three different types of participatory video projects can be defined, based on their goals (Shaw and Robertson, 1997; Huber, 1999): participatory video can serve a 'therapeutic' aim both on an individual and a group level. If used in that way, video helps to reflect on the needs of the participants and communicate those towards the others. In the therapy-type of participatory video projects the process is more important than the outcome and the videos are created more for the community and its members and less for the public. The project is owned by the participants. The second type of participatory video projects serves 'advocacy' aims. There is a broad range of participation of local community members in those processes. The video activists – often external actors – play an important, and often more active role in the video production than the members of the community. The videos address social injustice and oppression of the target group, which is usually a vulnerable and subordinate group of the society. The projects are typically owned by the external actors. The product and its public dissemination – as a channel of advocacy – is important in this type of participatory video project. The third type of participatory videos serve 'empowerment' of a community and its members, and is in between activism and therapy approaches. It is therapeutic in the sense of reflection and self-expression and activist in the sense of its dissemination to the stakeholders and due to its aim of personal and social development. External actors – participatory film directors, development practitioners and facilitators – are actively involved in the process. The community members often take part in the production of the videos, at least through giving feedback to the directors about the footage.

Academic interest towards participatory filming emerged in community development studies, anthropology and sociology, closely related to the action research approach, where participatory filming is one of the research tools. Reflective dialogues between local community members and external actors (community development practitioners, facilitators, researchers) accompany the filming process, with the intention to involve the 'local expertise' of the research subjects in the development and research procedure (White, 2003). In that respect participatory filming material – besides empowerment – also serves as a qualitative data source of social-scientific research. The approach of the ALTERNATIVE project regarding participatory filming was mostly related to the 'empowerment approach' and had the dual intention of community development and social-scientific research. The videos offered a new perspective on several aspects of the local reality that were captured and documented differently with other research methods on the field. For example, when a video footage about the Village Day was screened in the Hungarian action research site, the local Roma people revealed a new reasoning of Roma people's activity on official, local events that contrasted other interpretations the researchers built up when analysing interviews. While Roma participation on local events was interpreted as a sign of integration into the local society by the researchers, when watching the videos, Roma people marked that they participated in the local programmes through the motive of mocking and teasing the non-Roma people.

Filming in the ALTERNATIVE project

Filming practices in Northern Ireland, Serbia and Austria

The overall objective of the ALTERNATIVE action research project was to offer an alternative understanding of handling and transforming conflicts in an intercultural context. The research started with the creation of a coherent theoretical framework, that has been built around the alternative understandings of security and justice in four different intercultural settings. The four different settings were attached to four different countries: Northern Ireland, Austria, Serbia and Hungary. On the basis of the common theoretical framework and conceptual background, four different approaches of empirical action models for conflict transformation in intercultural settings have been developed in the four countries. These models included action based on restorative principles (including restorative approach-based community building, education and case management), reseach and filming of the process. On the one hand, local films in each country were constructed with different purposes, including conflict transformation, research, education and dissemination. On the other hand, a common final film was created from the local footages, to be used for educational and dissemination goals. Making one final film including all the various local stories, reflecting the whole project and synthetizing all the different approaches of the local film-makers was a great challenge. This endeavour showed the complexity and uniqueness of each research site and could have been achieved only to a limited extent in the end. Therefore, the final film gave a visual platform for the researchers to explain the action research process and some conclusions.[1]

Considering filming, the human resources and local conditions of the research sites resulted in different approaches of using visual representation as a research tool. The different approaches were characterized by different roles and extent of involvement by the local residents in the filming process. In Serbia and Northern Ireland, due to the distances of the research sites, coupled with the limitations of resources and time, action researchers adopted a more classical documentary approach of filming. Locals as well as researchers were involved as interview subjects. The videos represented the perspectives of locals and researchers on the field. In Austria and Hungary, more participatory approaches were implemented. All research sites borrowed some principles from the 'empowerment' approach of participatory filming when screening the footage to the people, asking for reflections and using the videos to strengthen the relationship between the local community and the action research team.

Northern Ireland

In Northern Ireland, the action research team recorded a series of narratives, stories from the people's own perspectives. In the researchers' interpretation, the videos had an impact on the action research in two ways: they served as a source of information and as research instruments. Moreover they influenced the researchers' knowledge construction. As Hugh Campbell, researcher in Northern Ireland phrased it:

> Videos made me see connections in a fresher way. Film is a medium that works for me better than papers. Especially when searching for common points among the issues of the four research sites, Serbia, Northern Ireland, Austria and Hungary.

In Northern Ireland, the films were mainly used on public platforms, including educational initiatives. These occasions with local and international audiences stimulated discussion about the communities' capacity to use restorative practices to address harm. A participatory aspect of filming in Northern Ireland was the film screenings that the action research team organized for the participants, who gave feedback on the edits and approval for publicly using the films.

Serbia

In Serbia, the main purpose of filming in their local research sites was to document the relevant points of the research and to gain information on things they would not have been able to capture otherwise. Filming helped the research team to get a deeper insight into the social context of the local communities. Second, filming was used as a specific way of introducing local participants into the action research project, building up and representing a community context in which the restorative approach was implemented. The filming crew saw a potential in filming as a restoration tool, since it was a way to tell the stories of past conflicts and their consequences, and it generated discussions related to conflicts in communities where different ethnic groups live together. The final local film was presented in the local communities. While watching the film, members of different ethnic groups could identify many similarities in the relations and conflicts in different regions that at first glance have very little in common. The three main characters in the film – one from each of the research sites – had formative roles in the construction of the film by giving feedback and comments on the footages.

Austria

In Austria the researchers experimented with participatory filming approaches and involved local citizens more actively in the creation of the local films as reporters and as co-directors. Both the professionals and the residents participating in the movie were excited about this opportunity and many of them got connected to the project through the film-making. In that way, film-making had a positive, motivational impact on local participation. The Austrian research team did involve the locals in the direction and production of the footage as well: they gave the camera to the women at a local, intercultural community setting, the Women's Café, where local women of 'Old Austrian' and 'Turkish' origin come together,[2] as well as to the youngsters in the Bassena Centre, a local community centre, related to the multi-ethnic housing estate of the Schöpfwerk neighbourhood.[3] In one occasion, for example, the women were holding the camera and shooting the material, which was included in the films. This had an intensive impact on the participants: for those who got involved, the film-making was the most vivid way of relating to the project.

According to the views of the Austrian action research team, film-making itself could be considered as an intervention: due to storytelling, it bears a lot of potential for alternative restorative justice processes, which was manifested in their film-making activity with the adolescents: 'Film-making was a door-opener for us in the field that helped to get in touch with the adolescents', as Katrin Kremmel, researcher in Austria described it. There were a lot of conflicts in the local housing estate of Schöpfwerk between adult residents and adolescents. The film-making with the action research team helped the adolescents to share their perspective about conflicts in the neighbourhood and their attachment to the housing estate. The adolescents participated in the editing process of the film with feedback and suggestions. The film was screened for local residents in an open-air cinema event at the housing estate, where about 100 residents got to see it and gave standing ovations for it. The adults got to see how difficult local life can be for the adolescents in the housing estate, the impact of stigmatization processes and the adolescents' high level of care for their neighbourhood. Similarly to Hungary, this way the video itself became a first step of a dialogue process between the adolescents and other local residents that otherwise could not have been reached.

The following part of the chapter will focus on the Hungarian example, describing how filming was defined and situated within the conceptual framework of the action research, as well as its impacts on the research. This concrete example clarifies both the advantages and challenges of using participatory filming as a research tool.

The participatory approach of filming as a research tool in Hungary

The relation between action, research and filming

The overall approach of our action research consisted of three components: restorative action, research and filming; the relation between these three was of great importance. Realizing restorative activities related to conflicts in an intercultural setting had the highest priority. Research was subordinate to restorative dialogues, and the objective of the research was to support the reflection on alternative understandings of justice and security, through the analysis of restorative interventions into actual conflicts. Based on the phenomenological paradigm (Berger and Luckmann, 1991), which derives the social order from everyday social interactions, knowledge on the field was gained through the interactions between local people and the research team. Local people were involved as active participants to give constant feedback in various forms and scenarios; the films were one among other platforms to share local reflections.[4] The camera was introduced at the very beginning as part of the research. It was not given to the research subjects, but the local people were treated as a critical audience of the films.

Film-makers also took part in the knowledge construction. Thus our approach was close to Jean Rouch's (2003) concept of 'shared anthropology', which puts the focus on the mutual self-reflexivity between the film-makers and the subjects, and refers to the constant feedback of those who are filmed. Shared anthropology as a concept was established by Rouch as a reaction to power positions in colonized countries, to give voice to the suppressed, whose viewpoints and interests were not represented before. In our understanding, filming was considered as a 'third eye', being subject to the first two components (restorative dialogues and research) in the sense that it accompanied the action and the research. Sufficient care was taken not to hinder the restorative dialogues or research activities.

We created three films in the Hungarian research site. Each film had a different focus, but tried to document and reflect on the phases of the action research, through the eyes of the different actors. The aim was to capture the local interpretations attached to restorative dialogues, as well as to the main analytic concepts: security, justice, conflicts and coexistence in intercultural settings.

The film-making crew

The film-makers – just like in all the research sites of other, participating countries – were the researchers themselves, which caused some role conflicts, since filming meant a basically different presence for the researchers than using other qualitative research tools, such as interviews or participant observations. Double roles of being a researcher and a film-maker at the same time made it more difficult for the locals to situate some members of the team as actors in the village. Negative stereotypes against the camera fuelled by the bad experiences with media caused some resistance when we filmed at the research site. In addition to the researchers, we had a professional cameraman, who helped to make the procedure of recording and editing fluent. The cameraman's Roma ethnic origin and local familiarity was an added value, which made it easier to approach local Roma people with the camera.

The place of filming within the action research

After a negotiation process with the mayor, the members of the village council and the local Roma Minority Government we signed a Memorandum of Understanding with the village council, as an official confirmation that they welcomed and allowed us to conduct the action research in the village. The Hungarian action research started with the 'problem analysis' (Szegő, Benedek and Győrfi, 2015), where we tried to identify the main local groups of interest, their interpretations of conflicts, reasoning behind disputes and conflict-management strategies through desk research, interviews and participatory observation. That phase intended to build trust between the research group and the local residents via personal conversations, informal meetings and workshops.

Formal presence in the village was realized through the regular meetings of the Local Support Group that we established from motivated locals who were willing to assist the research process with information and feedback. At the same time we started restorative case work with those conflicts that came out in interviews and where we saw any motivation from the locals to deal with the case. Based on the first experiences with conflict cases we started to deconstruct our efforts to build formal restorative case scenarios. We realized that informal methods, episodic interventions and actions that functioned in the realm of community development, capacity and skill building were more effective at that stage than formal restorative interventions.

We used participatory filming as a means of action research throughout the research phase of exploration (which was based on interviews, participant observations and discussions), action (which consisted of different forms of intervention, from restorative learning through informal discussions to formal dialogue situations) and evaluation (which meant a reflective dialogue on the process, together with the research subjects). We video-documented some of our activities, including the workshops of the Local Support Group and some of the restorative circles, and asked for the opinion of local participants, dialoguers and researchers about these activities.

The turn and its consequences

Although we as action researchers tried to involve all voices, local people interpreted our presence in a political power space. We were granted an approval to work in the village from the local village council, governed by the then mayor. He did not belong to a political party but was labelled as left-liberal by the locals. We slowly had to release the ethos of an independent standpoint as dialoguers and researchers: however hard we tried to take that position, local people labelled us very differently. Political-ideological preferences in the village determined people's cooperation with us: it was a characteristic of the whole action research that was manifest in the filming as well. Some people refused to tell their opinion in front of the camera, based on the political fault line. Due to the Memorandum with the then council, in some local people's interpretation the ALTERNATIVE research supported the mayor's interests. They were critical and distrustful towards the research and questioned its legitimacy.

In the last year of our action research, local governmental elections took place. The composition of the local council changed completely and a new mayor was elected. The new situation gave an opportunity for us to reconsider our activities' impact on the local community from a new perspective and to lay new foundations of cooperation with the new leaders of the village.

The local election made it reasonable to interpret local reactions in the framework of a political power-play: as Zoettl (2012, p. 217) argues in his article about participatory video, identity and empowerment, being visible and making others visible is a form of symbolic power. The state and its agents, as well as other institutions establish identities by assigning 'names' to social groups, but the power of exhibiting – or masking – certain groups within or from public discourse is an even more dominant component of exposing symbolic power. According to Bourdieu (1998, p. 52), to the same extent that words have a part in the creation of social entities, the state gains a quasi-divine power by stating with authority the 'truth' about what a being (thing or person) is in truth: the state gives a socially legitimate definition of what they are and what they have a right to be. These ideas correspond with our experience that after the new elite got into a power-position they started to open up and became motivated to express 'the truth' in the film. The new mayor phrased her disappointment in an official letter as feedback to the second film:

> Watching your film, our impression was that you intend to publish a film to the world that interprets our village as a hopeless, shabby, run-down village consisting of Roma slums. It makes a quite disappointing impression about us that you picture us as a locality where people ride horse carts, which is 50 years behind the times. People who live here and we, who represent them, refuse this proceeding. You have been working here for years, recording an incredible amount of raw material. We were shocked how impossible it is to get a credible picture of our village based on your edition.

A dialogue process had started with the new mayor and her supporters, where filming was the most significant means, next to personal negotiations and workshops, to create space for sharing dissatisfaction. We used the restorative approach in a conflict between the locals and the action research team, whereby local people experienced that criticism was respected and heard: we asked them to tell us more about what they did not like in the films, as we wanted to understand. In our understanding, this restorative reaction was the key that turned the new elite of the village from resistance towards cooperation. It gave us some hope for a wider understanding and legitimacy to restorative approaches and dialogue processes in the village. That dialogue was represented in the third film about the action research.

Ethical concerns of filming and the relation between filming and restoration

The main ethical concern of film-making that we faced from time to time was centred around the relativity of knowledge and representation: knowledge and interpretations were based on the relative position of the viewer. To what extent can we as film-makers function as a credible and legitimate channel to represent the various viewpoints of local people?

As discussed in international workshops organized within the framework of the project,[5] the other countries' action researchers faced the same dilemmas while filming within the framework of the action research, concerning the subjective standpoint of the researcher. As Katrin Kremmel, researcher from Austria phrased it:

> When making a movie, what we do is constructing a story. And just like with any other story, who speaks in a movie, who gets to represent whom, how personal statements are contextualized and edited into a story-line are also questions of representational politics.

Hugh Campbell, researcher from Northern Ireland, had similar concerns when filming: 'Bias arises from how conscious I was about the choices I made when film-making. Who to interview, how to visually portray them, what to edit.'

Negative reactions of the locals in Hungary highlighted the difficulty of this endeavour and underlined the ethical responsibility of the researchers when interpreting locality through film as a visual medium. After the videos were edited, locals got the opportunity to watch these. For many people the films were the only form of connection with ALTERNATIVE research; as a consequence, they constructed their opinion about the action research through the films. Although the restorative dialogues and research activities were prior to filming and the films accompanied and supported the dialogue and research activities, we experienced that by its very nature, the films, in the end, became the most visible result of our activity and left the most remarkable trace in the field. The overwhelming power of visuality compared to every other medium thus became obvious.

The nature of films compared to dialogues

A further important concern arose from the basic difference between the nature of film compared to dialogue processes. While the restorative approach believes in the continuous change of relationships through dialogue, film – by its nature –

can capture only snapshots of opinions and of conflict situations. 'Photographs are a way of imprisoning reality […]. One can't possess reality, one can possess images – one can't possess the present but one can possess the past', as Susan Sontag captures (1977, p. 163). Similarly to how photos conserve aspects of the reality, films also conserve and file opinions, which goes against dialogue processes in a certain sense.

If we filmed a dialogue process, we tried to bridge the gap between the nature of a dialogue and the snapshots of a film by accompanying the dialogue processes and capturing the transformation of opinions through the film. But dialogues have a natural, dialectic way of elaboration. Direct reflections cannot be realized when people state their opinion in films.

Recorded opinions can be displayed at any time and may not have a positive effect on the relationship between the people who are concerned. We experienced that tension, as is shown in the following example. As we mentioned previously, some locals refused to share their opinion and did not give interviews in the first two films. This led to the situation that the videos captured only a particular set of opinions, most of all about intercultural conflicts. Roma residents spoke about racism and discrimination against the Roma in the village. Poverty was also expressed. Some villagers did not see the legitimacy of these 'alternative narratives' about the village. When they saw the videos they became outraged and disappointed that the picture outlined in the films by others about the village was not corresponding with their own opinion and expectations. A recently elected local councillor expressed his indignation in the following way:

> I could have eaten you alive when I saw that film […] it was very biased. Those people who want to act for the village were not represented. I took it personally, since I was raised in the village, even my surname contains the name of the village. Whenever I go somewhere, I go with a smile and take the good reputation of the village with me. And my picture does not contain that people hate each other here, or that they are hostile towards each other, or discriminatory, or anything like that. You cannot draw a picture like that. It is outrageous!

Interpreting the outrage as a reaction to the films in a conflict-theoretical framework we can say that the representations about the village in the first two films that disturbed the conservative, middle-class villagers were mostly the opinions of the oppressed. Videos provided a platform to these subordinate narratives that have been perceived to pose a risk to the distribution of power: films, through highlighting power inequalities, challenging the status quo, became a means of advocacy. Unlike in many participatory film-making projects, in our case advocacy through videos was rather an unexpected impact than an original intention of film-making.

If no dialogue took place between the parties, we tried to create a dialogue platform with the means of the filming itself. That happened with the example of the disappointment of the new elite: although the new local leaders have not accepted us as 'independent' mediators in the village, our receptive attitude to their outrage transformed some of them from resistance towards communication via the film.

Interpretations and their consequences

As to participatory filming, Hungary faced the contradiction that despite the fact that filming is considered to be a platform where – compared to other mediums of research such as a qualitative analysis based on interviews and participatory observations – information goes through the lowest levels of interpretation and opinions are viewed in their 'original form', we received sharp criticism on how we represented the local reality in the films. This situation is described well in Geertz's (1973, p. 5) thick description[6] study, where he uses the following metaphor:

> Believing, with Max Weber, that man is an animal suspended in webs of significance he himself has spun, I take culture to be those webs, and the analysis of it to be therefore not an experimental science in search of law but an interpretive one in search of meaning.

We found it very important to be self-aware of the many-sided nature of interpretations. We considered that film is a platform, which might reflect back the typical labels and stereotypes about certain groups in the village, and reflects the research teams' own perspective about the site. Each scene could be interpreted differently by the filming persons, the dialoguers, the researchers and the critical audience. To give an example: the Hungarian filming crew filmed the governmental councillor in the library and the Roma Minority Government councillor in his horse stable. Although the reason behind these venue choices was the people's availability in those places, we experienced that the spectators associated alternative meanings with these scenes that we could not imagine before. Besides giving their own interpretations, some spectators supposed hidden intentions behind our selection of the scenes. For example, in the case of the horse stable, the members of the new elite expressed the opinion that by filming the Roma Minority Government councillor in a poor environment, we eliminated the fact that his house was renovated through governmental aid. Nothing was 'innocent' and everything we did or did not do had a local consequence. Parallel to silence[7] being as important as speech, what we had not captured in the films was at least as meaningful for the locals as details that we did capture. Some villagers questioned why we put poor neighbourhoods into the films at all. They interpreted that we wanted to show a negative image about the village, because we, according to such allegations, 'worked for the former mayor', who's intention was to defame the villagers and show a more distressing picture of the Roma people's poverty and exclusion in the village.

Filming as a tool to gain scientific knowledge and for building relationships

We participated with the camera on every local event where we were invited. These events were inexhaustible sources of data. They offered the opportunity for the researchers to engage in conversations with villagers, who interpreted these illustrious events. In some cases we even documented these conversations with the camera. As foreseen, we made much more footage, i.e. video material, during the 30 months of the action research than what we put into the videos. All these materials were considered as relevant to scientific knowledge, used in the research as target of analysis. The visual image of groups present and groups missing from the events, or the spatial representation of different groups on the spot – together with the verbal interpretations of the locals – revealed valuable information about the local division of the society.

A local charity ball serves as an example. The ball was organized by a civil association of the newcomers (those people who migrated to the village in the last decades, mostly from the city) and was among those few local events were Roma people were present. It could have been captured as an inclusion story by the camera, since compared to most events that the Roma do not even visit, here the Roma and non-Roma people were having fun together. But we initiated a dialogue with the representative of the local Roma Minority Government, who first asked us if we recognized that the Roma people sat at separate tables from the non-Roma's and then emphasized the separation of Roma people at the ball.

Participation in local events with the camera also offered unique social data for the research team. The organizers of balls, school events, festivals, etc. were pleased to have footages about these events and requested 'special editions' for their own purposes to document and store these videos. The filming crew was ready to accomplish these requests. That cooperation built relationships with the locals, supported trust and had a positive impact on joining dialogue processes.

Filming as a way to get a different insight into narratives

An additional yet very important aspect of filming was the screenings and the following dialogues about the videos with the locals. These dialogues with some groups of the local society contributed to a more comprehensive use of filming as a research tool. Film screening was used in some situations to improve our bonds with social groups where there was an inconvenient lack of connections between us and lack of information about one another. One of these groups was the villagers with a Roma ethnic background. While searching for a proper way to approach that community, we decided to do a special video edition, with the intention to draw attention to and fuel discussions about the village and how people live together. We made a 15-minute video sketch from our footage that captured spontaneous moments of different events, mainly local gatherings. Some parts of the video would capture events and venues that were unknown and strange to the local Roma people: their social and/or economic status did not allow them to participate.[8] We initiated a discussion through this video, enabling them to peep into unknown places of local reality. The facilitated group discussion around the video made it possible to reveal some aspects of the local narratives of Roma people that we had not been able to explore before. It provided us with an insight beyond the 'grand narratives'[9] and with a deeper understanding on the level of local realities. Personal stories revealed local wisdom, which seemed to exist only in ambiguous fragments. We revealed new perspectives that were different from those that we had experienced before in interviews and participant observations. For example, inspired by the video about the Village Day (a yearly organized summer festival in the village), Roma people told a story where they mocked the Hungarian band playing, that they disliked. The punch line of the story was the non-understanding of the non-Roma, who did not catch the irony but 'took it literally'. That discussion highlighted the role of irony to handle social gaps and discrimination. The following quotation represents the dialogue from which the story was reconstructed (quotation from the group discussion after the video was shown):

WOMAN 1: 'What did I say? Marcsi, Jani – all of us were there. Recently. The Hungarian band was playing very poorly. The instruments were moaning in a way as if there was a problem.'

MAN: 'It was like a punishment! Indeed!'

WOMAN 1: 'I started to dance … as a mockery. I called Marika in. His wife and her sister. About five people started to dance. But just to make a mockery of the band. We made such a dance that about 50 Hungarian people stood up from the audience. And everybody was dancing with us. Am I correct?'

MAN: 'Yes, the Roma started the party.'

WOMAN 2: 'And we elevated the good mood, although we only wanted to flout the band.'

QUESTIONER: 'But they didn't get it?'

WOMAN 3: 'No! They thought that we liked the music. Such a big party worked out that they did not let us go home. Ok, I know that some of you went home. But I carried on. So … by the end even such people came to me to dance who I would never have expected. […] About eight people were Roma, all the others were Gádzsó [synonym of non-Roma Hungarian).]'

MAN: 'Even less Roma by the end.'

WOMAN 3: 'Six or seven Roma women made 50 people to stand up.'

MAN: 'So from this story you can see how Roma people are!'

WOMAN 3: 'And by the end all the Hungarians came: "Dance with me! Dance with me!"'

WOMAN 4: 'This is an example that nothing depends on the Roma when the question comes to cooperation.'

The role of filming as a tool in the restorative dialogue process

The last 'chapter' of our dialogue process with the new mayor and the new elite about the third film brought a breakthrough. The new local stakeholders and their supporters finally shared their opinion about our films and research activity, as well as their points on local issues that were raised by other villagers in previous films, including intercultural conflicts and coexistence in the village with newcomers and with the local Roma.

However hard we tried to comprehensively reflect opinions, when we screened the first edited version to the new mayor and her supporters, the reaction was outrage and dissatisfaction with the context and ways they were presented in the film. That episode of our dialogue intensified their previous prejudice, namely that we edited their reports in a subjective way that gave a false, biased image of the village and of them as councillors and villagers.

Across the negotiation process about the film, we realized that there is a lack of shared understanding between the new local stakeholders and the action research team about the goals of the ALTERNATIVE project and of filming. While the research team facilitated dialogue through films and believed in dialogue processes as keys of development and change, the local leaders wanted a film that portrayed them as inclusive and tolerant and promoted their social development activities in institutions and infrastructure (e.g the Dedication Ceremony of the new Country House or those few local events where Roma families were represented). Based on the reflections of the new mayor and her supporters, we re-edited the film and screened the new version for them.

Our last screening worked as a stage of a restorative dialogue process. The re-edited version of the third film finally reflected the views of the new mayor and her supporters in a way that they accepted, that they could identify themselves with. In our interpretation, the three films became three sequences of dialogues among various local groups (the indigenous residents and the newcomers, the Roma and the non-Roma, the rich and the poor, the liberals and the conservatives). People, who otherwise had not communicated with each other, could have seen each other's standpoints and interpretations about several local issues – including intercultural conflicts – that had not been discussed before.

Filming was introduced as a means that accompanied and documented the action research, but by the end it became a main platform of a dialogical process about intercultural conflicts. Filming was similar to facilitation between the parties by listening to their stories, documenting it and showing it to each other. The local residents shared their stories and interpretations in the films and listened to other people's stories through the films. By the end, they started to 'hear each other' and accept the legitimacy of narratives other than their own.

That change was manifested on the screening of the third film to the participants. A scene of the film reported about a healing circle organized within the framework of the action research for the losing ex-mayor, his candidates and their local voters to process the harm related to the offensive election campaign and their loss. The new mayor, after watching the film remarked how difficult it must have been for the old leaders to lose the elections after 12 years of governance. Arriving to a phase of resonance through the film can be interpreted as an analogy to the second stage of a mediation process,[10] 'sharing individual perspectives' – when parties are asked to present their individual stories and the other party is not allowed to interrupt. If we imagine a dialogue process, after that stage come the reflections, the expression of common points and searching for possible solutions.

Experiences and lessons learnt on filming as an action research tool

The project as carried out at local sites in four countries taught us several lessons on filming as a research tool. Participatory film-making supported various levels of the action research: including the documentation of the research activities, creating and strengthening the relationship between the local community and the action research team, assisting the dialogue process through giving space for sharing and reflection in the camera and on local screenings. Besides those functions of participatory filming that took place on the field, the films were used in education about intercultural conflicts and restorative justice, as well as for dissemination.

Throughout the filming process we learned how difficult it is to keep a neutral position as action researchers, dialoguers and participatory film-makers alike. The locals interpreted our action research activities through the films and attributed unintended meanings to them. When an action research includes participatory film-making in a local community, researchers have to take into account the difficulty of adopting a non-biased position and the challenge of being credible for the various local groups. Moreover, they should be aware of the power of visual representation and the non-intended consequences of making complex social realities and conflicts visual.

In Hungary, the filming activity manifested the strong fragmentation of the local community that was experienced in the action research as well. People were not ready to sit down at a table and discuss deeply rooted conflicts, and they were not willing to participate in the same film as a 'visual platform' to talk about their issues. The best we could do was to share the different films that represented different voices from the locality and to ask for reflections. Critical opinions were welcomed and channelled into the next film.

We believe that the restorative dialogue starts from telling and listening to stories. Our films created a platform to share local stories and standpoints, which is an important step on the way towards a direct, face-to-face dialogue. By the end of the action research, filming led the restorative procedure until that stage, including telling and listening to the stories of the vulnerable, disadvantaged social groups of the village. Next steps towards a dialogue have to be taken by the villagers. We hope that people will do that for the sake of a more peaceful future of the village.

For the project as a whole, filming proved to be a great challenge for the action researchers who took on filming. Although the project's coordinator organized workshops to train the researchers and supported them throughout the project by offering advice on the script as well as the editing, filming and especially participatory film-making required specific skills and more time and budget than was foreseen. Furthermore, the original idea was to integrate the local films into one common documentary. This proved to be unachievable due to the different filming styles as well as local contexts. Therefore, creative solutions were found. First, an online platform was created for the different films and footages to be used more interactively together with the project's manual (www.alternativefilms.euforumrj.org). Second, all project partners were interviewed on the basis of a common scheme to reflect upon the project results, for other researchers and practitioners to learn from the common endeavour. This shows how action research is an open process: while certain actions and research tools may have been set up beforehand, the process needed to remain flexible in order to address obstacles and challenges encountered, as will be shown in the following chapters where we describe the actions on the field.

Notes

1 The final film is available on the online platform of the ALTERNATIVE project: http://alternativefilms.euforumrj.org/.

2 Frauencafé – Women's Café had been established in one of the housing estates of the 21st district of Vienna, by a local community development organization, wohnpartner, as a reaction to conflicts between 'Old Austrians' and mainly 'Turkish' residents. In the Frauencafé, women of the two groups come together in fortnightly breakfast meetings (Chapter 4, this volume).

3 The community centre 'Bassena Stadtteilzentrum am Schöpfwerk' has been running since 1982, when the first residents moved into the Schöpfwerk neighbourhood, 12th district of Vienna. Today the housing estate inhabits about 5,000 residents, who speak up to 20 different languages. The Bassena is a sub-organization of the NGO 'Verein Wiener Jugendzentren' (Vienna Youth Centres), which receives its funding from the City of Vienna, but the Bassena has gained a degree of financial independence through the years. The main objectives of the centre are to activate residents and create local networks and connections among the people, as well as to promote awareness raising, support political representation and help them overcome social exclusion. For more information, see Chapter 4, this volume.

4 For further information on the local platforms of participation see Chapter 5, this volume.

5 Within the project, a first workshop was organized to train the researchers on how to handle the camera and come to a common script. In the final year, another workshop was organized to support the researchers in their final editing.

6 Thick description is a term introduced by the anthropologist Clifford Geertz for an interpretative way of understanding the meanings of human behaviour.

7 The phenomenon of silence culture and the ways towards dialogue processes were discussed in Héra *et al.* (2014).

8 For more information about these events and venues see Héra *et al.* (2015) and Szegő *et al.* (2015).

9 For more information about the diffentiation between 'grand narratives' and personal stories, see Szegő *et al.* (2015).

10 The stages of a mediation process are the following: (1) the mediator introduces the process; (2) the parties tell their stories; (3) the mediator identifies and frames issues and sets the agenda for negotiation; (4) the parties discuss common points and search for possible solutions; (5) the parties select alternatives; (6) the parties may make and sign an agreement.

References

Berger, L.P. and Luckmann, T., 1991. *The social construction of reality*. London: Penguin Books.

Bourdieu, P., 1998. *Practical reason. On the theory of action*. Stanford, California: Stanford University Press.

Geertz, C., 1973. Thick description: toward an interpretative theory of culture. In: *The interpretation of cultures*. New York: Basic Books.

Héra, G., Benedek, G., Szegő, D. and Győrfi, E., 2015. *Comprehensive final report*. Public deliverable 5.5 of the ALTERNATIVE project. Budapest: Foresee. Available at: www.alternativeproject.eu/wp-content/uploads/2014/12/Deliverable-5.5-Comprehensive-final-report.pdf [accessed 16 March 2017].

Héra, G., Győrfi, É., Szegő, D., Balla, L. and Kelemen, K., 2014. *Problem analysis*. Non-public deliverable 5.2.a of the ALTERNATIVE project. Budapest: Foresee.

Huber, B., 1999. Communicative aspects of participatory video projects: an explanatory study. Master's thesis. Uppsala: Swedish University of Agricultural Sciences.

Rouch, J., 2003. *Ciné-ethnography*. Ed: Feld, S. Minnesota: University Minnesota Press.

Shaw, J. and Robertson, C., 1997. *Participatory video: a practical guide to using video creatively in group development work*. London: Routledge.

Snowden, D., 2011. *Eyes see, ears hear*. Newfoundland: Memorial University.

Sontag, S., 1977. *On photography*. London: Penguin Books.

Szegő, D., Benedek, G. and Győrfi, E., 2015. *Evaluation and follow-up report*. Non-public deliverable 5.4 of the ALTERNATIVE project. Budapest: Foresee.

White, S. ed., 2003. *Participatory video: images that transform and empower*. London: Sage.

Zoettl, P.A., 2012. Images of culture: participatory video, identity and empowerment. *International Journal of Cultural Studies*, 16(2), pp. 209–224.

4 Getting involved and remaining distant

On action research in Vienna

Katrin Kremmel and Christa Pelikan

Introduction

This contribution consists of two main parts. In the first part, 'The essence of action research', we refer to some of the basic considerations about action research we had developed in the course of the theoretical efforts of the first year of project ALTERNATIVE.

The other more lengthy part provides close descriptions of our action research activities in Vienna's social housing estates. Throughout, ALTERNATIVE researchers aimed at directly involving citizens in solving their conflicts and reaching out for justice as a means for promoting democracy and active citizenship. An objective of ALTERNATIVE was, coherent with restorative justice philosophy, to include citizens in various steps of the local research, but also to set up the whole project as an action research in which theory feeds practice and vice versa. Furthermore, there was the objective to give scientific input into the enhanced understanding and development of action research methodology.

In this contribution, reflections about specific topics that relate to action research are interspersed in these descriptions and quotations from the action researcher's logbook. They deal with 'transparency', 'community ownership' and 'dependence and independence'. The theoretical concept that served as a guiding star for carrying out action research in Vienna is first of all active participation and its more radical version 'community ownership'; an extract of the relevant theoretical discussion of this concept will precede the main section.

The basso continuo of the whole article is contained in its heading: it is about the tension between getting involved and remaining distant.

The essence of action research

In the very beginning of the ALTERNATIVE project, we had invested quite some thought on the particular methodological dimensions of action research. As Ivo Aertsen (2010, p. 2) states:

> The separation between practitioners and researchers is fading away to some extent in favour of a relationship of cooperation and a process of influencing

> each other. Researchers and researched are equal in the discussion, and a priori expertise from only one corner is not accepted. But expertise can be specific: knowledge about own experiences and insights on the one hand, and expertise about collecting, analysing and presenting data on the other hand.

See also Stringer (1999) and Reason and Bradbury (2001) for a discussion of this point.

During the first phase of the research project we discussed and further specified the contribution and the task of the researcher in the endeavour of action research.

First, the researcher is taking a specific point of view, a 'second order' observation point (Luhmann, 1984). The meta-perspective entailed in this second-order observation is to be understood as one that is apt to produce a perception of social phenomena that is adding something to the perceptions of the immediate actors. It is different, but not 'superior'. This addition of a different perspective makes for an enrichment, a broadening and a balancing of perception.

This perception is informed and guided by:

- knowledge of the societal ecology. The concept of 'societal ecology' can be characterized as a 'process-oriented' concept paying particular attention to the various sequences of a singular reform. It also recasts this singular reform within the sequence of changes taking place in the broader socio-political field (legal/criminal policy, scientific, media fields, for example). Such an approach allows understanding the rise and dawn of new ideas and of counter-ideas in recasting them in their context. It involves questions such as: 'under which conditions, at which stages of overall developments, does an idea take shape and appears to compete with other ideas and policies?'; 'when and how did reform efforts take which turn?'; 'on what did they focus and in which way did policy decisions influence the developments at later stages?' (Bolivar, Pelikan and Lemonne, 2015);
- knowledge of theoretical concepts and pieces of theory that offer – already at that stage – ad hoc interpretations of the phenomena observed.

Second, with conventional empirical research the knowledge generated is 'handlungsentlastet' a term created and used by Jürgen Habermas (1992), meaning that it is cognisance relieved (freed) from the pressure of immediate action. It thus remains outside the 'whirl of action' and – more important – outside the constraints of 'reality' of everyday life, outside organizational constraints and outside the constraints of acting in the arena of politics. Both characteristics, second-order observation and 'relief from involvement in action' (*Handlungsentlastung*), allow for perceiving phenomena and developments through a different lens – in the last instance this results in a distancing effect.[1]

This is decidedly different in action research. In action research, researchers do get involved in action at the research sites, they are initiating interventions that are to lead to change.

We would like to question whether – notwithstanding this involvement – it is necessary for research to maintain a certain distance in order to make its specific contribution. Does such distance open new paths to knowledge? Does such distance promote a contribution of research that is broader and more balanced, or does it rather introduce the pretence of objective and 'rational' knowledge that claims the kind of superiority we actually strive to overcome? In other words: is distance to be equated with staying remote and being reduced to a 'cold' rationality?

Finally, and of paramount importance, all the material produced by research activities through interviews, through the observation of discussions in groups, undergo the process of being analysed and interpreted by using and applying theoretical concepts. How can we reconcile this core task of scientific research with the aims and principles of action research?

The solution is a simple one: researchers have to become partners in a dialogue. The interpretations of 'reality' as guided by theoretical concepts have to be brought home and have to be confronted with the everyday understanding and the common sense interpretations of actions and of practices!

Reflection, as an interactive exercise to be carried out by the team of researchers and as a joint effort with practitioners, appears as the path towards a kind of distancing effect that surmounts the dangers of remaining remote and abstract but retains the quality of adding something: a different, a broader and more balanced cognisance.

What does this mean and imply? The researcher 'offers' the practitioner whom she has observed as a distanced second-order observer her interpretation, using theoretically based (relined) concepts. And she enters a discourse with the aim to examine the plausibility and the 'practicability' of these concepts. The concepts she introduces have to make sense for the practitioners and they should in the most favourable circumstance produce a surplus value of cognition, and finally be capable of impacting on the practice. The acceptance and the adoption of scientific interpretations, of explanations or of statements of causation cannot be imposed on the practitioners (nor on a general public); instead their becoming convinced may emerge as a result of confrontation and discussion.

Summarizing: the role and contributions of the partners in action research, of researchers and practitioners, are different. The rationale of cooperation is not 'we are equal and doing the same thing'; rather it is 'we are equal and we are engaging in a dialogue to which we contribute according to our different background and training'. We regard this attention to be paid to different tasks and orientations as important. Entering a dialogue instead of veiling the different contributions by pretending that we are all doing the same thing will be more effective in demystifying the perception of scientific research. This is not only about an increased acceptance of research and its results but also about seeing research in a realistic way, arriving at an understanding of what can be achieved by research and where it reaches its limits; in other words, in which way the considerations and restrictions stemming from the political involvement of other stakeholders afford adaptations of the goals and the practice designs proposed by the researchers.

Active participation: the guiding theoretical concepts

Restorative justice, a way of responding to crime, harm, conflict, injustice, and wrongdoing, has been articulated as a new paradigm of justice which challenges retributive justice mainly on three grounds: (a) it views crime as a harmful event for the people concerned rather than as a breaking of the law (lifeworld vs system orientation); (b) it gives back to those affected by a crime the power to participate rather than having the state deal with it (participation vs delegation); and (c) it emphasizes restoration of the harm caused in terms of mending broken relations, offering reparations to the victims, and restoring a sense of security, rather than applying punishment for the sake of inflicting pain (restoration vs retribution) (Pelikan, 2003, 2007).

Active participation – as opposed to delegation to institutionalized authority – is thus one of the defining features of restorative justice. The demand for active participation of 'the people', more specifically, of those affected by conflict or by incidents of 'crime' has been projected as the dream of a society where alienation can be overcome. Put more modestly, active participation is meant to counteract the detrimental effects of modernity, the effects of bureaucratization and of the abstractedness of criminal law and the criminal procedure on people's lives and ways of living together.

Applied and restricted to the field of criminal law it meant a more satisfactory, more sustainable, a more humane way of going about conflict regulation. Beyond that, the wider political implications of active participation of those concerned was expected to both promote democratic values and serve as an exercise ground for democratic practice.

In the context of ALTERNATIVE it is expected to lead to the participation of citizens in restorative justice procedures, in order to manage or resolve their own conflicts. Less obvious, yet still crucial, is the necessity of citizens and civil society to actively participate in the promotion of alternative ideas and thoughts on how society might deal with wrongdoing, conflicts and crime (prevention).

The re-appropriation of conflicts through parties, victims and offenders concerned, becoming active in the solution of 'their' conflicts was soon expanded to the call for the inclusion of wider circles of affected persons – the community. The importance of this concept was further enhanced in connection with the notion of crime prevention. The involvement of the community was perceived as necessary in order to prevent 'pre-criminal' behaviour. In this context community involvement means community control, relying on the strength of informal control mechanisms. In this respect critique was voiced. Community control is assumed to produce exclusion – of those not belonging, those who are not regarded as 'one of us'. That way, communities can act as social entities that informally enforce conformity and suppress diversity (Kremmel and Pelikan, 2013, p. 22).

Community ownership as espoused predominantly in connection with restorative circles and with those activities that strive for restoring the future as happens in the Zwelethemba model adds a new angle to the role of community in restorative justice. Pali and Pelikan (2014) have contended that in Zwelethemba 'resolution comes from inside the community and … arises as a consequence of deliberation'. Despite the fact that 'Ownership of the conflicts in RJ is always and heavily emphasised as belonging to the parties' (Pali and Pelikan, 2014, p. 152), practice in Zwelethemba tried to go a step further, sharpen active participation to become community ownership (Shearing, 2001; Froestad and Shearing, 2007).

In the action research in Vienna, the concept of community ownership came to the fore when working towards restorative circles. It meant insisting on residents' ownership of the process as different from professional ownership of restorative processes. Ultimately it meant arriving at an arrangement that allowed arriving for a new equilibrium of residents' ownership and service providers' tasks and interests. It can serve as an example of practice imprinting on theory-building.

Doing action research in Vienna's social housing estates

The set-up

Our action research was built on our relationship with two partner organizations that have been practising community work and conflict resolution work in the Vienna Gemeindebau for quite some time (almost 30 years in the case of the community centre 'Bassena am Schöpfwerk', since 2010 in the case of 'wohnpartner')[2] (Kremmel and Pelikan, 2014a).

Organizational set-up and steps of intervention in the community centre Bassena

During the second year of our research, we had established close working relationships with the Bassena through one of our researchers (Katrin) joining their team as a participant observer, 'officially' as an intern, and through two social workers of the Bassena adopting the roles of researching practitioners. This general set-up and the common meetings for reflection with the whole research team and the head of the community centre ensured close exchange between the practitioners' and the researchers' perspectives and allowed us to conduct a general field analysis with the active participation of our local partner organization.

At the beginning of the third year of our project, our action research interventions were supposed to start. In the Bassena, our first intervening steps consisted of 'communication capacity-building workshops'. During the preparation phase of these workshops, the roles of the professionals involved, changed significantly. One of the researchers (Evi) with extensive experience as a trainer and her colleague (Ela) who had been recruited for the ALTERNATIVE project were acting as trainers in these workshops. The other researcher (Katrin) stepped out of the role of an intern, but accompanied the workshops as a participant observer, while the two social workers Wolfgang and Johannes took over the responsibilities of hosting the workshops (inviting and mobilizing residents, preparing the facilities, being present during the workshops).

The 'restorative circles' workshops followed the communication capacity-building workshops and were conducted with the help of a facilitator (Gerda), who had been trained by Dominic Barter and had gained experience in the practical implementation of restorative circles in Viennese neighbourhoods, before the beginning of our cooperation.[3] During the restorative circles workshops, the IRKS researcher Katrin once more acted as an observer; occasionally she took part in a role-play.

Organizational set-up and steps of intervention: the Women's Café initiated by wohnpartner

Establishing similar work relations of confidence and trust with wohnpartner took somewhat more time, due to the significant difference of both structure and size between both organizations. After a long phase of qualitative interviews with about 18 wohnpartner staff members, we eventually got in touch with one particular wohnpartner team, who took great interest in our circles' initiatives and invited us to work with them within the Women's Café. The Women's Café was established following the initiative of Turkish women as a result of a long and complicated conflict resolution effort in a housing estate of Vienna's 21st district. It is a fortnightly event, a breakfast gathering of Turkish and Old-Austrian women, who meet to talk to exchange their joys and sorrows and to plan joint activities (Kremmel and Pelikan, 2014b, 2015a).

In the Women's Café, we also started out with a series of 'communication workshops' with a team consisting of Ela, the trainer we had recruited, Gerda, the circles' facilitator as an observer, and two IRKS researchers. Both communication workshops took place in the Women's Café, during its regular breakfast meetings. They were facilitated by a community worker of wohnpartner (Esra), who is the organizer of the Café, and the IRKS team. Each of these workshops involved all participants of the Café present.

Step two consisted of circle preparation sessions. For these sessions, a small number of women had been 'selected' and invited by Esra, the organizer of the Women's Café; they took place at a separate location and a time outside the regular breakfast meetings. A division of roles between wohnpartner community workers and the circles' facilitator had preceded the first session. The IRKS researcher Katrin acted as an observer.

The research effort

From what we have stated in the section on the essentials of action research we can easily delineate the steps followed when doing this kind of research. Its main ingredients are reflection and discussion. The material assembled consisted of detailed accounts of observations, of transcripts of interviews and of discussions, finally of the films (see Chapter 3 of this volume). This material was reflected upon individually by each of the researchers to then be discussed in reflection sessions involving the researchers and the facilitators/trainers. Reflection sessions also took place immediately after the interventions, the workshops and the pre-circle. At these sessions the social workers of the Bassena, respectively of wohnpartner, the trainers who had facilitated the workshops and the observing researcher participated. The dialogical approach to these sessions was winding up in self-referential circles, individual reflection, team reflection immediately after an intervention and reflection sessions taking a whole series of interventions into view, constituting an endless reflective loop and moreover a dialogical process that could stretch well beyond the finalization of the project.

Getting involved

Let us take a closer look at the researcher's involvement in the action research endeavours of ALTERNATIVE in Vienna, through the example of one of our action researcher's role at both of our research sites, the community centre Bassena and the Women's Café.

At the very beginning of our empirical research phase, the head of the community centre Bassena put forward the question whether participation as a group member in the residents' groups who met regularly at the community centre was reconcilable with the role of a researcher: 'Can Katrin retain her role as a researcher, or more concrete: can she observe herself "in action"?' After careful considerations we came to the conclusion that it would indeed be possible for our action researcher to become an active member of a residents' group. There would be differences though between her and other group members: Katrin was on the one hand not a resident of the research site and therefore would not be immediately affected by the outcome of the group activity. On the other hand, there was an interest in promoting living together peacefully that stemmed from the overall goals of ALTERNATIVE, namely 'to develop mechanisms to enhance communication between individuals and groups, in order to provide Europe with concrete tools to better handle everyday social conflicts' (Vanfraechem and Aertsen, 2016, p. 5).

Katrin's task would be the observation of group activities, of communication, and generally, of social processes taking place. She would be part of these processes and she would exert influence on them. She would have to be aware of this influence and she would indeed have to co-observe herself and this influence. But let us be clear about this: there is a researcher-effect in any kind of interactive research and this effect and influence always have to be observed and reflected upon (Steinert, 1984; Deppermann, 2003; and generally on the position of the researcher: Devereux, 1967).

Thus, in the beginning of March 2012, Katrin became a 'special intern' of the team of community workers at the Bassena and it was made transparent to the residents that she was also a researcher in a project focusing on social life in this neighbourhood. Working alongside the team meant that she participated in their weekly team meetings. She was present during daily shifts, where she spent time within the facilities of the community centre and in the semi-private[4] space of the neighbourhood itself: its parks, courtyards and passages. She talked to residents, sometimes about whether they would like to drink tea or coffee, sometimes about the loss of a father, a sick child or about uncertain future perspectives due to troubles at the workplace or due to not having a workplace at all. Apart from these at times quite mundane interactions, she also participated at sessions of residents' groups (the group 'Cultural Exchange', the group 'Respekt' and a committee organizing a neighbourhood party, etc.). These groups consist of approximately seven members each, who get together to network and discuss topics of common interest.

Katrin documented her experiences and observations in a research diary or logbook, which served as a basis for reflection within the team of researchers but also with the community workers of our partner organization Bassena.

In 2014 we started a series of capacity-building workshops at the Bassena that were carried out by two trainers cooperating within ALTERNATIVE. The last few workshops of this series, which took place in the beginning of 2015, were oriented towards making participants acquainted with the rationale and the potential design of restorative circles. There as well, Katrin was primarily present as an observer, but sometimes she also took part in role-plays that were part of each workshop.

The Women's Café

Starting in 2013, ALTERNATIVE became engaged in the Women's Café. There, Katrin became a 'Vertrauensperson', a person of trust for the women as well as for the wohnpartner community workers. She took part in the fortnightly meetings and she was present during the communication capacity-building workshops, where she had been talking to women in various groups, both in face-to-face communication and participating in the discussions of various small groups. The same occurred in the 'pre-circles', facilitated by Gerda, the restorative circles' facilitator. It was once more a multifaceted role, oscillating between that of a participant, but always a special participant and an outside 'researcher-observer'. After Gerda had to terminate her commitment in the Women's Café because of the lack of trust on the side of wohnpartner (for a further explanation to this, see below) we had to redefine Katrin's role. Once again the question of the compatibility of researcher and participant became urgent. Katrin decided not to become a facilitator (even less a replacement of Gerda), but to contribute to the planning and the design of working towards a restorative circle. And she would, of course, remain in her role as a researcher, observing and reflecting with the other researchers on the on-goings in the Women's Café. This was a further step in reconciling the tasks of participating in the action and of doing research. She succeeded in communicating her decisions to the leader of the wohnpartner team and to gain the acceptance of the two community workers from wohnpartner that took over the facilitation of the circles.

Preserving transparency while working towards a restorative circle

We will give an account of the tensions and dilemmas our action research faced by presenting parts of two sessions in the Women's Café. The comments made and the interpretations we have discussed will be interspersed into these descriptions.

Let us first recount the story of the Women's Café, in the district of Floridsdorf and the events preceding its set-up. The story of the Women's Café began with a lot of complaints coming to the attention of wohnpartner around 2010/2011 in a housing estate comprising about 3,000 flats. The incidents reported were serious: threats, attacks by dogs, even malicious arson in one case. There was thus a criminal law angle to it although no criminal procedure, even less an indictment and a sentence had come about. Addressing wohnpartner was predominantly done by the 'Old-Viennese' residents and consisted of complaints regarding noise, the aggressive behaviour of children and more generally Turkish women occupying the benches in the yards.

Wohnpartner worked for about two years preparing for large group mediation through individual talks, through discussions with the Turkish residents only, followed by big rounds called 'Hofpalaver' (courtyard-palavers) and a number of thematic preparatory meetings with groups of residents. This was followed by more intensive work in different settings. The group meetings were often very difficult, very emotional and put a lot of stress especially on the Turkish residents. There was the language problem and more than once people were emotionally seriously hurt and injured. The Turkish-speaking social workers of wohnpartner did a considerable amount of care-work, as they provided individual assistance and support. In addition there were round tables, there was coaching and various other settings used for preparing the large group mediation process. This group mediation took place with elected representatives of the so-called 'thematic working groups' that had done the preparatory work, with representatives of the housing agency 'wiener wohnen' and representatives of the district administration. With all the preparation that had happened it was now about arriving at agreements and solutions. We were told that it was not difficult to arrive at such a solution: there was a general sentiment and agreement that 'we want to live together peacefully and we really want to live together'. But then an Austrian voice was raised asking how this can be realized with so many Turkish residents not speaking German sufficiently well. At that point, an elderly Turkish lady walked up to the podium to take the empty seat of a fish-pool setting, where discussants could join a panel that marked the concluding part of the large group mediation. She was walking slowly and tediously and she was speaking with a trembling voice. She said: 'Yes, the Turkish residents will make an effort towards learning German – and we will start to have breakfast in the yards once a week and everybody and especially our Austrian neighbours are welcome to join us.' Following that an Austrian woman spoke up and said: 'And I will do German lessons for you and together with you!' These results were communicated to the whole neighbourhood. Wohnpartner states that as a consequence they saw a 90 per cent reduction of complaints in the community.

The courtyard breakfast did not survive very long: the Austrians did not join their Turkish neighbours. After the summer, breakfast was transferred to a room provided by the local youth organization and slowly the Austrians came as well; the so-called 'Women's Café', taking place fortnightly in the mornings, saw up to 50 women of all ages, ethnicity and social background. The Turkish-speaking community worker of wohnpartner is still the person mainly responsible for supporting the Café. The women attending decide on themes they want to discuss and often an outside expert is invited, e.g. on child rearing or health matters. The German courses were a success and found considerable media coverage (Kremmel and Pelikan, 2014b).

The story of the Women's Café having been told, we will now proceed with providing a short itinerary of our interventions in the Women's Café that focused on present tensions and conflicts within the group of women still participating at the fortnightly meetings. Through our interventions we aimed at working towards a restorative circle and more generally towards an increased capacity of the women to self-determine their common way of going about their own conflicts. Our interventions consisted of two sessions that were to function as 'pre-circles'. An important task of the first session was to agree on an 'action' that was to serve as the central issue to be discussed and thus as a starting point for the further circles.[5] This 'action' is central to Dominic Barter's approach, who insists that starting from a problem would not provide sufficient focus for the process; it might unravel and get out of hand. The participating women, the wohnpartner staff members present and the facilitating circles' practitioner settled on a – still troubling – 'incident' that had occurred several weeks before, during a special event of the Women's Café which had taken place before Christmas. An external expert had been invited to hold a lecture for the group of women – and especially for Muslims among them – about Austrian Christmas customs and festivities with their respective religious background. In particular one of the Muslim women had felt urged to walk out of the room and others had followed her. The remaining women were left behind with uncertainties and fearful assumptions about why these women had got up to leave the room during the lecture. From Katrin's logbook:[6]

> Gerda, Esra, Anna and I meet one and a half hour before the encounter with the women is supposed to begin to prepare ourselves. The women will arrive in about 60 minutes and still, nobody really knows what might happen once they will sit down together in the circle.

In a way this is a typical situation we faced throughout our action research. A process-oriented and open-ended workshop is not necessarily an unplanned or unstructured workshop, but preparations and pre-set structures for the meeting are different from a result-oriented workshop. The latter remark pertains to the situation of the trainers/facilitators and the requirement to reconcile planning and structuring with readiness and the 'courage' to 'let go', to dare to confront the unexpected. The qualitative analysis of the accounts of the workshops and the reflection sessions brings to light what is meant by this 'preparation for openness'. It is also depicted in the booklet produced, containing guidelines for setting up restorative circles, (Kremmel and Pelikan, 2015a, 2015b). We will see in the following that for the participants the open-ended character of these preparatory workshops is related to the requirement of transparency. Transparency provides the women with agency, the possibility to face openness and to find their place within an open process. Continuing with Katrin's logbook:

> We start to discuss central questions after some chitchatting. Who is present in which role? The four of us have different roles (Esra and Anna are part of the women's group with responsibilities regarding the organization of the meeting and having to support the others as professionals; Gerda is here because she has some experience with working with conflicts and I am here because I take a special interest in conflict resolution processes and in the women's group) but we all have something in common which we want to state openly: we are here because we like being with the women personally, because we already have spent some time with them and what is happening within the group also concerns us on an emotional level.

In a later remark, Katrin adds:

> Stating that we are here, because we are affected personally, might actually appear as the least professional, but the most honest introduction, which does not provoke an image of us being distant experts.

Thus, the avoidance of distance is declared a prime goal of this action research effort. The solution proposed to the dilemma of being involved and at the same time being an outsider, consists of the transparency about or the disclosure of personal affection and involvement. 'What is happening in the group concerns us on an emotional level.' And it is trust in the legitimacy of evoking the emotional level that grounds this kind of involvement. From Katrin's logbook:

> How will Gerda and Esra work together as co-facilitators? Gerda suggests that Esra should be the one to welcome everybody, since she had also invited the participating women, whom she thought would be good to 'work' with (the women had been invited to a 'working session', which was supposed to make very clear that this meeting was not going to be 'just' about breakfast and chatting). After that, Gerda would ask everybody in the group to state why they were here, what they were expecting from this meeting and what conflicts they were experiencing at this moment. Having agreed upon these steps, both women then start to wonder how they would proceed from there, since there might be different routes towards 'building the house'.[7] I (Katrin) suggest, that this might be something on which we cannot decide now, but we can discuss who (Esra or Gerda) will decide, which way to go and how the other one will follow that lead. Esra proposes

that Gerda and she might just as well point out the different routes to the group, discuss with each other which one to take, pick one and tell the group why they picked it. I point out that this means that the decision would eventually be taken by them – the facilitators – in a transparent way, of course. But the decision could be left open to the participants as well, by simply asking them where to go and what they think would be necessary next.

Promoting community ownership

Already at this point, a difference in approaches – which proved to be important – slowly emerges. Gerda's and Katrin's radical understanding of community ownership collides with the need for providing (at least some) guidance. We will see that this topic turned out to be the quintessential point of controversy or rather dissatisfaction for the wohnpartner team: they were convinced that 'their' women needed more guidance, while Gerda wanted to have a decision-making process that left (almost) everything open for the women to propose and to decide.

A following sequence of Katrin's logbook (which we cannot quote due to its length) relates the discussions taking place between the women at the first 'pre-circle' session, during which several important issues surfaced. The women referred to the intra-Islamic conflict that had made for the exodus of a part of the women earlier that year. The women who had left were now engaged in a mosque where a traditional brand of Islam is taught and practised. They discussed also the incident before Christmas mentioned above. Understanding was voiced for the Muslim women who were exposed to the rather long expert's lecture on Christian customs. The Austrian women expressed this understanding through statements like: 'We should not invite external experts for this kind of stuff anymore' and, as a conscious effort of stepping into the shoes of the others,

> Just think about it, how we would have felt, if things had been the other way around. If there had been an expert telling us this many things about Islam, maybe we also would have felt threatened, like they wanted to brain-wash and convert us.

The pre-circle session ended on a rather positive note with the statement of a Turkish woman who said: 'Human is human and comes first, faith and belief comes last' and an Austrian woman picturing her understanding of interreligious relations as the bridges that can be built and lived. The whole group of participating women left the meeting energized and willing to get in touch with the women who had reacted in an offended way during the expert's lecture.

In which way does this exciting and touching narrative relate to action research? First of all, this was just something to listen to and to observe. The dialogue was flowing, the stories told came 'naturally' as responses to questions which had been asked by others, e.g. the question of Hedwig, who wanted to know how the Turkish mothers had felt when the Austrian women gave Christmas presents to their children: 'Was that ok for you, that we gave your children presents?' No particular interventions on the side of the facilitator were needed.

But the already mentioned 'quintessential dissatisfaction' turned up in the reflection session including the facilitator, the community workers and the researcher that took place immediately afterwards. Katrin summarizes:

> Esra thought that the women had clearly been confused and a bit lost throughout the meeting, not always understanding what was happening and how to be constructive. She thus had made some attempts to structure the conversation more (collect certain points on the flip chart, etc.).

Katrin commented on this by formulating two hypotheses: (a) the women would be less confused, the more they practised and indirectly learned about the communication structures in a (pre-)circle and (b) the women would be less confused the more the facilitators explicitly provided structures. These structures would need to be coherent with the logic of restorative practices and action research, what eventually means that these structures would have to serve the women and the process, not the other way round. From the logbook:

> But later, during the reflection session, the same Esra remarks: 'There already was quite a lot of ownership and self-reliance on behalf of the women. I think this has worked very well. What the women have experienced here today was a whole lot of recognition. I don't think the two Turkish women have felt seen this way before in the group. They were so happy when they left, they told me. And I overheard how Cemre stepped up to Hedwig and asked her whether she could practise German with her individually. They both agreed on times when they will meet. Cemre actually understands everything, but she does not speak fluently and at home her family keeps making jokes about the way she talks, so she is really embarrassed to speak in public. That she's now approaching Hedwig on her own account, really means a lot.'

Uneasiness as to the lack of structure on the one hand and appreciation of the power of recognition that was visible and tangible in this session on the other hand, are kept in balance in Esra's assessment and evaluation of the encounter. We will see below when and why this changes and the balance is tipped towards decisive critique and reproach of the unstructured mode of moderating followed by Gerda. In a similar line, the appreciation of the principle of the enfolding conflict espoused by Gerda is addressed in the reflection session. From Katrin's logbook:

GERDA: 'The question that we need to keep in mind is, whether what is happening at any moment still contributes to helping the conflict unfold. That is what is important, that the conflict is not blocked. As long as that is not the case, what actually happens is ok, even if it does not comply with what we would like to see in an ideal case. Maybe things just need a little more time until they get to being more balanced, for everyone to participate.'

KATRIN: 'But how do you check whether what is happening is still helping the conflict to unfold? What criteria do you have there?'

GERDA: 'I have my map in mind and as long as what is happening is somewhere on the map, I as a facilitator am fine with what happens.'

More on transparency

At this point, Katrin as an equal member of the team is exercising her task as researcher predominantly by asking questions. Gerda clarifies what her primary goal is: letting the conflict fully unfold, so it can be worked out and ultimately resolved. She takes the criteria for this to happen from the 'map in her mind'. We will see that this raises once more the question of transparency, or rather the question of how and when this 'map' necessarily needs to be convincingly conveyed to the participants and cannot remain hidden in the facilitator's mind.

A complete turn-around – fear and xenophobia

The second pre-circle session took place without any of the Turkish women being present, but with only Austrian women attending and it was to put the questions mentioned above to the test. No definite reasons for the Muslim women staying away were known; at least at this point it was not interpreted as an act of deliberate resistance. We quote from the logbook:

> Hedwig who had also had the opening statement on behalf of the women last time, begins: 'After the last time, I went home and I really kept thinking about this. I have travelled to Arabian countries before. Wherever I got to, I went to a mosque with the tourist group I was travelling with and we sat down together with the tourist guide of that country and he would tell us about the mosque itself and about Islam. This has nothing to do with brain-washing, this is about taking interest in the country where you are at. And I think the lecture on Christmas customs taking place in Advent was just like that. The women should not have been offended, they should take an interest in our culture as well, so they don't feel so foreign here. This is just about informing them. I don't understand how this could offend them. Especially for the mothers among them, these things are important, to open up their horizon, so they know where their kids are growing up.'

These utterings make for a complete turn-around of the first session. At the first session, participants departed from the quest of how the Muslim women might have felt at the expert's lecture before Christmas and they closed the session with the resolution not to provide information of this kind through external experts again. At the second session, however, the participants arrived at a perception of the events marked by the conviction that the Turkish women should actually embrace events of this kind. From Katrin's logbook:

> The second session continues with the participating women expressing resentment and fear. Esra leaves her role as a co-facilitator and reacts directly, partly recognizing the emotional pressure behind these utterances, but at one point also exhorting the women to consider the situation Muslim women might find themselves confronted with in their daily lives.
>
> Gerda introduces an important listening exercise by going into role-play and taking the position of a Muslim woman who feels offended and not listened to. She asks the women to repeat what they heard for as long as she, in her role of a Turkish woman, feels understood. One of the women at first displays a high capacity for empathy as she repeats in detail what she hears from Gerda, to then get back at uttering more fears regarding the increase of Muslim political presence in Vienna, and especially of women wearing the headscarf. Further attempts on behalf of Gerda to change the course the conversation is taking, get stuck again.
>
> Towards the end of the session, one of the women addresses Esra.
>
> FANNI: 'Esra, are you angry about what we said before.'
>
> MITZI: 'Ah, Esra, no, she is never angry about these things.'
>
> ESRA: 'It is ok for me, I think it is good that we talk about these things here, that we get rid of them.'

There was no reflection session taking place after this pre-circle session due to time constraints of the wohnpartner team members. This deviation from the preconceived research design caused conflicts and misunderstanding with the leader of the wohnpartner team that became relevant for further developments.

At the surface there is an astounding change of the ways in which the (Austrian) women did perceive the events of the 'Christmas lecture'. As Hedwig now states: 'The women should not have been offended, they should take an interest in Austrian ('our') culture as well, so they don't feel so foreign here.'

Of course, one wonders what had happened during the 10 days which passed between both pre-circle sessions – and why it happened. We think that this 'turnover' is mainly owed to internal dynamics of communication. At both pre-circle sessions participants probably 'meant' what they say. In the first meeting they got carried away with the understanding: we should not have invited an external person, it is understandable that the Muslim women felt 'overwhelmed'. While at the second meeting, their simultaneously existing and somewhat self-contradictory opinion prevailed that there was no reason for the Muslim women to be offended at all. The fact that there happened to be no Muslim woman participating at the second meeting further opened space for the Austrian women to express their resentment. At one point Mitzi clearly stated that she would 'never say these things in front of Cemre, because she would not want to hurt her!' At both meetings, there was mutual reinforcement of perceptions voiced initially by one of the participants.

As a reaction to the second pre-circle session, the head of the wohnpartner team decidedly declared that she regarded further cooperation with Gerda impossible. According to the head's understanding, the whole group of women had been highly disturbed by what had happened, they had felt lost and disoriented. Gerda had failed to provide guidance and safety to them. In addition, she feared that giving vent to xenophobic attitudes and feelings the way it had happened during this session was putting the existing processes and previous achievements in the Women's Café (of deconstructing existing stereotypes) at risk. These worries were grounded in experiences she had: 'Once you open this valve, an unstoppable torrent of xenophobia and racism enfolds that leaves no space for anything else.'

During an extended reflective team meeting, the researchers and Gerda tried to come to a better understanding of what had happened during the pre-circle sessions on the one hand and of Gerda's work, her intentions and the processes she envisioned, on the other hand.

As we have announced in the paragraph on the theoretical framework, the tensions and contradictions emerged as a result of our practice, of the concrete intervention taking place. They became manifest as two themes. First, a radical understanding of active participation and community ownership as a core requirement of restorative circles had become prevalent and was at odds with wohnpartner's perceptions of the scope of active participation. As it became manifest also in the openness of the process and the facilitator's attitude of following the lead of the participants, wohnpartner experienced this as disquieting, as not adequate for 'their' women at least. Second, the question of transparency popped up again: does it suffice for the facilitator to have a map in her mind and to carefully steer the process of the conflict 'enfolding' – intervening only when this process appears blocked? Regarding Gerda's work following Dominic Barter, the master plan 'behind' slowly emerged in the course of the two sessions and got contours for the researcher, who had been in constant exchange with Gerda – even after meetings with the women and wohnpartner staff members. However, it had remained opaque to Esra and Anna, the two community workers of wohnpartner and therefore also to the head of wohnpartner, who had only received information on the ongoing events from both staff members. We would now say that this contributed to the impression that Gerda did not provide the kind of structure that would convey safety or at least transparency not only to the women, but also to both Esra and Anna.

Gerda concluded that the group was on the way after the second pre-circle session, because she was able to actually 'see the way', but Esra and Anna were not able to see what she saw and she could not communicate this in a reflection session (see above). What they saw scared them and made them think that they were on a dangerous track, since it ran counter to their strategy of not tolerating xenophobic utterings.

We now come to see these different strategies; the wohnpartner strategy on the one hand and the restorative-circles strategy on the other, as being concerned with two different ways of providing containment.[8] Wohnpartner is used to provide containment by excluding certain themes, questions, yes, indeed 'feelings'. One could rightly question the adequacy and the efficacy of this practice, but it is there, due not least to certain political constellations. Gerda was on the way of providing containment, meaning safety for the women by making them acquainted with a tool for dealing with these feelings and of giving them space by training listening capacities. We still believe that transparency as to the place of this 'training' within the whole process was lacking. And it is also clear that it would really require a lot of time to prepare the ground for an understanding of this way. The hurdles that appear on this way were too difficult to bear for wohnpartner, especially in its present situation of an election campaign where the right-wing 'Freedom Party' has set out to overthrow the Social-Democratic regime of the City of Vienna.

Remaining independent

This makes us consider another pivotal dilemma of action research: striving to remain independent.

Researchers have, of course, to be independent. What does this independence imply? In line with the principles and the rationale of action research it is *not* about remaining detached from any involvement with stakeholders or 'players' in the field of conflicts that mark the intercultural setting of Vienna's social housing estates. Independence in this regard means preserving the specific standpoint/observation point of the researcher (albeit it is action research). And being freed from the burden of action (*Handlungsentlastung*) is *not* realized fully as we have explicated above: 'Researchers do get involved in action at the research sites, they are initiating interventions that are to lead to change.'

Katrin's refusal to adopt the role of the facilitator points to the limits of possible involvement. Through both the history of the Women's Café and the decision to discontinue working with Gerda – because she was perceived as providing insufficient guidance and containment for the women – it became clear that a facilitator working in the Women's Café would have to work 'in line' with the expectations of wohnpartner. This would have led to a form of dependence on our partner organization, which we found we could not work with. For Katrin to get into the role of a facilitator would have meant to be exposed to the same kind of expectations that Gerda had been confronted with. She would have to act within the limits of the wohnpartner's rationale, and moreover, its place within the political power-play. Also, departing from a restorative rationale, it was important for us to respect the needs of all stakeholders involved in the process, which also includes wohnpartner. Since wohnpartner would remain in the field and wanted to work with the women in the Women's Café beyond the end of the project, protecting their relationship with the women was a central necessity to them, which meant that they wanted to keep ultimate decision-making power within their confines. Opening towards the notion and the practice of community ownership would require a long process and ongoing discussions beyond the closure of the project.

In the first instance, the ALTERNATIVE team does not depend on any of the local political players. We have entered contractual partnerships though and our partner organization wohnpartner belongs to the extended net of administrative agencies under the roof of the City of Vienna (*Gemeinde Wien*), more specifically it is a special branch of the large housing agency. The deference to political calculation and political strategy these partner organizations have to attend do impact on our work. We could not disregard them. The decision of wohnpartner to terminate working with Gerda in preparing restorative circles because her approach ran counter to their strategy of completely banning any xenophobic utterances, had to be accepted.

As already said, we were left at that point with the task of negotiating an adaptation of Katrin's role as a member of a team of process planners and designers. We achieved this and it has proved to the advantage of the project's goals, namely to further advance an enhanced practice of active participation. Her careful contributions to the planning process of the steps which were to follow made it possible to move a bit closer towards the 'ideal' of community ownership, while respecting wohnpartner's limits and responsibilities.

The community workers of wohnpartner who were supposed to take over the moderation task and to develop a specific design for circle work in the context of the Women's Café, based on Gerda's concepts and strategies, went about this task with a lot of dedication. Katrin did comment on first plans and entered into discussion as to their further adaptation. On the one hand, she succeeded in carrying through the main tenets of active participation and community ownership, insisting on decision-making power as to the incidents to be addressed and the goals to be attained resting with the women. On the other hand, the requirement of transparency was taken care of in a more pronounced and competent way. 'Guidance' was thus translated into practical steps by the wohnpartner staff members, which intended to explicitly make the women acquainted with the course and the sequence of steps that could be followed in the conflict resolution process of a restorative circle.

Once more: getting involved and remaining distant – on leaving

Apart from the dependence on the partner organization and the political calculations and strategies followed by them, we are dependent on the people we work with: the residents in the Bassena and in the Women's Café. Trust was established by the researcher (as well as by the trainers) and expectations were raised. Although the participatory principle of restorative justice was never left and no prospect of any action to be taken 'on behalf' of the residents was ever entering the dealings with the residents, the sheer presence of the intervention team, including the researcher, was a stimulating and driving factor. We are back at the initial question whether in action research one can become involved and remain distant. We would like to discuss this further by turning attention to the problem of 'leaving the scene'. This happens in any kind of research, but with action research it is different. The action researcher is definitely leaving people behind she has established a relationship with. In the case of ALTERNATIVE, this relationship has lasted for about three years. Although from the very beginning it was clear that the project is an endeavour that was going to end at some point, it turns out that, as concerns the complicated intervention we have started in the Women's Café, it did not come to a closure. But we do find promising signs that we did approach the prime intention of this intervention, namely to convey the capacities to initiate and to carry out circles in the neighbourhoods of social housing estates as intercultural settings on the residents' own initiative. We have been told that the women started an initiative to collect useful articles for refugees. At least, after the last meeting in the Women's Café a new way of relating to each other, of discussing and addressing difficult topics became visible and tangible. We think though that some more attempts to spread the idea of this possibility and the trust in people's own capacities to follow this path will be required. The researchers continue their cooperation with the organization wohnpartner and have started to prepare more round tables, and other formats for spreading the experiences gained through ALTERNATIVE. This will require a common effort, based on intensive ongoing communication.

Notes

1 Habermas has used the term 'handlungsentlastet' also in connection with his concept of deliberation, and deliberative democracy (Habermas, 1990; Ottmann 2006).

2 The community centre 'Bassena Stadtteilzentrum am Schöpfwerk' is active in the neighbourhood of the Schöpfwerk in Vienna's 12th district ever since the first residents moved in in 1982. Unlike wohnpartner our other partner organization, the Bassena's link to the administrative and political structures to the City of Vienna is less direct, as the community centre is a sub-organization of and thus financed by the NGO 'Verein Wiener Jugendzentren' (Vienna Youth Centres). This NGO receives its funding from the City of Vienna, but the Bassena has gained a degree of financial independence through creating an additional legal entity in cooperation with other social institutions active in the neighbourhood. 'wohnpartner' is a branch of the large organization of Wiener Wohnen, respectively 'wohnservice'. This is, in fact, a huge hierarchically organized structure where wohnpartner has been fitted in. The advantages that go with this structure – general availability, consistency and equability of services – is thus balanced against a certain bureaucratization and the public perception as part of an administration that offers services as well as control.

3 Restorative circles are one of the procedures through which a restorative approach is followed. It rests on the inclusion of all parties affected by a particular conflict, the circle keeper is responsible for taking care of the extensive preparatory work ('pre-circles') to be organized whereas in the circle itself he/she restricts her interventions to putting the key questions – it is the parties themselves that are supposed to work through the circle and eventually arrive at an understanding and a plan to transform the conflict. Dominic Barter has developed a design for restorative circles working in South American neighbourhoods that found wide attention in Europe. He himself has become wary though of an uncritical take-over of the model without paying sufficient attention to the necessary preparatory steps (personal communication of facilitator Gerda).

4 Especially the courtyards 'belong' to the housing estates but are open to the general public; this is sometimes difficult to convey to the residents.

5 A term, which Dominic Barter started to use for the phase that precedes, accompanies and outlast actual circles. It encompasses all the measures necessary to build a community-based conflict resolution.
6 The quotations from the logbook are always indented.
7 Another term put forward by Dominic Barter that denotes the activities required before the 'circle' itself can take place. It was adopted and further developed by the social workers of wohnpartner.
8 We borrow the concept of containment from Anton Obholzer (1997) who himself refers to psycho-analysts Donald Winnicott (1971) and Wilfred Bion (1961).

References

Aertsen, I., 2010. A few words about 'action research' in social sciences. Unpublished paper for ALTERNATIVE. Leuven: KU Leuven.

Bion, W.R., 1961. *Experiences in groups*. London: Tavistock.

Bolivar, D., Pelikan, C. and Lemonne, A., 2015. Victims and restorative justice: towards a comparison In: I. Vanfraechem, D. Bolivar and I. Aertsen, eds. *Victims and restorative justice*. London: Routledge, pp. 172–201.

Deppermann, A., 2003. Interview als text vs. interview als interaktion. *Forum Qualitative Sozialforschung*, 14(3), Art.13.

Devereux, G., 1967. *From anxiety to method in the behavioral sciences*. The Hague: Mouton & Co.

Froestad, J. and Shearing, C., 2007. Beyond restorative justice – Zwelethemba – a future-focused model using local capacity conflict resolution. In: R. Mackay, M. Bosnjak, J. Deklerck, C. Pelikan, B. van Stokkom and M. Wright, eds. *Images of restorative justice theory*. Frankfurt/Main: Verlag für Polizeiwissenschaft, pp. 16–35.

Habermas, J., 1990. Drei normative Modelle der Demokratie: Zum Begriff deliberativer Politik. In: H. Münkler and R. Saage R., eds. *Kultur und Politik. Brechungen der Fortschrittsperspektive heute*. Festschrift für Iring Fetscher zum 65. Geburtstag. Opladen: Westdeutscher Verlag, pp. 11–24.

Habermas, J., 1992. *Faktizität und Geltung. Beiträge zu einer Diskurstheorie des Rechts und des demokratischen Rechtsstaates*. Frankfurt/Main: Suhrkamp.

Kremmel, K. and Pelikan, C., 2013. *Theoretical research report on activating civil society*. Public deliverable 4.1 of the ALTERNATIVE project. Vienna: IRKS. Available at: www.alternativeproject.eu/assets/upload/Deliverable_4.1_Theoretical_report_on_activating_civil_society.pdf [accessed 8 June 2016].

Kremmel, K. and Pelikan, C., 2014a. *Living together in the Gemeindebau in Vienna: on tensions, conflicts, fears and hopes*. Public deliverable 4.2 of the ALTERNATIVE project. Vienna: IRKS. Available at: www.alternativeproject.eu/assets/upload/Deliverable_4.2_Research_report_on_the_sociological-legal_description.pdf [accessed 8 June 2016].

Kremmel, K. and Pelikan, C., 2014b. *Ways towards the resolution of conflicts? A study of the existing ways of handling conflicts in social housing estates in Vienna*. Non-public deliverable 4.3 of the ALTERNATIVE project. Vienna: IRKS.

Kremmel, K. and Pelikan, C., 2015a. *Towards restorative circles: action research interventions in Vienna's social housing estates*. Non-public deliverable 4.4 of the ALTERNATIVE project. Vienna: IRKS.

Kremmel, K. and Pelikan, C., 2015b. *Towards restorative circles: inspiration and guidelines for practitioners*. Public deliverable 4.5 of the ALTERNATIVE project. Vienna:

IRKS. Available at: www.alternativeproject.eu/wp-content/uploads/2014/12/Deliverable-4.5-Follow-up-materials.pdf [accessed 8 June 2016].

Luhmann, N., 1984. *Soziale systeme. Grundriss einer allgemeinen theorie*. Frankfurt/Main: Suhrkamp.

Obholzer, A., 1997. The residential setting in psychotherapeutic work with adolescents. In: D.M. Piazza, ed. 2013. *When love is not enough. The management of covert dynamics in organization that treat children and adolescents*. New York: Routledge, pp. 5–13.

Ottmann, H., 2006. Liberal, republican and deliberative democracy. *Synthesis Philosophica*, 21(2), pp. 315–325.

Pali, B. and Pelikan, C., 2014. Con-texting restorative justice and abolitionism: exploring the potential and the limits of restorative justice as an alternative discourse to criminal justice. *Restorative Justice. An International Journal*, 2, pp. 142–165.

Pelikan, C., 2003. Different systems, different rationales: restorative justice and criminal justice. In: F. Moyano Marques, ed. *Project DIKÊ: protection and promotion of victim's rights in Europe*. Lisbon: APAV, pp. 223–227.

Pelikan, C., 2007. The place of restorative justice in time and space. In: R. Mackay, M. Bosjnak, J. Deklerck, C. Pelikan, B. van Stokkom and M. Wright, eds. *Images of restorative justice theory*. Frankfurt/Main: Verlag für Polizeiwissenschaft, pp. 5–56.

Reason, P. and Bradbury, H., 2001. Inquiry and participation in search of a world worthy of human aspiration. In: P. Reason and H. Bradbury, eds. *Handbook of action research. Participative inquiry and practice*. London: Sage, pp. 1–14.

Shearing, C., 2001. Transforming security: a South-African experiment. In: H. Strang and J. Braithwaite, eds. *Restorative justice and civil society*. Cambridge: Cambridge University Press, pp. 14–34.

Steinert, H., 1984. Das Interview als soziale Interaktion. In: H. Meulemann and K.-H. Reuband, eds. *Soziale Realität im Interview – Empirische Analysen methodischer Probleme*. Frankfurt/Main: Campus, pp. 17–59.

Stringer, E.T., 1999. *Action research*. 2nd edn. London: Sage.

Vanfraechem, I. and Aertsen, I., 2016. *Justice and security through restorative justice approaches to conflicts in intercultural settings*. Final report. Leuven: KU Leuven.

Winnicott, D.W., 1971. *Playing and reality*. London: Tavistock Publications.

5 Turning resistance to cooperation

Action research in Hungary

Dóra Szegő, Gabriella Benedek and Éva Győrfi

Introduction

Foresee Research Group, the Hungarian partner of ALTERNATIVE, was responsible for implementing the action research focusing on intercultural conflicts in a Hungarian village with approximately 2,800 inhabitants. This chapter presents the general tendencies and conclusions of this action research process with concrete cases illustrating the experiences.

The action research started with a 'Problem Analysis' phase, where we tried to identify the main local groups of interests, their interpretations of conflicts, reasoning behind the disputes and conflict-management strategies. We used desk research, interviews and participatory observation. This phase intended to build trust between the Foresee Research Group and local residents via personal conversations, informal meetings and workshops. The problem analysis resulted in a map of the local groups of interests, such as 'native villagers' and 'newcomers', members of the Catholic church and non-religious, Roma and non-Roma, the supporters of the previous and present regime, poor and rich residents, representatives of the different political ideologies – and typical conflicts between these groups (Héra *et al.*, 2014).

Action research methodology: relation between research and dialogue

Our fundamental aim in the action research was to test the legitimacy and functioning of the restorative approach and formal conflict resolution processes in intercultural conflicts of a local village community, considering what the local interpretations are of security, justice and community and whether experiences in restorative ways of conflict resolution had an impact on these interpretations. We have put in intensive efforts to harmonize that dual aim: keeping with the research focus on the one hand and building pathways to restorative interventions on the other hand. All activities on the field intended to serve that dual aim. The action research team consisted of dialoguers and researchers. The dialoguers prepared and carried out interventions based on restorative principles, including formal and informal restorative dialogues (circles, peacemaking circles, shuttle mediation, group discussions and workshops) and trainings. The researchers observed and examined these interventions with participatory observations and interviews. Dialoguers and researchers were in a continuous dialogue with the locals and we tried to involve so-called 'local researchers', residents acting as observers, bringing their local knowledge and expertise to the debate. Our interpretations of the intercultural setting were fed by formal, regular meetings for reflection, where the locals, the dialoguers and the researchers discussed insights from their different perspectives.

We were searching for a village that matched the criteria of 'intercultural setting', but we tried not to narrow the focus exclusively to conflicts between Roma and non-Roma citizens. A continuous reframing of the local understandings of interculturality took place based on the information and experiences that we gained on the field. Conflicts had several, different layers that sometimes overlapped. A conflict that might seem at first sight to be related to ethnicity and cultural differences, turned out to be filled with tensions related to the differences of social and economic status.

Approaching the village and facing the local culture of conflict resolution

After several meetings and conversations with the members of the village council, the mayor and the Roma Minority Government, we signed a Memorandum of Understanding. This statement was the official confirmation that the council of the village welcomed and allowed us to conduct the action research in the village. We followed a 'top down' approach in that respect and we only realized later the significant impact of that decision on the whole action research process. On the one hand, the lack of a call for assistance was a very distinctive feature of our two-year long fieldwork. Although the local decision makers gave legitimacy to the research team in the village, the local people had not asked for help in their conflicts. This manifested in a lack of motivation as well as resistance to participate in restorative dialogues. As one of the Foresee dialoguers phrased it:

> If at least they would have stated: 'Listen, I got to my limits. How do you see this issue?' But here very few people had questions about their conflicts. With the others we hardly have had the chance to offer new ways of conflict resolution; local conflict cases rather offered the possibility to understand the ways of conflict resolution in the village.

On the other hand, the distrust against the political elite and against any external actors and unknown initiatives are a general phenomenon in Hungarian society (Kornai, Rothstein and Rose-Ackerman, 2005; Tóth, 2009), that also determined the attitudes towards the action research. Getting approval for our work from the mayor and building relationships through local institutions appointed our position in a local political power space. The vision of taking an 'independent' position as dialoguers and researchers, as much aspired as it was, was not a realistic aim in the village setting. The research team was viewed in a certain way by the locals based on our Memorandum of Understanding with the then mayor and was therefore labelled as left-liberal. Even our choice of issues on 'intercultural conflicts' determined our being judged in the village. Relations between Roma and non-Roma was considered as a leftist topic and caused resentment and insecurity in some local people, who thought that focusing on that issue served the interests of the local Roma minority and went against the majority interests.

The terms related to interculturality, such as 'Roma', 'minority' and 'racism' were delicate issues. Sometimes people on the one hand used those words very consciously and cautiously, as a means of political communication or as a representation of their own ideological standpoints. On the other hand, people were very sensitive to those issues; in some situations the usage of words became a basis for conflicts. For example, the local Roma people used the term 'racist' very often to label local people whom they did not agree with. They presumed racism in most of those situations where they suffered harms regardless of the background circumstances. The sensitivity of the intercultural issues had manifested itself in the majority villagers' tendency to avoid using the term 'Roma' or 'minority' and was substituted many times with 'poor people' or 'cultural differences' by the local non-Roma, although it became obvious that they referred to Roma people or to conflicts between Roma and non-Roma. In such a sensitive power space, political-ideological standpoints of the local people determined their attitudes towards the research: cooperation or aversion. The fact that we researched 'intercultural conflicts' made it more difficult to open up people to relate their narratives and to frame these often conflicting narratives into 'stories' that we could have addressed by restorative dialogues.

Even those people who were more trustful and open to cooperate with the research had expectations that the action research could hardly fulfil. People were expecting experts who offer exact, rapid results and give solutions to their problems. They had not easily understood the action research approach, where development intended to take place with the active contribution of the locals, based on a reflection process with the researchers. We could not integrate restorative practices into existing local realities since we had not found local roots of dialogue-based communication. Open communication was not on the local people's table: most people considered 'debates' as pitfalls to avoid. Thereby our action research undertook the task of introducing an entirely new culture of communication. We had to start with the basics: gaining legitimacy for dialogue processes, creating platforms for sharing and building pathways between the different groups of people. We experienced that there was a great need for storytelling. Most of the people were ready to share their opinion on local issues in personal discussions. A further step towards dialogue processes were local workshops that we held, where different groups of people met and started a discussion, people who would otherwise not talk to each other: native villagers and newcomers, Catholic and non-religious people, conservative and liberal, Roma and non-Roma.

A transformation and 'reframing' process of the research started at that point. While the original plan was to use dialogues as a means of restoration, dialogue itself finally became a goal: we widened the focus from concrete conflict cases towards building communication within the local community as well as between the community and the research team. The emphasis was put on building trust, overcoming obstacles to participation and empowerment with informal practices based on restorative principles. The next challenge was to transform these episodic, single discussions into platforms for dialogue processes.

The action research process: framing and reframing

Since our project was first of all a research project, the social development aspect was subordinated to the research goals. The aim of the research was to understand local perceptions of security, justice, community and conflicts, and moreover to map the possibilities of restorative justice approaches and methods in conflict transformation. We built upon the local capacities and did not want to force the improvement of dialogue processes by all means. That 'cautious evolution' characterized the course of our action research. The main question at the beginning was to what extent we could build trust and evoke knowledge, capabilities and motivation for the sake of involvement into formal restorative dialogues.

After the problem analysis phase we tried to further build trust. Formal presence in the village was realized through the 'support group' that we established, consisting of motivated locals who were willing to assist the research process with information and feedback. Informal presence at local events and feasts was also an important platform of the fieldwork. At the same time, we started restorative case work with those conflicts that had been revealed in the problem analysis interviews and where we encountered any motivation from the locals to deal with the conflict. Cases referred by locals covered issues of social exclusion, discrimination, justice and security, whether neighbourhood conflicts or personal harms against each other. We mapped several local groups of people during the problem analysis and 'big narratives' as general interpretations of conflicts that belonged to the identified group and its members. In certain cases these narratives served as 'cover stories' to hide the deeper layers of conflicts. We tried to go beyond those narratives, dislocate people from that level of 'framing conflicts' and facilitate dialogues among 'people concerned' instead of 'groups of interests'. Individual discussions and small group work provided a platform for alternative interpretations that went deeper about conflict issues and local problems. But however hard we tried, people were not likely to undertake their personal narratives in restorative dialogues (conferences and circles). These classifications, group memberships and power dynamics had a great impact on the lifecycle of the cases. It happened for example in some cases that the local power-relations in the village interfered with the case work. An example for that phenomenon was the charity distribution case (see the case description after Figure 5.1), related to a conflict about the distribution of food packages, provided by the Red Cross, through local volunteers. Locals phrased criticism towards the volunteer organizers concerning the fair distribution of packages. The leader of the local Roma Minority Government[1] started to intervene in the preparation procedure by approaching Roma people who we invited as participants into the dialogues, intending to influence their opinion. We experienced that many people from the Roma community whom we invited into the restorative circle stayed away. We heard back in the form of rumours that the local Roma Minority Government leader convinced the Roma not to join the circle. When we tried to interpret his gesture, we found that we might have violated the conventional local ways of representation of interests when addressing local Roma people without the assistance of the 'gatekeeper', namely the local Roma Minority Government leader.

Several local narratives ran parallel about each conflict that even determined the 'framing' of the issues. In some cases it was hard to get to a common understanding about the main theme of the conflict. In the Butcher festival case (see the case description after Figure 5.1), the Roma people framed the case as a discrimination issue (namely that the organizers raised the entrance fee of the festival to exclude the Roma people), while the organizers refused that accusation and referred to financial explanation in their argumentation (they are motivated to target rich people to increase the income of the festival). Nevertheless, the issues and labels of the conflicts were continuously changing, which made it more difficult to circumscribe a conflict, to define a focus and to reach the people concerned. When we started to reveal the conflict within the local Roma community about the representation of interests by the Roma Minority Government, it turned out that the tensions covered various other layers of conflicts in the background. The roots of the conflicts were related to personal family debates and had a long history across generations.

While the first year of the action research was characterized by the notions 'look' and 'think', the upcoming period was rather a diverse and less predetermined 'action'. To keep the flexible work in line with the logic of the cases and also with the main concepts of the ALTERNATIVE research (justice, security, intercultural settings and restorative approaches) we made a design for a research protocol. The research protocol was meant to enable reflective contributions to the interventions on different levels (researchers, conflict parties, other locals and dialoguers) and gave a wide space for flexibility in terms of framing, participation, methods, occasions and time frames. Every action and intervention had its own research team, which consisted of a researcher, a dialoguer and, in conflict case-centred interventions, a local volunteer-researcher. The research protocol laid down the basic principles and practical framework of their discussions. A regular, mutual reflection accompanied the process, which made it possible to gain information and knowledge and to discuss issues from three different perspectives: the researcher's viewpoint, the dialoguer's viewpoint and the 'local expertise'. Both the locals and the research team gained different viewpoints and ideas from each other concerning restorative practices and interpretations of local conflicts.

Researchers had to deviate from the research protocol. Local actions needed an even greater demand for practical and conceptual elasticity – not only to grasp, but simply to realize thoughtful and reasonable interventions. We describe in the following the typical patterns of our restorative interventions. Figure 5.1 gives an overview about the scope of cases from the point of the involvement of the facilitators, while Figure 5.2 represents the cases from the degree of willingness of the conflict parties to face and hear each other within the framework of a facilitated dialogue process.

Case descriptions[2]

Butcher festival case

A Butcher festival has been organized for a few years in the centre of the village, on the soccer field, as a private initiative of a local entrepreneur. Several villagers felt discriminated: due to the high entry fee to the festival they could not participate on the event. Poor villagers were standing outside the fence and were watching the show from there. They referred to the event as the 'festival of the rich people'. Some Roma people perceived the high entrance fee as a targeted discrimination against the Roma villagers. The organizers argued that this is a private, business-oriented event, where the entrance fee is the main source of income. Foresee was not asked to help in that case and no restorative intervention took place. Nevertheless, we got an insight into the conflict through visiting

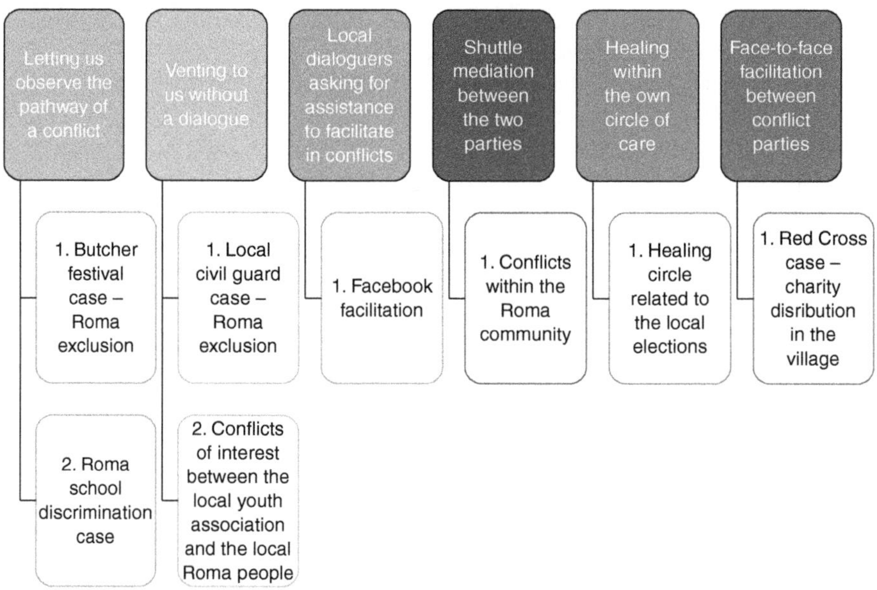

Figure 5.1 Type of cases from the point of involvement of the Foresee facilitators.

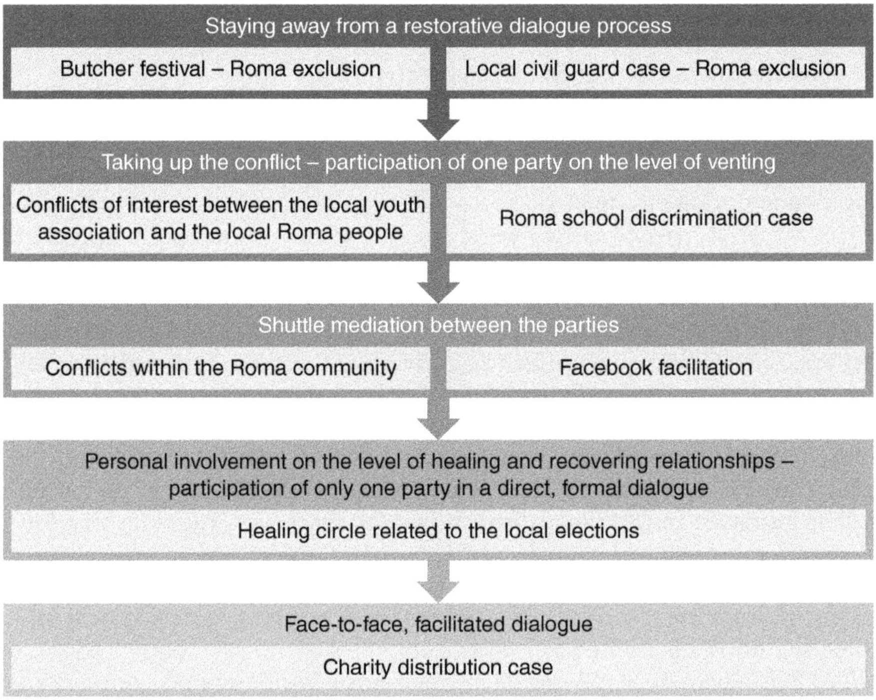

Figure 5.2 Readiness of the parties concerned to get involved in an assisted dialogue process.

the festival, interviewing local stakeholders and being invited as observers to a governmental meeting where the locals tried to discuss the conflict.

Local civil guard case

Members of a local NGO initiated the establishment of a civil guard in 2009. At that time, members of the civil guard were against involving Roma residents into their group. Some members of the organization invited the local Roma Minority Government leader to join the civil guard, but no other Roma from the village were welcome although for the local Roma security was an important issue. In the interpretation of the Roma Minority Government leader the conflict, which arose due to the Roma's exclusion from the civil guard, was not discussed. Neither he nor other local Roma joined the group. As the number of burglaries increased in the village at the end of 2013, the Minority Government Leader criticized the current civil guard's efficiency and initiated the establishment of a new civil guard. He and his supporters informed the members of their informal network and advertised the plan on Facebook and in one of the local newspapers. They tried to mobilize some Roma residents as well. The Minority Government

Leader asked the dialoguers of the Foresee Research Group to assist a discussion about this initiative with the current civil guard, to dissolve tension and get to a common understanding. Finally, a dialogue was not carried out, due to the lack of volunteer interest in relation to the new civil guard.

Charity distribution case

Distribution of charity food packages had been organized in the village since 2010. So far the village carried out six charity actions, provided by the central office of the Red Cross, through local organizing work, mostly done by the local nurse. These charity actions were organized randomly, depending on the extent of support by the central Red Cross office. After several charity distribution actions, some Roma people addressed criticism towards the organizers regarding the principle and criteria of eligibility, the way of distributing the packages and information provision. Some Roma expressed that this action was unfair as they thought people who did not deserve support or aid received packages, while the people in real need were excluded. Others thought it would be the organizers' task to guarantee an egalitarian distribution of the packages. The main organizer, who is working voluntarily in the charity project, felt the criticism to be unfair in many respects. The category of 'to be in need' was not defined by her in terms of any measureable criteria, but was defined based on one's own self-assessment: there is a declaration for every participant to be signed, who claims a package. When the amount of charity that the village gets is really small, there is no way to distribute the packages in an optimal allocation. A Roma woman, who is an opinion leader among Roma women, undertook the role of referral person and initiated a restorative dialogue about the conflict. A peacemaking circle was organized with the participation of the local volunteer organizer, the Roma woman representing the Roma community, the director of the kindergarten and a community participant representing a local NGO. The volunteer organizer, the Roma woman and the community representatives all agreed that the charity action is failing to be fair and righteous when distributing the packages, as there are no widely accepted criteria to define who is poor. All parties reflected on the issues, took some responsibility and understood the other people's concerns. Participants were able to detect causes of getting into conflict and to bring ideas about how to reduce the likelihood of a conflict. They agreed on the channels and ways of facilitating the information flow about the charity event and to give wider access of the local community to the organization process of the charity events.

Roma school discrimination case

The conflict that happened in the local elementary school was reported by different actors, parents and teachers alike. A student's puppet has disappeared in a classroom. Three Roma students were accused of theft. They were summoned to the director's office and their backpacks were searched for the puppet. They had to wait for the director after school time; they could not go home. Their parents were not informed and the children had not arrived home after school, which made the parents stressed. Later the puppet was found not in the students' backpacks, but somewhere else. The parents became very upset about the case and perceived it as a discrimination against their Roma kids. They asked for help of the local Roma Minority Government leader. They went into the school to complain about the unfair treatment and invited the school director to a conversation at the mayor's office. The school director, the parents affected, the Roma Minority Government leader and the mayor of the village participated in the meeting. Quite different interpretations were reported to us about the incident itself, as well as about the meeting, where Foresee was not invited as an observer. The only common point of the actors was that nobody felt relief at the end and there was still no agreement about how to handle similar situations and how to prevent similar cases in the future. Based on the reported displeasure on both sides, Foresee started to prepare a restorative dialogue between the school and the parents. The dialogue was not realized, since none of the actors who vented about the case wanted to face the issue with other people. Moreover, the school (represented by the director) did not take any responsibility for the case, but took the victim's position. The dialoguers decided to prepare a separate meeting for the teachers where the teachers could express their arguments about handling conflicts with students and parents in general. The director was not open to that separate meeting either. The meeting was neither refused nor realized.

Healing circle related to the local elections

Local elections took place in the village in 2014. The former mayor who had governed the village for 12 years lost the election, together with most members of the village council. Not only the results of the election but the campaign itself raised tensions. People told several stories about the 'unjust' and 'incorrect' campaign of the team that won the election while spreading gossip about the private life and defaming the former mayor. The non-empathetic reactions of the rivals after the results intensified the harms of the former mayor and the defeated council. As a consequence of these attacks the former mayor even moved out of the village to the neighbouring city a few months after the election. A supporter of the former mayor initiated a restorative dialogue to support the recovery of the mayor. The healing circle involved the mayor, the former city council and their supporters to address the grief and disappointment related to the elections.

Conflicts within the Roma community

One of the local Roma, an informal leader figure of the local Roma community who was participating in the peacemaking circle about the charity distribution, approached us and requested help. According to her opinion, several Roma families had a problem with the Roma Minority Government leader, who was also a member of the local governmental council. They complained that he was not helping all the Roma families of the village, only the ones that were close to him. Many local Roma people perceived discrimination in the village based on their social status and ethnicity. The Minority Government is meant to be the means for Roma in the village to represent their interests and to have a voice in local affairs. Due to the minority governmental leader's chair in the local village council the local Roma community had particularly high expectations towards him and his activities. The request for a restorative dialogue was close to the time of the local governmental and minority governmental elections, which had a role in the outcome of the case. Finally, the local Roma Minority Government leader resigned from his position in the minority council and was not elected to the governmental council either. Due to that circumstance, he was not motivated to discuss the conflict with the woman and refused to join the facilitated conversation in any way.

Getting involved in conflict cases

Letting us observe and follow

The research team observed conflicts from the widest distance when locals let us get an insight into and follow the pathway of a conflict case, but we were not requested to be of any kind of assistance. We accepted these boundaries and have not forced involvement in those cases. These occasions gave us the chance to observe and understand local ways of conflict resolution even though in many cases these solutions were far from restorative, and were based on the avoidance of communication and living with the problems without talking about them.

Give a space for venting without a dialogue

The most frequent local scenario was when people concerned in a conflict were ready to open up and vent privately (e.g. in interviews or in informal conversations with the researchers), share their individual narratives on conflicts, but they were not motivated to refer cases, to meet and talk with the other affected people. These cases got stuck at the stage of referral or preparation. But the forceful aspiration to vent about conflicts underlined the interpretation that the 'silence culture'[3] is not a fully effective strategy of problem solving.

At the beginning, the action research team treated the phenomena of venting as an unsatisfactory phase of a dialogue process and wanted to get further with those cases. But as the action research has gradually opened up towards less formal processes, our interpretation of venting was also reframed. Matching it with an analogy of 'sharing individual perspectives', the second stage of a mediation process[4] helped the team to recognize that venting is a necessary milestone of dialogue processes. Although the parties might yet be very far from ready to join dialogue processes and we could not reach the dialogue within our time frame, venting served as a preparatory step towards dialogues.

The conflict related to Roma discrimination in the school is an example of those cases where our activity was limited to the observation of the local ways of conflict resolution and finally we arrived at the phase of individual venting. Although Foresee was already working with conflicts in the village, no one informed us about the negotiation meeting that took place: we heard of the conflict retrospectively. Both parties were ready to vent about the events in private discussions with us. In the Roma parents' interpretation, the teachers made a racist discrimination when accusing three Roma kids of theft without reason. By not being informed about the conflict they perceived it as not being treated as partners by the school and expressed the lack of being heard on the meeting that was organized. The parents were supposedly afraid of the power-position of the director and wanted to avoid possible negative consequences of taking up the conflict while in the interpretation of the director thefts are a persistent problem in the school and the school tried to take an action with completing a fair process related to the theft. The teachers perceived themselves as victims of stigmatization when being labelled as racist by the parents and by lacking means related to thefts in school. The parents and the teachers agreed that the meeting had not led to a satisfactory, comforting outcome. Nevertheless we could not continue the dialogue with restorative methods, since none of the actors were willing to take on their opinion publicly and to pursue the dialogue. They withdrew and handled the situation through a silence culture. Although we could not continue the dialogue process, the dialoguers found it on the one hand promising that at least the parents' reaction to the harm they suffered was an initiative of a negotiation. On the other hand, by collecting different narratives of the same conflict we got the chance to learn about centralized and closed communication patterns as characteristics of the school and the lack of horizontal, inclusive dialogue among the actors. This was in a sharp contrast with the students' attitudes and way of communication as we experienced it in the restorative school classes held by the Foresee dialoguers.

Assisting local dialoguers to facilitate in local conflicts

After widening the scope of the action research towards less formal processes we initiated different actions on the field as a means to learn about restorative approaches, to develop people's conflict-management skills and – as an indirect aim – to get closer to conflicts. Three actions were built up on that logic: we held restorative school classes for students in the local elementary school, we organized a restorative learning group for future facilitators and we assisted local dialoguers to manage conflicts in virtual community media surfaces (e.g. local Facebook pages). These initiatives also departed from venting, but the learning processes in safe environments empowered local people to transform their perspectives on conflicts and in some cases adopt restorative elements in conflict resolution. In a few concrete conflicts people even requested advice and mentoring.

One party alone in a dialogue process

A big step towards dialogue processes was that in a few cases the referral persons – and people being on their side – became motivated during the venting process to take up their narratives publicly and requested our help. But they were alone with their desire for an intervention. Usually the powerless, marginalized people were more ready to join dialogues, e.g. newcomers who were marginalized in the community of the village or Roma who had financial and social disadvantages. As a possible interpretation, those people who were in power (socially and financially) were not interested in any change in the distribution of power that might have been initiated by dialogue processes.

One of those cases where we could work only with one party was the healing circle related to the local elections. The aim of the circle was the expression of feelings and the restoration of relationships within the former mayor's own circle of care. The members of the circle of care, including the case referee, who considered themselves as support persons of the mayor recognized during the circle their own disappointment, grievance and victimization related to the events.

Face-to-face facilitation between conflict parties

Only one conflict case ended up in a formal restorative dialogue with the participation of all parties. The case where we could hold a formal peacemaking circle (Fellegi and Szegő, 2013) was the charity distribution case, where the fact of a dialogue as a symbolic gesture got more emphasis than the outcome and the formal agreement.

Although the cases were characterized by a wide group of people being concerned, we found it very hard to involve them into the dialogue process. Only a small group of people was ready to join. Many important community-related cases died away during the preparation process, got stuck on the level of venting or were handled with the participation of only one side. We interpreted this limitation with the lack of open communication culture that we faced from the beginning. Typical, local ways of conflict resolution were built upon avoidance and lack of dialogue.

As Héra (2018) argues in his theoretical article about the phenomena of exclusion in relation to the ALTERNATIVE fieldwork,

> participants of these groups have vivid and intense discussions about the 'others'. However, hardly any of them share their opinions – and feelings, harms or criticism – with members of the 'other group'. Instead, most of them voice their ideas, feelings, harms or criticism only within their own group.

In a prevalent local interpretation, the 'culture of silence' instead of confrontation was a guarantee for peaceful coexistence. As the new mayor[5] phrased it, the effective policy of handling conflicts was a silent attitude. In that model, talking about conflicts causes more tension and conflicts are going to be solved on their own if people are patient enough:

> most people in the countryside are modest people. They know really well that these conflicts exist but they won't talk about the conflicts. Primarily not because of being afraid to lose positions, but rather because they don't want to hurt people. Even if they know that talking openly about conflicts would not cause trouble for themselves. They consider: 'what will happen if they tell their standpoint about conflicts?' They will always have their own opinion but they won't take the risk of publicity. (…) It is not useful to force anything. A sense of patience is needed. Leave people alone with their issues. Don't talk about conflicts. It is useless to hurt people who don't want to behave like you expect it. The only thing that solves these situations is time.
>
> (Interview with the new mayor, elected in 2014)

Local advocates of the silence culture interpreted restorative justice as a threat to peace. They expressed the concern that 'the research group threw a stone into the still water' with putting conflicts to the focus. In many cases these people were against the dialogue processes. They vented about conflicts in private discussions, but they were not ready to get into a dialogue process and rather accepted the 'status quo' although their interests were not properly represented.

Informal activities

Based on the lessons learnt during the first period of the action research, we started to deconstruct the efforts to build formal restorative case scenarios. We realized that informal, episodic interventions and actions that were related to conflicts more indirectly worked better on the field than our efforts to formal and continuous interventions. At that point we drew inspiration from community development approach and methods. Among the actions, separate group discussions were organized for different local groups representing diverse and opposing viewpoints related to conflicts. The aim of these discussions was to open a platform for sharing individual perspectives on conflicts with the hope to depart on the way towards dialogues (at least in the form of shuttle mediation). We established a restorative learning group where those people joined who wanted to gain facilitator skills and aspired for assistance in their own conflicts. We organized restorative school classes for elementary school students to disseminate a restorative communication culture among the children and to empower them in their own good practices.

We borrowed the model of the Whole School Approach (Hopkins, 2003; Morrison, 2005) that categorizes the levels of restorative interventions in schools to describe the development of our practices in the village (see Figure 5.3 below). In the second phase of the action research, our practices hardly functioned in the 'tip of the iceberg' namely intensive interventions with formal

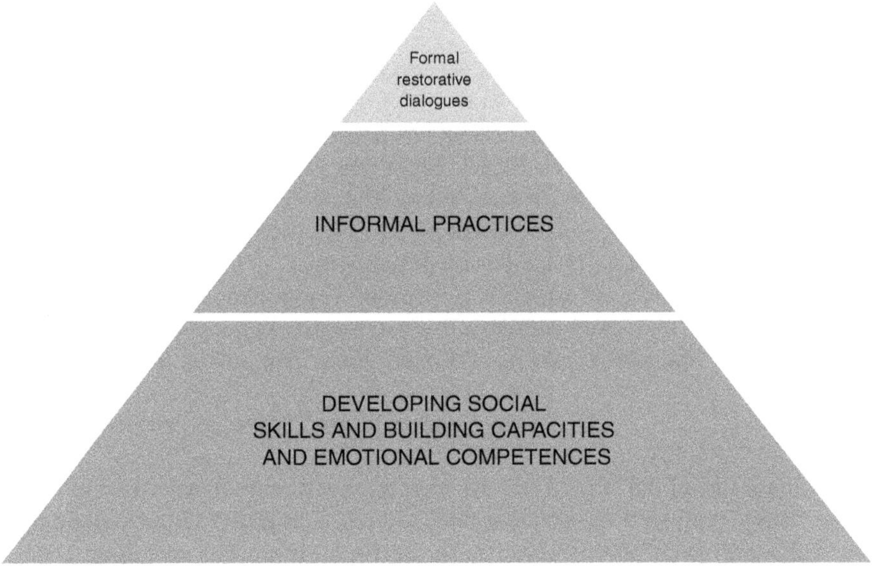

Figure 5.3 Levels of restorative interventions within the framework of the action research.

restorative practices. We rather put efforts into the development of conflict-management skills of locals and to sensitize them and involve them in informal restorative practices through e.g. group discussions and workshops.

The initial intention behind the less-intensive interventions was to build pathways towards formal restorative dialogues. Although conflicts came up at all levels of the activities, finally most of the actions remained at a low level of intervention intensity and have not led to direct, formal restorative dialogues in conflicts. Believing in the power of formal restorative methods (conferences, circles) we interpreted that circumstance as a deficiency of the field work, although at the same time we acknowledged the power of capacity building and informal practices. We kept searching for answers to the question, 'What are the supportive and hindering circumstances for people to get closer to restorative dialogues?' Figure 5.4 summarizes those conclusions that the research team formulated about circumstances supporting or hindering dialogue processes.

Conceptual and methodological dilemmas throughout the action research

While continuously replanning the activities during our field work and getting away from direct, formal restorative interventions, some professionals in our research team argued for the necessity of quantitative changes: they advocated for more mapping and trust building in the community and working with

Supportive circumstances to join a restorative dialogue process

- acknowledging the existence and legitimacy of conflicts
- previous experiences of conflict-related dialogues
- lack of means in handling a conflict
- exceeding the threshold: getting in touch with a restorative approach in informal activities grows the likelihood of engagement with conflict-focused dialogues
- marginalized position in the community grows the likelihood of being motivated in a change through a dialogue process

Hindering circumstances to join a restorative dialogue process

- previous negative experiences with conflicts
- being afraid of the judgement of the community
- labelling mechanisms
- fear of losing social position
- the 'culture of silence' as a communication pattern
- believing in the legitimacy of only 'one truth'

Figure 5.4 Supporting and hindering circumstances of formal restorative dialogues.

informal methods before inviting the locals to conflict-focused, formal dialogues. Other team members argued that a qualitative change is needed: we should base our activities on a different paradigm.

The failure of formal dialogue processes in most cases made the team reconsider some of the basic methodological principles of restorative interventions. This transformation was supported by the experience that in many situations empowerment, and competence- and community-development methods seemed to be more effective in approaching conflicts in the village than formal restorative methods. This circumstance made us rethink our interpretation of capacity and competence building, community development as well as of the informal restorative practices.

We attached greater importance to these actions that – if based on restorative principles – became alternatives to formal restorative interventions and not preparatory steps of restorative dialogues. Dialoguers reported that going beyond the limits of their methodological boundaries as restorative professionals, using skill- and capacity building, and community development methods was the key for local participation and cooperation.

The 'glass-half-full' viewpoint

As a main tendency on the level of 'general discourses' we faced the limits of the restorative approach as a means to handle intercultural conflicts, but we experienced the power and efficiency of the approach in individual stories. We reached people through personal relationships. Personal experience with the restorative approach in any of our activities worked as a motivational factor and increased the likelihood of cooperation in other restorative activities. It happened in some cases that we could build on the different levels of interventions: after participating in informal activities some people asked for advice on how to handle conflicts on their own, they were ready to be involved in workshops and film screenings. In a few cases after participating in a restorative circle they approached us proactively as case referees or with needs to learn about the restorative approach.

At the closing phase of the action research we faced a conflict with the new local leadership of the village. Based on the political-ideological fault line the new local leadership and its supporters refused any cooperation with the research. After gaining power, they expressed distrust towards the research team and questioned the impartiality of our work. Finally, in such an adversarial situation the restorative approach functioned as a 'life belt' that kept us on the field: we reacted to their harms by giving space to express their dissatisfaction in informal dialogue situations about our local participatory video footages that arouse tension, disappointment and anger in their group. In our interpretation, addressing their needs turned them towards cooperation. The restorative reaction made them ready to share their viewpoints about our fieldwork and videos, as well as about local conflicts. The dialogue process around the conflict between the research team and the new local leaders built bridges between a wider group of local people and the research team, and led to a broader acceptance of the restorative approach in the locality.

Conclusions

Conclusions concerning methodology

At the end of the research, we formulated questions and considerations for further research rather than conclusions (Héra *et al.*, 2015). The validity of focusing on conflicts in an intercultural setting and approaching them with formal restorative methods has been put into question. The question was raised whether only the pathways towards the outcomes should be replanned or the fundamental goal of the action research had to be reconsidered, whether our experiences about the obstacles and limitations of restorative approaches in intercultural village settings are a state of affairs or a 'station' on a long journey towards becoming more effective with direct, formal restorative practices.

The team members were divided in that respect. Practitioners rather believed in 'staying within the paradigm' and framed the more universal interventions as steps on the way to formal restorative dialogues. They were searching for answers on how the formal restorative dialogues could benefit from skill- and community-building activities. Researchers were more sceptical about the effectiveness of focusing directly on conflicts with formal restorative interventions in an intercultural context.

The need for less formal and more universal interventions raise the importance of interdisciplinary cooperation between restorative professionals and community development professionals. We asked whether we should 'pass over' the field for community developers and intervene with a restorative approach only in case of a formal call for a restorative intervention related to a conflict case. Or should we widen the limits of restorative approach and integrate community development, capacity building and empowerment into the repertoire of restorative methods? The dilemma of to what extent our results and conclusions are specific to the particular features of the intercultural settings remains a key issue for a further project.

Conclusions concerning the nature of intercultural conflicts

We experienced many times that the local conflicts had several layers and we often only saw the 'tip of the iceberg'. These layers were often rooted in long-term, personal debates that had a history transcending across generations. Another scenario was when the conflicts were related to entrenched positions that were rooted in the prejudices of certain social groups towards each other, based on ethnicity or on political values. In these cases, the concrete conflicts activated these 'positions' and prejudices; people were not reacting to the actions and events that happened actually but rather to what they supposed about the 'others' due to their prejudices, sometimes confirmed by past experiences. These two scenarios were sometimes overlapping, strengthening the 'culture of silence' and pushing away people from joining dialogue processes. The most important mark we left on the field was that we thematized conflicts and framed their existence as a valid condition of a settlement. Local understandings of diversity were reconsidered and acquired a higher legitimacy through the action research project. People belonged to various different groups with very different values and interests, but commitment and care for the village was a common characteristic they shared. We hope that commitment and care in the village will be a base strong enough to open up and share.

Notes

1 After the change of the regime, local minority self-goverment bodies were established. The minority self-government bodies, among them the Roma Minority Government, gain financial support from the state and are entitled to establish and maintain institutions in the field of local education, media, and culture. The Minority Government representatives and leaders are elected every four year.
2 For the detailed description of the cases see Benedek (2015).
3 The phenomenon of silence culture was discussed in detail in Szegő *et al.* (2015).
4 Stages of mediation are the followings: (1) opening-introduction, (2) sharing individual perspectives and understanding, (3) reflections, finding common points and (4) agreement and seeking sustainability (Lederach, 1997).
5 In the last year of our action research local governmental elections took place. The composition of the local council changed completely, and a new mayor was elected. The new leaders of the village were those people who were distrustful towards the research team based on the political fault line. We had to lay new foundations of cooperation with the new leaders.

References

Benedek, G. ed., 2015. *Problem analysis*. Non-public deliverable of the ALTERNATIVE project. Budapest: Foresee.

Fellegi, B. and Szegő, D., 2013. *Handbook for facilitating peacemaking circles*. Budapest: Foresee Research Group.

Héra, G., 2018. Counteracting social exclusion through restorative approaches. In: B. Pali and I. Aertsen, eds. *Restoring justice and security in intercultural Europe*. London: Routledge, pp. 93–109.

Héra, G., Győrfi, É., Balla, L. and Kelemen, K., 2014. *Building the bridges of trust with and within the communities*. Non-public deliverable 5.2.a of the ALTERNATIVE project Budapest: Foresee Research Group.

Héra, G., Benedek, G., Szegő, D. and Győ fi, É., 2015. *Comprehensive final report*. Public deliverable 5.5 of the ALTERNATIVE project. Budapest: Foresee. Available at: www.alternativeproject.eu/wp-content/uploads/2014/12/Deliverable-5.5-Comprehensive-final-report.pdf [accessed 25 May 2016].

Hopkins, B., 2003. *Just schools. A whole school approach to restorative justice*. London and New York: Jessica Kingsley Publishers.

Kornai, J., Rothstein, B. and Rose-Ackerman, S. eds., 2005. *Tisztesség és bizalom a posztszocialista átmenet fényében. A társadalmi bizalom megteremtése a posztszocialista átmenet időszakában*. Budapest: Nemzeti Tankönyvkiadó.

Lederach, J.P., 1997. *Building peace: sustainable reconciliation in divided societies*. Washington D.C.: United States Institute of Peace Press.

Morrison, B., 2005. *Building safe and healthy school communities: being responsive and restorative*. Sidney: Federation Press.

Szegő, D., Benedek, G. and Győrfi, É., 2015. *Process analysis and follow up report*. Public deliverable 5.4 of the ALTERNATIVE project. Budapest: Foresee. Available at: www.alternativeproject.eu/wp-content/uploads/2014/12/Deliverable-5.4-Evaluation-and-follow-up-report_revised_201512_01.pdf.

Tóth, I. Gy., 2009. *Bizalomhiány, normazavarok, igazságtalanságérzet és paternalizmus a magyar társadalom értékszerkezetében. A gazdasági felemelkedés társadalmikulturális feltételei című kutatás zárójelentése*. Budapest: Tárki.

6 Conflicts, victimization and restorative justice in intercultural settings

An example of action research in Serbia

Vesna Nikolić-Ristanović, Sanja Ćopić, Nikola Petrović and Bejan Šaćiri

Introduction

Within the ALTERNATIVE project, the Victimology Society of Serbia (VDS) implemented a research entitled 'Fostering victim-oriented dialogue in a multi-ethnic society' with the aim to identify, propose and implement a restorative model of conflict transformation in multi-ethnic contexts. The VDS research team intended to look for the potential that exists in Serbia for using alternative restorative approaches; to arrive at ideas of how to involve citizens from multi-ethnic communities, particularly victims, in democratic processes for peace building and conflict transformation; and to stimulate cooperation of citizens and state institutions at the local level in order to develop long-term human and civil security, as well as justice solutions for multi-ethnic communities, based on restorative justice principles and values.

In order to achieve these objectives, we started in 2012 with theoretical research, i.e. a literature review and qualitative research of civil society's and state's dealing with interethnic and related political and intercultural conflicts in Serbia in the period 1990–2012 (Ćopić, 2013; Nikolić-Ristanović and Ćopić, 2013, 2016; Nikolić-Ristanović and Šaćiri, 2013).[1] This provided a basis for developing and operationalizing the empirical study on conflicts, victimization and justice in multi-ethnic communities in the border regions of Serbia as a preparatory phase for the action research (Nikolić-Ristanović *et al.*, 2014, 2015).[2] The empirical study was conducted in three multi-ethnic communities: in Medvedja (South Serbia, near the border with Kosovo), Prijepolje (South-West Serbia, near the border with Bosnia and Herzegovina) and Bačka Palanka and Bač (North-West Serbia, near the border with Croatia). These are communities which were most affected by ethnic conflicts in the former Yugoslavia during the 1990s. We explored relations and conflicts between Serbs and Croats, Serbs and Bosniaks/Muslims, and Serbs and Albanians. This was followed by the action research, which consisted of two main parts: participatory seminars entitled 'From the conflict towards peaceful life in the community' (intervention phase), which were implemented in the same multi-ethnic communities as the empirical study (Nikolić-Ristanović, Srna and Ćopić, 2015a, 2015b),[3] and the participatory process of developing the 'Manual on best practices of applying restorative justice approaches in intercultural settings' (Ćopić and Nikolić-Ristanović, 2016) that should serve for raising awareness and education on restorative approaches in conflict transformation in intercultural settings.

This chapter presents the methodological approach of the action research, as well as some of the main findings and lessons learnt. The chapter starts with providing the main theoretical departing points of the research. It continues with a description of the methodology of the empirical study on conflicts, victimization and justice in three multi-ethnic communities, and a discussion of the main findings. Thereafter, it presents the main methodological approach of the action research in three multi-ethnic communities in the form of participatory and process-oriented seminars with testing the applicability of restorative approaches. The chapter ends with main conclusions and lessons learnt. Additionally, in the concluding part we bring the findings of the action research back to the theoretical framework, reconsider the concepts that are in the foreground of the research and propose a possible restorative approach to be used in the intercultural context of Serbia for conflict transformation and the increase of overall security of citizens.

The main theoretical departing points

After the formal ending of the wars in the former Yugoslavia, numerous unresolved problems, tensions and conflicts remained in Serbia, which impact the dynamics of interethnic relations, particularly in multi-ethnic communities (Domonji, 2008; Nikolić-Ristanović and Ćopić, 2013). Even today, relationships and conflicts between members of different ethnic groups in Serbia are still very much affected by the legacies of the wars from the 1990s and the way the Serbian state dealt with them (Nikolić-Ristanović and Ćopić, 2016). We started from a very broad understanding of the concept of interethnic conflict: it includes a wide range of problems in relationships between members of different ethnic groups in Serbia. Additionally, in line with the overall aim and general context of the ALTERNATIVE project, the concept of conflict was considered to be multifaceted, thus encompassing different forms of problems or behaviour on different levels (micro, meso and macro): armed conflict, societal conflict, violent conflict, cultural conflict, religious conflict, political conflict, interpersonal conflict, group conflict etc. (Foss *et al.*, 2012, p. 29), which was used as a basis for operationalizing the concept of conflict in the empirical study.

Post-conflict societies often lack mechanisms and institutions for upholding the rule of law and for dealing with conflicts, tensions and divisions in a constructive way, which provides a fertile soil for further eruption of lawlessness, corruption, discrimination, violence and crime (Rohne, Arsovska and Aertsen, 2008; Nikolić-Ristanović and Ćopić, 2013). Theoretical research conducted in 2012 suggested that in dealing with both past and present interethnic conflicts by the state in the period 1990–2012, the security discourse prevailed and state institutions focused primarily on judicial mechanisms to deal with those conflicts. Therefore, we may argue that justice in post-conflict settings (transitional justice), as is the case in Serbia, is primarily identified with legal approaches (legal justice). Criminal justice is quite often seen as the best and necessary means to 'undo past state justice and to advance the normative transformation of these times to a rule-of-law system' (Teitel, 2000, p. 28), but, as correctly noticed by some authors, it suffers from retroactivity, politicization and selectivity (Minow, 1998, pp. 30–31), which is visible in Serbia. There is a permanent increase of repression in the name of protecting victims and citizens in general, which fits well in the global policy of penal populism (Garland, 2001). Unfortunately, the effects of such a policy are not visible: conflicts still exist and they become even deeper. Additionally, victims are not actively involved in conflict transformation; they rather stay passive observers of the processes, particularly of the criminal justice procedure (Nikolić-Ristanović and Ćopić, 2013). Trials generally give no space for 'interaction between dissimilar voices', which is in the essence of 'dialogical/restorative justice' (Foss *et al.*, 2012, p. 47), and which is particularly important in the process of recovery and restoration of the victim. Therefore, legal justice or legal truth is of limited nature and is not sufficient to restore relationships disturbed by wars or other conflicts (Nikolić-Ristanović, 2003, p. 240).

To summarize, theoretical research undertaken at the very beginning of the project implementation suggested a predominance of an inefficient and mostly counterproductive use of retributive justice and security discourse in Serbia. This impacts on citizens' feelings of security and has particularly negative consequences on victims from ethnic minorities, whose prospects of protection and support are in doubt (Biro *et al.*, 2002; Helsinki Committee for Human Rights in Serbia, 2004; Savković, 2010). The lack of security and the fragmentation along ethnic diversity often result in strengthening of social inequality. Social inequality and conflicts in intercultural settings are often interrelated and can be (mis)used to preserve social injustice. In such a context, the state is not seen as a guarantor of security, but is rather perceived as a source of insecurity and unsafety.

Finally, as suggested by the theoretical research, although they are existent, a restorative justice discourse and restorative practices are not visible, used and recognized enough in dealing with past and present interethnic and other related conflicts in Serbia. Therefore, there is a need to work on promoting the rule of law, but also on promoting restorative approaches for solving existing and preventing future conflicts and promoting social justice in intercultural settings in Serbia, which can contribute to a closure of the cycle of violence and to the increase of overall security and safety of citizens.

Taking the abovementioned into account, in developing the action research we started from Allport's (1954) intergroup contact hypothesis, its revisions (Amir, 1998; Pettigrew, 1998; Janoff-Bulman and Werther, 2008) and further elaborations in relation to the use of constructive communication for overcoming divisions and reaching reconciliation in post-conflict societies (Lederach, 1997; Bloomfield, 2003; Forbes, 2004; Justad, 2006; Nikolić-Ristanović, 2015). Theoretical departures for the action research also included restorative and transformative justice literature, including on restorative dialogue, restorative practices/approaches (primarily circles) (e.g. Liebmann, 2007; Fellegi and Szegő, 2013; Törzs, 2013; Bannink and Walker, 2014; Galtung, 2000 and Lederach, 2003, 2011, quoted in Srbova 2015), as well as experiences so far of using yoga as part of restorative justice and reconciliation programmes (Franklin, 2001; Rucker, 2005; Nikolić-Ristanović, 2014; Srbova, 2015; Walker and Kobayashi, 2015). Finally, the action research presented a continuation, and a very important re-examination and upgrading phase of what the Victimology Society of Serbia has been doing since 2005 within the 'Association Joint Action for Truth and Reconciliation' on developing the 'Third way' model of dealing with past and present conflicts in Serbia (Nikolić-Ristanović, 2015). The 'Third way' model is defined as a non-conflict, inclusive, two-way communication of people with different experiences of war and other conflicts about the past, which implicates dealing with all crimes, victims and perpetrators regardless of their ethnic or other belonging, affiliation or personal features (Nikolić-Ristanović and Srna, 2010).[4] This model has been recognized by some authors as a possible way of applying restorative justice in post-conflict societies (Nikolić-Ristanović, 2006; Liebmann, 2007; Aertsen *et al.*, 2008).

Existing literature suggested and previous research on the development of the 'Third way' model confirmed that optimal contact, constructive communication and (restorative) dialogue play an important role in overcoming divisions, hostilities and conflicts between members of different groups in general, and particularly in post-conflict societies (Nikolić-Ristanović, 2015). Communication and dialogue are considered as essential to restorative (justice) approaches, particularly those considered to be dialogical processes (e.g. mediation, conferences, circles). The main potential of restorative approaches in the intercultural field is seen in promoting active participation of citizens in conflict transformation, creating possibilities for encounters and for including all stakeholders, including victims as key actors in democratic intercultural (restorative) dialogue,[5] as well as for networking and cooperating with different agencies in promoting social justice (Törzs, 2013). Similarly as in conflict transformation literature (Galtung, 2000 and Lederach, 2003, 2011, quoted in Srbova, 2015), it refuses binarism and advocates for an inclusive and comprehensive approach.

Research on the development of the 'Third way' model (Nikolić-Ristanović, 2015) suggests that conditions need to be set for both optimal contact and for the gradual change from authoritarian to democratic ways of communication, as well as for further development and maintenance of democratic (inclusive) communication. Conditions that need to be met for the contact to be considered as optimal include: balanced power relationships, safe space, common goals and interests, intergroup cooperation instead of competition, as well as close connections between members of different groups (Allport, 1954; Amir, 1998; Pettigrew, 1998; Nikolić-Ristanović, 2015). Additionally, institutional support is also seen as one of the key conditions for optimal contact (Allport, 1954). All these conditions seem important for enabling different people to recognize not only their differences, but also similarities (similarities in different experiences), which may contribute to individuals or groups coming closer to each other, preventing estranging. In order to enable two-way communication, it is necessary to set a communication framework that allows both sides to speak and to be heard, to get to mutual understanding and respect, to refrain from mutual blaming and to overcome divisions (Nikolić-Ristanović and Srna, 2010, p. 51). This necessarily leads us to the concept of restorative dialogue.

Restorative dialogue is inclusive, grounded on restorative principles and values, and it fosters communication between participants who are sharing experiences, perceptions, emotions and perspectives (Ray and Roberts, 2007). It is in the essence of the main restorative practices/approaches, namely mediation, conferences and circles. In developing the action research we explored different circle models, such as peacemaking circles (Fellegi and Szegő, 2013; Törzs, 2013) and solution-focused restoration circles (Bannink and Walker, 2014), which have two main characteristics. First, circles put emphasis on the interconnectedness of all humans and are based on a holistic approach, which means that they 'consciously engage all aspects of human experiences – spiritual, emotional, physical and mental' (Pranis, 2005, quoted in Törzs, 2013, p. 31). Second, a circle format enables equal participation, symbolizes inclusion and interconnectedness, and creates a special dynamic in the dialogue during the process (Fellegi and Szegő, 2013).

Finally, recent research suggests possible synergetic effects of combined use of restorative justice with yoga (Rucker, 2005) and mindfulness (Walker and Kobayashi, 2015), healing and empowering effects of yoga on victims (Franklin, 2001; Nikolić-Ristanović, 2014), as well as the use of yoga as a conflict transformation, conflict prevention and community-building tool, particularly in post-conflict societies (Srbova, 2015), which also was a starting point in developing this action research.

Setting the scene: empirical study on conflicts, victimization and justice in multi-ethnic communities

In order to enter the field and test the applicability of restorative approaches in the local multi-ethnic communities, we conducted the empirical research first. It was important for trust building, networking and establishing cooperation with people from the local research sites, who were involved in the action research (as interviewees, in collecting the data within the survey, in organizing and participating at the seminars, in the process of developing a practical tool for application and raising awareness and education on restorative approaches). The empirical research also enabled us as researchers to get familiar with the societal ecology of the research sites, which was relevant for understanding and interpreting the research results, and for developing and operationalizing the action research. Thus, the empirical research was a preparatory phase for the intervention.

The empirical research dealt with conflicts that have been evolving since 1990 between members of different ethnic groups in three multi-ethnic communities in Serbia and the way people have been solving them. We also studied how victims are treated, how security and justice are perceived, and what role restorative justice approaches have in dealing with conflicts and security. The empirical research consisted of a qualitative and quantitative part, and had a strong action dimension. Within the qualitative research, data was collected through interviews with 17 persons of different ethnicity, from both local NGOs and state institutions in the research sites. A victimization survey formed the basis for collecting data about victimization and conflicts in the quantitative part of the research. A semi-structured questionnaire was conducted on a sample of 1,423 respondents: 610 in Prijepolje, 431 in Bač/Bačka Palanka and 382 in Medvedja.[6] A respondent-driven sampling was used bearing in mind the social context of the post-conflict society (Klinger and Silva, 2013).[7]

The data was collected by local people (mostly NGO activists), who were our interviewees within the qualitative part of the research. They have a long-term experience in interethnic dialogue/cooperation projects and enjoy trust in their communities. This proved to be important for approaching respondents from different ethnic groups, establishing trust and distributing questionnaires. Apart from that, an action dimension of the quantitative research was visible in that its aim was not only to collect data on the subject of the research, but also to inform citizens (respondents) about existing NGOs, institutions and independent state agencies that could provide certain services (assistance, support, information, legal aid, mediation) to victims of violence, discrimination and other forms of human rights' violations, including those that are ethnically motivated. Additionally, the aim was to raise awareness about interethnic relations and conflicts, victimization, security issues and restorative justice through the questionnaire and/or conversations with persons who distributed and administered questionnaires. Moreover, the research findings were presented to and discussed by the participants of the seminars in the three local research sites within the intervention phase. Thus, the empirical research results served as a basis for developing the methodology of the action research in the form of participatory seminars.

The main findings of the empirical research

About a quarter of respondents (26.9 per cent or 383/1,423) from the survey sample suffered some form of victimization in the period from 1990 until the time of the survey (2013). Respondents who answered that they had been victimized reported a total of 1,367 victimization incidents. Around two-thirds of them (264 or 68.9 per cent) suffered from repeat victimization. Similar to victimization surveys carried out in other countries not affected by armed conflicts, the findings suggest that a small number of people is affected by most of the victimization incidents (Doerner and Lab, 2002; Croall, 2007). The most frequent forms of victimization according to the respondents' answers were: insults, threats and inability to realize one's rights. Most victimizations were interethnic by nature. Additionally, the finding that about one-third of the respondents knew someone from their own as well as from another ethnic group who was victimized by a member of another ethnic group, suggests that interethnic victimization is much more widespread in the society.

Data suggest that Albanian respondents were the most often to answer that they had been victimized compared to respondents from other ethnic groups (χ^2=323,359, df=3, p=0.001). The highest proportion of victimizations occurred during the 1990s, coinciding with armed conflicts in Croatia, Bosnia and Herzegovina, and Kosovo, while the smaller part occurred after 2000, being primarily related to the current political situation in the research sites (such as the inability to realize one's rights and pressures because of political affiliation).

The research findings suggest that both restorative and retributive measures/mechanisms were recognized as solutions that may bring justice in cases of interethnic and other conflicts in which the respondents were victimized. Punishment is still very much seen as an important form of reaction in the aftermath of different forms of victimization: it composes 25.3 per cent of all answers about mechanisms suitable to achieve justice in the concrete cases of victimization. Contrary to this, mechanisms of restorative justice or restorative approaches (dialogue, to know why what happened has happened, which also requires some form of an encounter and communication, apology, compensation, return or repair of property, community service) compose more than two thirds (71.6 per cent) of all mechanisms suitable to achieve justice according to the respondents. The research findings also suggest that for the great majority of the respondents (80.5 per cent) justice in the concrete case of victimization is attributed to restoration (restorative justice), either alone (46.8 per cent) or in combination with punishment, i.e. retribution (33.7 per cent).

Respondents' answers prove to open the space for a broader use of restorative approaches even in cases of victimization where a power imbalance exists. Respondents were introduced to the case scenario in which a young man was approached in the street by a police officer, who asked for his ID and concluded that the young man was of a different ethnicity, and then started to insult and humiliate him. This case was followed by a list of possible solutions, including both retributive (punishment) and restorative mechanisms (dialogue, mediation, community meeting/conference, apology, victim support, approaching peace council, compensation). The majority of respondents considered punishment as an excellent solution in the given case. Compensation holds the second place and is followed by: the apology of the police officer, mediation, dialogue, approaching a victim support service, organizing a community meeting/conference to solve the problem and approaching a peace council.[8] It is interesting that although there were fewer respondents who considered dialogue, mediation or a community meeting individually as a good or excellent solution compared to punishment, the number of respondents who said that one of these three solutions was good or excellent was still more than half of the total number of respondents. On the one hand, respondents who experienced victimization considered community meeting/conference and compensation to be solutions suitable to bring justice more that those who did not have such an experience. Respondents who did not have an experience of victimization tended to be more open towards the use of dialogue and apology. It is interesting that there were no differences between these two groups when it comes to mediation, approaching peace councils or the use of victim support services.

To summarize, although punishment is still seen as an important mechanism suitable to bring justice in cases of victimization, respondents' answers prove to open the space for the broader use of mechanisms of restorative justice, including restorative processes (dialogue, mediation, community meeting/conference) and restorative outcomes (apology, compensation, repair). It is particularly important to stress the need of those victimized to actively participate in the process of conflict transformation and not to be left on the margins of the social reaction. Therefore, we may argue that restorative approaches based on active participation, dialogue, respect, inclusion, empowerment and restoration (Vanfraechem, 2012, p. 14) could be mechanisms that are suitable for achieving justice in cases of victimization. However, people should be more aware of restorative justice mechanisms and approaches and the fact that they actually use them in everyday life.[9]

Taking this as a starting point, the core part of the action research (the intervention phase) focused on raising awareness and working towards capacity building of representatives of the three multi-ethnic communities for dealing with conflicts with the use of restorative approaches and dissemination of the gained knowledge in their social networks. This process started with bringing back the findings of the empirical research study to the local multi-ethnic communities and reflecting on them during participatory seminars.

Participatory seminars in multi-ethnic communities: testing the applicability of restorative approaches

Participatory seminars entitled 'From the conflict towards peaceful life in the community' were conducted in three research sites during 2014. They presented a process of bringing together citizens, representatives of civil society organizations and state institutions on the local level into a democratic intercultural dialogue (Council of Europe, 2008, p. 17) (an inclusive process that fosters active participation). The main aim of the action research was to test the applicability of the 'Third way' model of dealing with past and present conflicts in multi-ethnic communities in Serbia, which are more directly affected by the wars in the former Yugoslavia, and to further upgrade it, both theoretically and practically. Additionally, the aim was to elicit ideas about future steps on the promotion and implementation of restorative approaches in local multi-ethnic communities, and to develop a practical tool, which would serve these purposes (Nikolić-Ristanović, Srna and Ćopić, 2015a).

Given the aim of the action research, we defined four main objectives of the participatory seminars: (a) to introduce participants to the empirical research results in order to get their feedback, i.e. comments and explanations of the survey findings from the perspective of their own experience of living in a multi-ethnic and multicultural community; (b) to engage in participants' capacity building for dealing with conflicts with the use of restorative approaches and for dissemination of the knowledge on restorative justice in their social networks; (c) to test the applicability of different restorative approaches; and (d) to elicit ideas about restorative approaches suitable for dealing with conflicts in the given local communities and ideas and suggestions for further steps to be taken, which were used for developing the 'Manual on best practices of applying restorative justice approaches in intercultural settings'.

Methodology and content of the participatory seminars

The core part of the seminars consisted of three mutually linked workshops: 'Communication about conflicts, victimization and security'; 'Injuries and needs: Recognizing similarities in different experiences'; and 'Restorative justice and conflict resolution: testing a restorative circle model'. The workshop approach was chosen as a fruitful method of learning (active learning, experiential learning, interactive learning and learning in line with the model), but also as a method of change (psychological and psycho-social) that is inspired and initiated with this kind of learning (Janković and Kovač-Cerović, 1995, p. 51), which leaves a space for flexibility.

Apart from the overall objectives of the seminars, each workshop had its own aims. The workshop on communication about conflicts, victimization and security had the following particular aims: to identify communication patterns about conflicts, victimization and security which were used by the participants; to make participants familiar with the potential that communication in the spirit of the 'Third way', as a form of restorative dialogue has for the resolution and prevention of conflicts; to test the 'Third way' communication/restorative dialogue in a multi-ethnic community in order to learn how useful and acceptable this way of communication is for the participants in their everyday, personal and professional life; and to learn whether and how the principles of restorative communication should be further developed and/or adjusted to the need of local communities. Additionally, being the first workshop in order, it also aimed to give us as researchers first impressions about how acceptable/attractive restorative justice is for the participants in a concrete community, and, thus, to help us decide about the optimal direction and/or necessary modifications of a further seminar implementation and its adjustment to the context and participants.

The second workshop 'Injuries and needs: Recognizing similarities in different experiences' focused on deepening initial communication between participants, initiated in the first workshop, by moving to a more delicate and direct plan of psychological and relational aspects, and on the enrichment of participants' communication by introducing non-verbal forms (drawings, touching each other, plays). The other focus was on experiential learning (cognition) of participants about themselves, about others and about their mutual relations. In addition to these general objectives, this workshop had three specific aims on the individual, relational and social level. At the individual level, it aimed to encourage participants to understand themselves through awareness of personal injuries and needs arising from them. At the relational level, the workshop intended to encourage the participants to understand others (members of the group), through knowledge of their injuries and empathic understanding of their needs; to understand mutual relations, i.e. recognizing similarities in the experiences of different people; and to develop personal safety and mutual trust and to consider the way in which these were developed. At the social level, the aim was to develop motivation for further cooperation of group members in their local communities, which was also one of the objectives of the entire seminar.

Finally, specific aims of the third workshop entitled 'Restorative justice and conflict resolution: testing a restorative circle model' were: to learn what place restorative justice has in conflict resolution through mapping the potential for the use of restorative approaches for each group of seminar participants; to identify examples of good practice that are based on restorative justice principles, which could be useful for conflict resolution in intercultural settings; and to find out in which way restorative approaches impact on accountability and if they were empowering for the participants, particularly victims. In addition, this workshop also sought to introduce participants to different restorative approaches and their usefulness for conflict prevention and resolution in intercultural settings. Additionally, the workshop aimed to make participants aware of different uses of restorative approaches, in order to enable them to recognize restorative approaches they already use in their everyday life. Finally, during the workshop one restorative approach – the restorative circle – was tested; thus, one of the aims was also to learn whether the tested restorative approach is an adequate form of conflict resolution for the three communities.

During the final seminar session, participants could discuss and exchange ideas and enlist suggestions on the possibilities of using information and knowledge from the seminar in practice, as well as how they saw the use of restorative approaches in their local communities. This was used as a starting point for the participatory process of developing the 'Manual on best practices of applying restorative justice approaches in intercultural settings' in the continuation of the action research.

The main methodological approach of the participatory seminars was setting the laboratory/experiment conditions for optimal contact and communication between members of different groups as the seminar participants, which allowed for exploring the applicability of the 'Third way' model in three multi-ethnic communities and coming to ideas about its possible further development. This included three main components. First, we took care that most of the conditions for optimal contact are met (Allport, 1954; Amir, 1998; Pettigrew, 1998; Nikolić-Ristanović, 2015). Second, the communication framework was set as the part of the ground rules, with elements of mindfulness included.[10] Third, different relaxation and empowering techniques, including yoga-breathing techniques and meditation, were used throughout seminars as the generator of inner peace and positive personal and intergroup change. Therefore, we intended to explore how seminar participants communicate/change their communication patterns about difficult topics, including their own conflicts/victimizations and related needs, when conditions are controlled and space is created for them to feel safe and relaxed. In this way, the seminars also provided a space for experiential learning, further networking, and building relationships and cooperation.

During the workshops the following concrete methods and techniques were used: observation, individual and group work (both in small groups and in big group/plenary), questionnaires, drawings, meditation/relaxation and other exercises, presentations and discussions.

Seminars involved 45 participants in total: 14 participants in Medvedja, nine in Prijepolje and 22 in Bačka Palanka. Seminar participants were selected based on three main criteria:

1 The field/sector they work in or are actively involved in. Therefore, participants were representatives of civil society organizations (including victim support organizations, victims' and war veterans' organizations, women's organizations, organizations of young people, peace organizations), local governance, state agencies and institutions at the local level (police, social welfare service, schools, pre-school institutions), and of religious organizations.
2 Existing networks and 'the web of relationships' (Lederach, 2005).[11] It was relevant to include persons who have their own networks and who could contribute towards dissemination of knowledge, ideas and the new models of dealing with conflicts based on restorative justice and to (re)building the web of relationships in the wider society.
3 Socio-demographic characteristics, which meant to have participants from ethnic groups that were in the focus of the research (Serbs, Albanian, Croats and Bosniaks depending on the research site) and to have, within each ethnic group, participants of different age and gender. This kind of diversity was important in order to introduce different perspectives into the discussion and work, and 're-categorization' if and when needed (Justad, 2006).

Seminars were evaluated content wise and in terms of the achieved aims both by seminar participants and VDS research team members. As for the participants, evaluation was done on two levels: after each thematic workshop and at the end of the seminar, by filling in the evaluation questionnaires reflecting on the particular workshop and the seminar in general and sharing their impressions. VDS team members evaluated each seminar through sharing their impressions, observations, good things and noticed shortcomings, which helped in improving the seminar throughout its delivery. Therefore, developing and implementing the seminars in general and each workshop in particular was a process, which turned out to be a valuable learning experience for both members of the VDS research team individually and the Victimology Society of Serbia in general. Finally, an evaluation of the seminars was organized for the VDS research team members. We used the restorative circle format during the evaluation workshop and we applied the same communication framework as the one set forth during the seminars. This was a valuable experience for us, which suggested there are some necessary steps and standards for successfully implementing restorative approaches, which seem important for our further intervention and future work.

Main conclusions and lessons learnt

The research conducted in Serbia within the ALTERNATIVE project suggests that conflicts existed or still exist in all three multi-ethnic communities on different levels: conflicts between citizens; conflicts between citizens and the state, i.e. state institutions; and conflicts between citizens and the state's representatives (e.g. police officers). Conflicts with the state have a prominent place, which is tightly connected to the non-functioning or inadequate functioning of the state and the lack of rule of law. Thus, the state is not seen as a guarantor of the security, but is rather perceived as one of the main sources of insecurity. This is also confirmed by the empirical research findings that perception of security goes much beyond physical safety of people (in terms of freedom from crime, war or violence); it also refers to social, economic, legal and political safety.

In Serbia, as a post-conflict society, there is a continuity of conflicts from the war to the post-war period, but new conflicts have emerged as well. Apart from interethnic, there are also intra-ethnic conflicts. Thus, conflicts do not exist only along one particular line, e.g. ethnic belonging, but they are also based on religion, gender, age or other personal characteristics, or are tightly connected to the political situation in the multi-ethnic communities encompassed by the research and the political and economic transition in the country in general. Therefore, the research confirmed the need to speak about 'conflicts in intercultural settings' rather than of intercultural conflicts (Foss *et al.*, 2012, p. 24; Vanfraechem, 2012, p. 36). Otherwise, naming all conflicts as intercultural or interethnic may lead to the construction of conflicts or 'maintenance and escalation of conflicts' (Foss *et al.*, 2012, pp. 23–24). Additionally, both empirical and action research confirmed the findings of our theoretical research (Nikolić-Ristanović and Ćopić, 2013) suggesting that for the security/safety of citizens in Serbia it is necessary to deal with both past and present interethnic, but also other (intra-ethnic) conflicts, while taking care of their very complex interconnectedness and in an inclusive way. In sum, through the action research we made a shift from dealing with conflicts between particular ethnic groups to conflicts between individual citizens (not always of different ethnicity), and between citizens and the state (state institutions) based on unequal power-relations.

A potential for restorative justice in conflict transformation exists in Serbia. Both respondents in the empirical research and seminar participants in the action research gave relevance to restorative approaches for conflict transformation in their local communities, in particular for those that are based on encounters and dialogue. Additionally, seminar participants within the action research became more aware of the potential of restorative approaches, so that they could recognize the use of these approaches in their everyday private and professional life and even advocate for their broader use. These findings are important if we consider restorative justice as an important social force that contributes to the revival of participatory democracy, which ought to be more inclusive, responsive and just, promoting active and responsible citizenship and cohesion of different interests, mutual respect and solidarity, as well as treating opponents in deliberative processes not as enemies, but rather as 'fellow travellers' who are stemming towards constructive solutions and common interests (Walgrave, 2008, pp. 194–195). This finding is also relevant when bearing in mind that Serbian society is predominantly authoritarian and punitive.

The action research suggests that the 'Third way' model of communication as a form of restorative dialogue, and the restorative circle model, are applicable and appropriate approaches for multi-ethnic communities in Serbia for conflict prevention and transformation. Meeting conditions for optimal contact contributes to changes of communication patterns and enables constructive communication (dialogue). The action research suggested that participants found setting the communication framework to be important since it allows for mutual respect and trust, which fosters openness, mutual understanding and support, providing people space to communicate about difficult issues in a more easy way. Recognizing similarities in different experiences may contribute to a better understanding of one's own self, for understanding others, and for making people feel closer to each other and preventing estranging. The importance of using different aspects of yoga that contribute to concentration on present (mindfulness) as well as to inner peace and balance (e.g. breathing techniques, relaxation and meditation), was also recognized by the seminar participants.

Since the change of the state policy towards dealing with conflicts, tensions and discrimination in intercultural settings is a long-term task in post-conflict societies, working on (re)building relationships, trust and mutual understanding, and developing restorative approaches on the local community level (bottom-up approach) seem more realistic and effective. Participants of the seminars within the action research showed interest and readiness to work together, to share their experiences and to communicate, which is an important condition for further networking and joint work on promoting and implementing restorative approaches in multi-ethnic communities. Moreover, they initiated the creation of inter-sector bodies which they called 'restorative teams', which should serve for promoting, developing and implementing restorative approaches in their communities. Additionally, based on the ideas elicited during the seminars, joint work of VDS research team members and representatives of the local multi-ethnic communities resulted in the 'Manual on best practices of applying restorative justice approaches in intercultural settings', which shall serve for the promotion of and education on restorative approaches to conflict transformation in multi-ethnic and multicultural communities in Serbia. Therefore, initiating local restorative teams and developing the Manual could be considered as two main outcomes/results of this action research.

However, the action research suggested that institutional support is still missing in Serbia and it presents an obstacle for the 'Third way' model as well as for other restorative approaches to be more widely recognized and used within society. Therefore, in order for these approaches to be more visible, recognized and used within the wider society it is necessary to further strengthen, enhance and develop the legal, professional and institutional framework, i.e. to secure institutional support, but also to work in synergy with state mechanisms. It is also important to continue raising awareness of citizens and professionals on restorative approaches, and to work on developing and implementing education programmes on restorative justice and restorative approaches on different levels.

Finally, this action research was a valuable learning experience for us as researchers as well. It helped us to learn more about restorative justice and to become more aware about the potential role restorative approaches have to play in a much wider context of people's everyday life and in various relationships; much broader and much more complex than interethnic relationships and divisions. We started to think of restorative justice in a much broader way, not only as a form of justice, but rather as an approach, intervention, practice or as a way of life. Our work in the ALTERNATIVE proved how important it is not to look on restorative justice only in connection to the criminal justice system and as a way of responding to crime, or to identify it with one particular form of application, such as mediation, which is the case in Serbia, nor to see it only as a way of reaction, but also as a tool for prevention of future problems, tensions and conflicts.

Based on the results of the action research implemented within ALTERNATIVE, as well as on the work and experiences so far within the 'Association Joint Action for Truth and Reconciliation', we defined crucial elements of the restorative approach to conflict prevention and transformation applicable in intercultural settings: conditions for optimal contact, communication framework in the spirit of restorative justice, yoga and mindfulness, peacemaking/restorative circle model (a circle format) and a solution-focused approach. These elements would make it a unique and original model of conflict transformation in intercultural settings not only in Serbia, but also in the region. Therefore, our future work would be oriented towards strengthening cooperation with local restorative teams in the local research sites and working on the promotion of restorative justice and raising awareness on restorative approaches in these local communities on the basis of the developed Manual. In addition, we would also stem towards testing the restorative approach developed within the ALTERNATIVE project in other intercultural settings both in Serbia and the region, in order to give local people a kind of a tool to be able to think about conflict transformation differently and to try to deal with tensions, problems, discrimination and divisions in a more constructive way with the use of restorative approaches. Thus, while the action research has formally come to an end, we continue the endeavour of sustaining the project results within the field.

Notes

1 The research report on dealing with conflicts by NGOs and the state *Dealing with interethnic conflicts in Serbia and the place of restorative justice and victims* is available at the ALTERNATIVE website www.alternativeproject.eu/assets/upload/Deliverable_6.1_Research_report_on_dealing_with_conflicts_by_NGOs_and_the_state.pdf, and the

website of the Victimology Society of Serbia www.vds.org.rs/File/Deliverable_6_1_Research_report_on_dealing_with_conflicts_by_NGOs_and_the_state(.pdf.

2 The research report *Conflicts, security and justice in intercultural context of Serbia* is available at the website of the project ALTERNATIVE www.alternativeproject.eu/assets/upload/Deliverable_6.2_Research_report_on_interethnic_conflicts_and_citizens_security_perceptions_.pdf and the website of the Victimology Society of Serbia www.vds.org.rs/File/Deliverable_6.2_Research_report_on_interethnic_conflicts_and_citizens_security_p.pdf.

3 The research report *Action research report on the application of restorative justice in intercultural settings* (Deliverable 6.3 of FP7 project ALTERNATIVE – Developing alternative understandings of security and justice through restorative justice approaches in intercultural settings within democratic societies).

4 The 'Third way' model rests upon the following key principles: mutual recognition, support and non-accusation; inclusive relationship towards crimes, victims and perpetrators and inclusive discourse about the past (speaking about all victims, perpetrators and witnesses regardless of their ethnic and other identification and features); care about human rights, empowerment and reintegration of all persons affected by conflict; using a wide range of restorative methods for establishment of the truth and reconciliation; and a proactive approach in dealing with the past (Nikolić-Ristanović and Srna, 2010).

5 As pointed out by the Council of Europe (2008, p. 17), intercultural dialogue

> fosters equality, human dignity and a sense of common purpose. It aims to develop a deeper understanding of diverse world views and practices, to increase cooperation and participation (or the freedom to make choices), to allow personal growth and transformation, and to promote tolerance and respect for the other.

6 The ethnic structure of the sample was as follows: in Medvedja 243 (63.6 per cent) respondents were Serbs and 139 (36.4 per cent) Albanians; in Prijepolje, there were 304 (49.8 per cent) Serb and 306 (50.2 per cent) Bosniak respondents, and in Bač/BačkaPalanka – 346 Serb respondents (80.3 per cent) and 85 Croats (19.7 per cent).

7 In this way we intended to decrease the number of refusals, because, keeping in mind the findings of the qualitative research, we were aware of still existing distrust and fear among citizens, in particular among those belonging to ethnic minorities. By choosing the respondent-driven sampling we tried to avoid some limitations and problems in applying standard sampling techniques when using random sampling in surveying vulnerable populations in post-conflict societies (Klinger and Silva, 2013). This was particularly applicable to South Serbia, where some of Albanians who left Serbia at the end of the 1990s now only occasionally live there. In addition, there are no precise data about the number of Albanians in Medvedja; the residential layout is chaotic etc.

8 Peace councils are bodies usually composed of several (mainly three) respectful members of the local community. The role of these councils is to develop good relations between citizens and to solve conflicts and problems they might have. These councils exist in some local communities. The work of these bodies used to be regulated (in the former Yugoslavia) by the law on courts. Today, the law on the organization of the courts in Serbia stipulates that establishment and the work of peace councils is to be regulated by separate acts. This is done by the decisions of the authorized bodies in the municipalities (local self-government).

9 This is supported by the findings that the majority of the respondents (897 or 63.0 per cent) experienced solving any problem in their lives through a dialogue, while one third of the respondents (428 or 30.1 per cent) turned to a person who was respected by other members of the community in order to mediate and to assist in solving a concrete problem (informal mediation).

10 Including the following rules: listening and respecting each other, regardless whether one agrees or not; mutual recognition and self-respect; allowing/accepting existence

of different understandings/experiencing of the same events by different people; no accusation of others and self-blaming – empowering I talk instead of YOU, THEY talk; acceptance of responsibility for what one says; understanding ourselves and others through the awareness about the connection between a personal sense of grievance, exclusiveness and aggressiveness in communication; the focus on the present moment and mindfulness: full consciousness about oneself and others, about the place where we are and what is going on, about own feelings and reasons for them as well as about reasons behind feelings and deeds of other people which often are not directly related to us; proactive instead of reactive approach (proposing solutions instead of self-defence and attack of others).

11 Lederach (2005) uses the term 'web of relationships' in the context of peace-building. As he points out, peace-building 'must experience, envision, and give birth to the web of relationships' (p. 34), while 'the essence of peace-building requires us to explore in much greater detail the inner makeup of creativity as embedded in understanding the dynamics and potentials of networking – the arts of web making and web watching' (p. 35). Therefore, for peace-building it is important to increase the capacities of both individuals and communities to network and to be able to (re)build relationships with others, including even their enemies.

References

Aertsen, I., Arsovska, J., Rohne, H.C., Valiñas, M. and Vanspauwen, K. eds., 2008. *Restoring justice after large-scale violent conflicts: Kosovo, DR Congo and the Israeli–Palestinian case*. Cullompton: Willan Publishing.

Allport, G., 1954. *The nature of prejudice*. Reading: Addison-Wesley.

Amir, Y., 1998. *Contact hypothesis in ethnic relations.* In: E. Weiner, ed. *The handbook of interethnic coexistence*. New York: Continuum Publishing, pp. 162–181.

Bannink, F. and Walker, L., 2014. Solution focused conflict management and restoration circles. Available at: www.lorennwalker.com/articles/banninkwalkerSFscript0514.pdf [accessed 20 September 2015].

Biro, M., Mihic, V., Milin, P. and Logar-Djuric, S., 2002. Da li su drustveno-politicke promene u Srbiji promenile nivo autoritarnosti i etnocentrizma gradjana? *Psihologija*, 35(1–2), pp. 37–47.

Bloomfield, D., 2003. Reconciliation: an introduction. In: D. Bloomfield, T. Barnes, and L. Huyse, eds. *Reconciliation after violent conflict: a handbook.* Stockholm: International IDEA, pp. 10–18.

Ćopić, S. and Nikolić-Ristanović, V., 2016. *Priručnik o najboljim praksama primene restorativnih pristupa u interkulturalnom kontekstu.* Beograd: Viktimološko društvo Srbije i Prometej.

Council of Europe, 2008. Living together as equals in dignity. White Paper. Strasbourg: Council of Europe. Available at: www.coe.int/t/dg4/intercultural/source/white%20 paper_final_revised_en.pdf [accessed 3 February 2014].

Croall, H., 2007. Victims of white-collar and corporate crime. In: P. Davis, P. Francis, and C. Greer, eds. *Victims, crime and society.* Los Angeles, London, New Delhi, Singapore: Sage Publications, pp. 78–108.

Doerner, W. and Lab, S., 2002. *Victimology.* 3rd edn. Cincinnati: Anderson Publishing Company.

Domonji, P. ed., 2008. *Vojvodina's multiethnic identity: challenges in 2007–08. Helsinki files no 27.* Belgrade: Helsinki Committee for Human Rights in Serbia.

Fellegi, B. and Szegő, D., 2013. *Handbook for facilitating peacemaking circles*. Budapest: Foresee Research Group. Available at: www.foresee.hu/uploads/tx_abdownloads/files/peacemaking_circle_handbook.pdf [accessed 3 September 2015].

Forbes, H.D., 2004. Ethnic conflict and the contact hypothesis. In: L. Yueh-Ting, M. Clark, M. Fathali and S. Worchel, eds. *The psychology of ethnic and cultural conflict*. Westport: Praeger, pp. 69–88.

Foss, E.M., Hassan, S.C., Hydle, I., Seeberg, M.L. and Uhrig, B., 2012. *Report on conflicts in intercultural settings*. Oslo: NOVA. Public deliverable 2.1 of the ALTERNATIVE project. Available at: www.alternativeproject.eu/assets/upload/Deliverable_2.1_Report_on_conlicts_in_intercultural_settings.pdf [accessed 3 September 2015].

Franklin, C., 2001. Physiotherapy with torture survivors. *Physiotherapy*, 87(7), pp. 374–377.

Garland, D., 2001. *The culture of control – crime and social order in contemporary society*. Oxford: Oxford University Press.

Helsinki Committee for Human Rights in Serbia, 2004. National minorities in Serbia: in conflict with a state ethnic identity. Annual Report.

Janković, S. and Kovač-Cerović, T., 1995. Osnovne pretpostavke radioničarskog postupka., In: T. Kovač-Cerović, ed. *Učionica dobre volje*. Beograd: Most, pp. 49–68.

Janoff-Bulman, R. and Werther, A., 2008. The social psychology of respect: implications for delegitimization and reconciliation. In: A. Nadler, T. Malloy and J. Fisher, eds. *The social psychology of intergroup reconciliation*. Oxford: Oxford University Press, pp. 145–170.

Justad, L.O., 2006. Post-conflict peace-building: social reconstruction and reconciliation through dialogue. Master's thesis. Oslo: Oslo University. Available at: www.duo.uio.no/bitstream/handle/10852/13993/33708.pdf?sequence=1 [accessed 15 September 2015].

Klinger, J. and Silva. R., 2013. Combining found data and surveys to measure conflict mortality. In: T.B. Seybolt, J.D. Aronson and B. Fischhoff, eds. *Counting civilian casualties: an introduction to recording and estimating non-military deaths in conflict*. New York: Oxford University Press, pp. 147–163.

Lederach, J.P., 1997. *Building peace: sustainable reconciliation in divided societies*. Washington, D.C.: United States Institute of Peace.

Lederach, J.P., 2005. *The moral imagination: the art and soul of building peace*. Oxford: Oxford University Press.

Liebmann, M., 2007. *Restorative justice: how it works*. London: Jessica Kingsley Publishers.

Minow, M., 1998. *Between vengeance and forgiveness – facing history after genocide and mass violence*. Boston: Beacon Press.

Nikolić-Ristanović, V., 2003. Possibilities for restorative justice in Serbia. In: L. Walgrave, ed. *Positioning restorative justice*. Cullompton: Willan Publishing, pp. 239–255.

Nikolić-Ristanović, V., 2006. Truth and reconciliation in Serbia. In: D. Sullivan and L. Tifft, eds. *Handbook of restorative justice*. Oxon: Taylor & Francis, pp. 369–387.

Nikolić-Ristanović, V., 2014. Joga i žrtve. *Temida*, 17(1), pp. 47–64.

Nikolić-Ristanović, V., 2015. Communication about the past and reconciliation: lessons from the Western Balkan. *Restorative Justice: An International Journal*, 3(2), pp. 188–211.

Nikolić-Ristanović, V. and Ćopić, S., 2013. *Dealing with interethnic conflicts in Serbia and the place of restorative justice and victims*. Belgrade: Victimology Society of Serbia. Public deliverable 6.1 of the ALTERNATIVE project. Available at: www.alternativeproject.eu/assets/upload/Deliverable 6.1_Research_report_on dealing_with_conflicts_by_NGOs_and_the_state.pdf [accessed 15 September 2015].

Nikolić-Ristanović, V. and Ćopić, S., 2016. Dealing with the past in Serbia: achievements in the past 20 years. In: M. Fischer and O. Simić, eds. *Transitional justice and reconciliation – lessons from the Balkans*. Oxon: Routledge, pp. 141–168.

Nikolić-Ristanović, V., Ćopić, S., Petrović, N. and Šaćiri, B., 2014. *Conflicts, security and justice in intercultural context of Serbia*. Belgrade: Victimology Society of Serbia. Public deliverable 6.2 of the ALTERNATIVE project. Available at: www.alternative-project.eu/assets/upload/Deliverable_6.2_Research_report_on_interethnic_conflicts_and_citizens_security_perceptions.pdf [accessed 15 September 2015].

Nikolić-Ristanović, V., Ćopić, S., Petrović, N. and Šaćiri, B., 2015. Viktimizacija i pravda u interkulturalnom kontekstu Srbije. *Temida*, 18(2), pp. 31–58.

Nikolić-Ristanović, V. and Šaćiri, B., 2013. Bavljenje međuetničkim konfliktima od strane organizacija civilnog društva u Srbiji: aktivnosti i diskurs. *Temida*, 16(3–4), pp. 27–60.

Nikolić-Ristanović, V. and Srna, J., 2010. Pomirenje sa sobom i drugima: od pristupa ka modelu. *Temida*, 13(1), pp. 43–58.

Nikolić-Ristanović, V., Srna, J. and Ćopić, S., 2015a. *Action research report on the application of restorative justice in intercultural settings*. Belgrade: Victimology Society of Serbia. Non-public deliverable 6.3 of the ALTERNATIVE project.

Nikolić-Ristanović, V., Srna, J. and Ćopić, S., 2015b. Primena restorativnih pristupa u interkulturalnim sredinama u Srbiji: Teorijska polazišta i metodološki pristup akcionog istraživanja VDS u tri multietničke sredine. *Temida*, 18(3–4), pp. 81–102.

Pettigrew, T., 1998. Intergroup contact theory. *Annual Review of Psychology*, 49, pp. 65–88.

Ray, B. and Roberts, A.W., 2007. Restorative processes. In: G. Johnstone and D.W. Van Ness, eds. *Handbook of restorative justice*. Devon: Willan Publishing, pp. 211–227.

Rohne, H.C., Arsovska, J. and Aertsen, I., 2008. Challenging restorative justice-state based conflict, mass victimisation and the changing nature of warfare. In: I. Aertsen, J. Arsovska, H.C., Rohne, M. Valiñas and K. Vanspauwen, eds. *Restoring justice after large-scale violent conflicts*. Devon: Willan Publishing, pp. 3–46.

Rucker, L., 2005. Yoga and restorative justice in prison. *Contemporary Justice Review*, 8(1), pp. 107–112.

Savković, M., 2010. Kontekst i implikacije huliganskog nasilja u Srbiji. *Bezbednost Zapadnog Balkana*, 5(18), pp. 91–99.

Srbova, K., 2015. Yoga for peace. Master's thesis, Brussels School of International Studies of the Department of Politics and International Relations in the Faculty of Social Science.

Teitel, R., 2000. *Transitional justice*. Oxford: Oxford University Press.

Törzs, E., 2013. *Report on restorative justice models*. Leuven: KU Leuven Institute of Criminology. Public deliverable 3.1 of the ALTERNATIVE project. Available at: www.alternativeproject.eu/assets/upload/Deliverable_3.1_Report_on_RJ_models.pdf [accessed 15 September 2015].

Vanfraechem, I., 2012. *Work document on operationalisation of theoretical concepts*. Leuven: KU Leuven. Non-public deliverable 8.1 of the ALTERNATIVE project.

Walgrave, L., 2008. *Restorative justice, self-interest and responsible citizenship*. Cullompton: Willan Publishing.

Walker, L. and Kobayashi. L., 2015. Rituals. restorative & therapeutic reentry rituals. In: M. Herzog-Evans, ed. 2015. *Offender release and supervision: the role of courts and the use of discretion*. Oisterwijk: Wolf Legal Publishing, pp. 351–371.

7 Working across frontiers

Community-based restorative justice in Northern Ireland

Tim Chapman, Hugh Campbell, Derick Wilson and Philip McCready

Introduction

Since the peace process in Northern Ireland was agreed in 1998 (Northern Ireland Office, 1998), the violence has been greatly reduced though not eliminated. The process has achieved a power-sharing democracy and the strengthening of human rights and equality. Arrangements to protect equality of esteem for cultural expression, such as the Irish and Ulster Scot's languages, have been established.

However, in an effort to ensure that the two main identities are represented in government, the settlement has institutionalized a politics, in which power is derived from maintaining balanced but separate identities rather than transforming inter-communal relationships. This form of identity politics tends to prioritize contentious cultural issues over economic or social problems. This sustains conflict at community level. As a consequence, while serious violence conducted by armed groups has significantly reduced, street disorder and riots continue to disrupt social and economic life.

To deepen our understanding of the problems facing Northern Ireland we reviewed the literature on community and identity and their relationship to violence. The resulting analysis prior to engaging in the action research presented us with some fundamental problems in theorizing a restorative justice response to conflicts in intercultural settings in Northern Ireland.

1. People tend to identify with a community to experience a sense of belonging and security (Agamben, 1993; Bauman, 2001; Esposito, 2013).
2. Modern state and market systems are eroding this sense of belonging and security (Habermas, 1987).
3. Resisting this erosion, people seek out some common, often ethnic, identity (Young, 1999).
4. Other communities may be seen to threaten the community's security and culture (Staub, 2001; Atran, 2010).
5. This may cause scapegoating which can be expressed in a form of identity politics that leads to harmful conflict (Girard, 1986; Staub, 2001).

We use the metaphor of 'frontiers' as a way of conceiving conflict in society. Wright (1987) referred to Northern Ireland as an 'ethnic frontier society' in that it was characterized by an uneasy tension between two competing nationalisms within its boundaries. In such societies, antagonism and fear dominate most relationships and shape the character of how security and justice are understood and experienced.

There is also a class frontier: most of the violent conflict is both perpetrated and suffered by people from working-class areas. Those most involved in violent conflict are predominantly young men suggesting that there is a strong gender and intergenerational dimension to be taken into account. One additional new reality is that many people from new ethnic minorities have settled in Northern Ireland.

An important product of the reform process was the introduction of restorative justice at the heart of the youth justice system in Northern Ireland. Restorative youth conferences are offered to virtually every young person who admits to an offence and to their victims (Zinsstag and Chapman, 2012). Restorative justice schemes had actually emerged prior to the state's initiatives in local communities as a means of reducing the brutal physical punishments that were being inflicted on offenders by armed groups during the civil conflict. The organizations who were most engaged in restorative justice in the field of conflict in intercultural settings were the community-based restorative justice projects.

To summarize, we believe that the Northern Irish state has demonstrated its ability to manage political conflict and violence but it is limited in its potential to transform conflict in intercultural settings. Does this present an opportunity for community-based restorative justice?

The ideas and practices of community relations and peace building have much in common with restorative justice. They emphasize building and healing relationships, dialogue and storytelling. The principles developed by Future Ways (Eyben, Morrow and Wilson, 1997), equity, diversity and interdependence, were of particular relevance to the ALTERNATIVE project's focus on intercultural contexts. However, the focus on specific harmful events and the engagement of people thrown together in relation to these events distinguishes a restorative approach from more general peace-building or community relations practices.

Community is both an important value and participant in restorative justice but it is also a contentious concept (Walgrave, 2002; Pavlich, 2004). Does this analysis mean that the concept of community has not only little relevance to a modern, democratic society but also represents a risk to a stable, intercultural society?

Restorative justice is generally employed as a means of addressing individual acts of harm. Most definitions of restorative justice methods such as conferencing speak of the offender, the victim and the community of support (Walgrave, 2008; Shapland, Robinson and Sorsby, 2012). For example the UN Handbook (2006, p. 6) states: 'Restorative justice refers to a process for resolving crime by focusing on redressing the harm done to the victims, holding offenders accountable for their actions and, often also, engaging the community in the resolution of that conflict.'

What if the harm caused by conflicts in intercultural conflicts cannot or should not be defined as criminal offences? What if the groups engaged in the conflict do not accept the label of offender or victim? If restorative justice is to be a relevant and appropriate way of approaching conflict in intercultural settings, there need to be new ways of understanding not only what restorative justice is but also what it means to experience security and justice.

The action research methodology

This analysis stimulated key research questions. Can restorative justice contribute to building a pluralist society at peace with itself? In doing so, how does restorative justice offer an alternative understanding of how justice and security can be delivered to people living in communities experiencing conflicts in an intercultural context? What would then be the relationship between communities and the state, particularly the criminal justice system?

In addressing these questions, the Ulster University team were not attempting to produce an independent and objective evaluation of community restorative justice in relation to conflicts in intercultural settings. We were interested in discovering what worked in practice and what discourses supported what worked. While factual data was used to ground theory and practice, the research focused more upon narrative and dialogical truth than forensic truth (Habermas, 1990; Shriver, 2007).

The project is an action research methodology, which fitted well with the principles and practices that the Ulster University team had been developing in their pedagogy and their engagement with civil society. Ulster University has provided a safe space for people engaged in or affected by conflict to meet and enter into dialogue, reflect and learn about each other. As a result the team has developed a way of building relationships and engaging people in learning which is very compatible with action research (Reason and Bradbury, 2006).

The sites that were chosen for the research included some of the most deprived communities in Northern Ireland. The locations of the research were consciously chosen so as to get close to the conflicts as they are experienced by those most affected by them. Many residents in these areas live precarious lives surviving on social security payments or poorly paid jobs that offer little or no financial security. The process of 'precaritization' (Lorey, 2012) generates a significant section of the population who are preoccupied with security.

The community-based restorative projects are also subject to precarity. They receive low levels of funding over short periods with no commitment to continue to fund. As a consequence, practitioners are often unpaid and have to seek temporary work elsewhere. This precarity makes it extremely difficult to plan a sustainable restorative justice service in the communities.

We did not, however, want to define these communities in terms of deprivation and precarity. The cultural and social theorist, bell hooks (1990) writes of her resistance to being referred to as the 'Other'.

> Often this speech about the 'Other' annihilates, erases: 'No need to hear your voice when I can talk about you better than you can speak about yourself. No need to hear your voice. Only tell me about your pain. I want to know your story. And then I will tell it back to you in a new way. Tell it back to you in such a way that it has become mine, my own. Re-writing you, I write myself anew. I am still author, authority. I am still the colonizer, the speaking subject and you are now at the center of my talk'.
>
> (hooks, 1990, p. 152)

The prevailing political and cultural discourses further simplified by mass media do not provide the nuances and possibilities that the examination of complex conflicts require. These discourses produce 'thin' or one-dimensional stories (White, 2000). We wanted to adopt a method, which uncovered 'thick' (Geertz, 1973), multi-dimensional narratives that reflect the reality of parties to a conflict.

Conflicts between groups, especially those that result in violence, will almost always generate the need for justice to be done. We wanted to test the belief that justice does not reside solely within the domain of the criminal justice system and that it can be restored through people actively participating in restorative processes within local communities. We were particularly interested in whether people felt safer if they had experienced justice.

The discovery of the truth is important both to justice and research. Shriver (2007) has usefully written about a process of discovering the truth or a series of truths. 'Forensic truth' captures the facts of what happened. However, it is important to people that they have the opportunity to tell their stories, the 'narrative truth'. As people tell their stories and listen to others' stories, they ask questions of each other and enter into communication thus producing a 'dialogical truth'. Our action research followed a similar process. The starting point in an inquiry, for example into a conflict between neighbours, may be a factual account. What interested us more were the narratives or subjective experiences of the conflict that different parties articulated and how these narratives could be transformed through dialogue from fixed positions based upon the past to more nuanced, 'thicker' discourses, which were open to different possibilities in the future.

Our approach to action research was based upon dialogue rather than on interviewing people. Dialogue (Isaacs, 1999) requires people, their experiences and ideas to meet and interact and in doing so to generate new knowledge of each other and their worlds. Some key principles underpinned the University's interactions with organizations and individuals:

- Inclusion: a willingness to make the effort to understand and respect the history and perspective of each group and to begin from where they are in reality;
- Relating as a critical friend: to ally with each group's struggles and support them through engaging and challenging them to think critically and creatively;

- Participation: to engage with people democratically by respecting their knowledge and expertise and facilitating active participation in learning from real situations and problems.

These principles are reflected in the participatory action research methodology (Reason and Bradbury, 2006) that the team adopted in the field. We were less interested in proving hypotheses than in participating in an emergent process that changes and develops according to unanticipated events and in understanding how people reflect, understand, develop their capacity and respond to these events.

It is important to emphasize that in collaborating closely with our partners, the Ulster team did not take the lead in any direct restorative practice: the approach was to enter into dialogue with each partner on the conflicts that they were addressing, to observe their practices where appropriate and when requested to support the building of capacity to engage in restorative processes. At no time did we choose to be the expert and take over or steal the conflict from the community (Christie, 1977).

Similar to our teaching on restorative practices, we did not put our action research methodology in the foreground preferring it to be virtually invisible. While clear memoranda of understanding, specifying the purpose, process and ethics of the research, were agreed with each partner, we chose to stage meetings and dialogues rather than structured enquiries or interviews. We allowed the outcomes to emerge rather than work towards planned results. Our action was communicative rather than strategic. Inevitably some of the hopes of the partners were not realized. This may have been disappointing but failure generates useful information, reflection and learning about realities. In each site we adopted an approach designed to generate the understandings and knowledge appropriate to the partner's interests regarding the specific conflict that was being addressed.

Derry/Londonderry

In Derry/Londonderry we worked with a Centre that supports and offers treatment to addicts, the Northlands Centre. Two researchers along with a representative of Northlands spoke with a range of people representing those who have a stake in the harms associated with drug use and dealing in the city. This led to two community conferences in local areas where people entered into dialogue in groups to share their understandings and responses to the problem. Not only were these conferences a demonstration of how a restorative process can mobilize local people to express their views on a harmful problem, but they also served an opportunity for action research, which generated meaningful data.

The approach adopted by Ulster University in partnership with Northlands was designed to achieve two objectives: (1) to listen to what people have to say about the issue; and (2) to enable local people to find a way to contribute to the improvement of community life through an increased sense of security and justice. The key questions put to the people whom we met individually included the following:

- What is your understanding of the nature of alcohol and drug use in Derry?
- What is the impact of this and in what ways have you come to believe that?
- What is being done that helps address harm?
- What more could be done and by whom?

The team's approach at the meetings was to develop a conversation around these questions in which experience and meaning were explored rather than adopting a semi-structured interview technique. This reflected the narrative dialogue approach that Ulster has developed within its teaching of restorative processes; through listening to people's narratives and entering into dialogue about them a 'thicker description' of their experiences, concerns and ideas emerge. This process also prepared people to participate in the community conference.

The format of the conferences was to invite a wide range of stakeholders to local community centres. The conferences were opened by local representatives and then one of the ALTERNATIVE researchers would outline the issues to be addressed and explain the process of the conference. Participants were seated around tables in the room (about eight people per table). Each table had a University facilitator who asked the questions, encouraged dialogue and clarified what conclusions were being made. The facilitator also kept a record of the key points made. The questions were simple:

- How would you describe the issue of drug use in the community?
- What do you think of current responses to it?
- What should be done?

Once the dialogue had been completed at each table, the facilitator summarized the conclusions to the whole conference. These conclusions were then used to develop an action plan to engage local people further in addressing the problem through participation in a training course organized by the University and the engagement of community activists, from communities in which armed groups are inflicting violent punishments on drug users, in training in restorative and non-violent responses.

South Belfast

In South Belfast we worked with a community project, CARE, which aspired to become a community-based restorative justice project so as to address anti-social behaviour restoratively as an alternative to paramilitary punishments. We had several roles in this site: (1) to observe and tell the story of the struggles of this project to establish itself; (2) to support it to build its capacity to become the service to the community it wishes to provide; and (3) to observe and understand its restorative practices.

Two researchers developed a strong relationship with the CARE activists in this community and were invited to observe them as they participated in events, attended meetings and engaged in restorative processes. The University also actively supported CARE to produce a strategic plan, to consider its governance arrangements, to gain access to funding for its restorative practices, to be trained in restorative practices and to design training programmes that its workers could deliver to the community.

The CARE offices are based at the heart of their community and the practitioners also live within the neighbourhood. Over three years, the researchers could observe how CARE responded to critical events in their community and also engage the activists[1] in honest reflections of their responses.

West Belfast

In West Belfast we were in partnership with a mature community-based restorative justice project, Community Restorative Justice Ireland (CRJI). With them we wanted to capture the narrative of their relationship with the state and their struggles to find and sustain a space in which they could both serve their community restoratively and be supported rather than dominated by the state system. We had a longstanding relationship with CRJI dating back to 2008 when they participated in the University's Certificate in Restorative Practices course.

The research involved many in-depth conversations about the history of the project and their current practices. Due to the relationships we had built, the CRJI activists spoke openly and honestly about their dilemmas and struggles. Due to the University's previous engagement with a range of state agencies, we were also able to conduct dialogues with judges, prosecutors, senior police officers, senior managers in the probation service, lawyers, and senior Department of Justice officials about their views of community-based restorative justice.

Research findings

Derry/Londonderry

Context

Derry/Londonderry was chosen as a site for the ALTERNATIVE research as local people had been concerned for many years about the use of drugs by young people and about the dealers who supply the drugs. Drug use can be perceived as an intergenerational conflict between young people who consume illegal substances (though also increasingly so-called 'legal highs') and the older generation's moral panic (Cohen, 1972) over the effects drug use has on their children and community life. In 2014 the Commission for Victims and Survivors (Northern Ireland) research into the trans-generational consequences of the violent conflict in Northern Ireland revealed that a significant number of individuals, particularly young men, have developed serious mental health and substance disorders. It is clear that many young men are using both drugs and alcohol as a way of dealing with the difficulties that have arisen from the Northern Irish conflict.

The criminal justice system has responded through Operation Torus led by the Police Service of Northern Ireland. It measures its success through the monetary value of its drug seizures and through the number of people arrested, charged and convicted for drug use and dealing. By 2008 an armed Irish Republican vigilante group calling itself 'Republican Action Against Drugs' (RAAD) had become active in Derry and neighbouring areas. It targeted people who it claimed were drug dealers and inflicted beatings, forced expulsions from the community and shootings, which included both wounding and killing. In addition to these two security-oriented responses to drug use and dealing in Derry, the National Health Service offered medical and therapeutic interventions delivered by skilled professionals.

Activating the community

In spite of the attention that the problem of illegal drugs was receiving in Derry, ordinary people's concerns persisted and yet they had had very few opportunities to articulate their concerns. The purpose of the ALTERNATIVE research was to discover whether by listening to those in civil society most closely involved in the problem an alternative narrative might emerge which would address these concerns more directly and more satisfactorily. The action research was undertaken in two stages:

1 Conversations with individuals in a range of community organizations directly involved in responding to the harm caused by alcohol and drugs as well as those with an active interest in community life.
2 Two community conferences.

Key narratives in the conversations

The conversations generated some key narratives arising from the problems associated with drug use and dealing in the community.

- The legacy of the Northern Irish conflict: many felt that significant experiences of loss and trauma combined with a lack of trust in state authority facilitated the use of drugs as a means of coping and the use of violence as a means of controlling behaviour.
- The 'hidden harm of drugs': this referred to the many harms associated with the use of drugs that were ignored by the prevailing security or medicalized discourses. Someone who had an overview of public health issues in Derry said: 'There are a lot of people suffering who have no contact with officials, there is no community in Derry which has not been affected.'
- The normalization of drug use: 'You need to get a grasp of the scale of it, there is a changing scene, the legal highs are becoming as normalized as a night out and a bottle of beer' (Health Worker). Indeed, the use of drugs was linked to the culturally acceptable practice of binge drinking. In spite of this normalization there remained a stigma attached to the use of drugs.

- The irrelevance of current short-term policies and practices: 'Very few decision makers are around to see the outcome of their decisions – the political pressure is to "make it happen" ', as one interviewee put it.
- The need for a better strategy: several people thought that there should be more relevant data to inform a coordinated strategy. However, there was little faith in professionals. One of the experienced health workers interviewed offered this perspective: 'Addiction services from the statutory side are dominated by middle-class language and professionalization.'

These interviews enabled the Ulster team to make contact with a wide range of people and organizations concerned with the problem of drug use in Derry. It allowed the team to build relationships on the basis of respecting local knowledge rather than as experts coming to offer our solutions and it generated information on which to base the next stage of the project, the community conferences.

Community conferences

Prior to the community conferences Ulster University invited Professor David Kennedy to deliver a seminar in Derry. Kennedy (2011) is the author of a successful strategy to address the problem of drugs in inner-city USA. His approach links the narratives of community concern with law enforcement and meeting social needs. In particular he emphasized the power of mobilizing both community disapproval of harmful activities such as drug dealing and violence and community support for those who choose to desist from such activities. He also stressed the need for a closely coordinated approach by a partnership between community, rehabilitation services and law enforcement.

There were then two community conferences. At first the Ulster team were keen that the local community should have ownership of the conferences by hosting each meeting, organizing it and leading the dialogue. However, the community organizations felt there would be greater impact if the University were to be seen as the convener. This arrangement meant that, although the conferences were located in community venues, invitations came directly from the University. This confirmed the idea of the University offering a safe, neutral space for difficult conversations.

The conference participants defined the problem on the basis of their direct experience. They said that it was important to stop talking about addictions in isolation. Drugs are varied and often linked to alcohol abuse. They can have a ripple effect of harming family and community life. The services that are available are too often uncoordinated and there is insufficient collaboration. Education on drugs is available but may be counter productive for some young people who use the knowledge to their advantage in choosing which drugs to use so that they do not get detected.

They stated that young people, who face a daily struggle with exclusion and deprivation throughout the city, are easily exploited by the drug dealers. The availability of drugs is a critical issue. People do not even need a drug dealer any more as they soon learn that they can get drugs from the internet. Some young people appear willing to openly defy the efforts of armed groups to control their behaviour.

The conference participants believed that the current reduction in public spending and the practice of competitive tendering resulted in a lack of sharing information and of collaborating on services. The demand for services outstrips the resources of providers who then control access to treatment. The users and their families need immediate intervention and rapid assessment, not a lengthy bureaucratic process. Several stories of delays in waiting for treatment were recounted as well as feeling abandoned by statutory services. They stated that when working with addictions a small window of opportunity may open where the users want to help themselves and which can close if the service is not immediately available. There was a high level of scepticism generally regarding the system's control over who receives a service and in what circumstances.

Interestingly, the security response to the drug problem was not supported. Participants asked: how can people safely get out of drug use without being attacked by an armed group or labelled by the system? Young people do not always need an expert coming in to help them. Sometimes they just need space and someone to listen so they can work things out for themselves.

It is clear from these conferences that drug use is seen by the community as causing a great deal of harm, much of it 'hidden' and/or ignored by the appropriate statutory services. While some people would support stronger law enforcement, most people want more user-friendly, better coordinated and relevant services. The lack of responsiveness and effectiveness of the medical and treatment services caused a significant level of frustration, anger and injustice to be felt. Neither the criminal justice system nor the paramilitary attempt to control drugs was perceived as delivering a sense of security to local people. Neither the medicalized nor the securitized narrative address the 'hidden harm' that causes so much anxiety and suffering among local people.

These conclusions formed the basis of further action in Derry supported by Ulster University. A community education programme on responses to drug use has been delivered to 60 people in Derry by the Northlands Centre and supported by the University who will accredit the course. The University is delivering its Certificate in Restorative Practices to a group of community activists working in areas where there are armed groups involved in punishing users and dealers.

South Belfast

In this section we relate how a new community-based restorative justice project, CARE, emerged from a Loyalist community and how Ulster University played a part in helping to build CARE's capacity to respond to conflict in its community. We describe critical incidents which demonstrate the effectiveness of community-based restorative justice in conflicts in intercultural settings.

CARE

CARE works in a Loyalist working-class area, which has been associated with the Ulster Defence Association (UDA) in the past. Like many community organizations in Northern Ireland they adopted restorative justice to reduce the incidence of paramilitary punishments in their area. The project engaged with Community Restorative Justice Ireland (CRJI) who initiated a development process with a series of facilitated workshops carried out by a director of CRJI for members of the community associations and a number of leading paramilitaries and ex-paramilitaries. This was significant: previous enemies were being brought together to cooperate through a common commitment to restorative justice. This collaboration has continued. The CARE manager sits on the management board of CRJI.

Fourteen members of CARE completed a course on restorative practices, facilitated and funded by CRJI. The CARE staff then enrolled in the University's Certificate course in restorative practices on the recommendation of CRJI. Around this time CARE developed a partnership with Colin Safer Neighbourhoods (which represented an adjacent Catholic community) and the Welcome Project from Lisburn. This partnership has proved very effective in resolving intercultural conflict by demonstrating how two previously antagonistic communities are cooperating to keep the peace.

Two challenges faced CARE: how to obtain funding to pay for staff and how to raise their community's awareness of and support for a restorative response to conflict and anti-social behaviour. The Ulster ALTERNATIVE team supported CARE in contacting a funder and helped the project to develop a strategic plan and funding proposal.

To overcome the lack of awareness within the community of the concept of restorative justice, CARE began a process of engagement with the community through various methods including leaflet drops, drop-in clinics, public discussions at venues throughout the estate and wider area. Ulster University helped the project design a community awareness presentation on human rights and restorative justice, a volunteer training course in restorative practices and Restoring Respect, a personal development for young people involved in anti-social behaviour.

CARE found it difficult to apply aspects of the restorative process that they had learned at the University:

> The relationship with the university has been one of the anchor stones to the development of CARE but sometimes it is hard to reflect the academic side of things onto the real coalface. The whole idea of the conference type approach … we have never actually done that type of formalized conference, it seems more of a youth justice agency type role. Our conferences or mediations or whatever you want to call them are a lot more informal because we are dealing with people that don't like formality.
>
> (Mark Black, Project Manager)

This led to the realization that restorative processes, which work in one context (the criminal justice system), do not necessarily work in a different context, local communities. The ALTERNATIVE team fundamentally rethought its approach to the practice of restorative justice and designed new practice manuals and training courses covering simple mediations, community restorative circles and multi-agency strategies (Chapman, Campbell and Wilson, 2014). An action research approach thus not only builds an organization's capacity but can also challenge and generate innovations within the existing body of knowledge.

The many observations of the events over a three-year study are here organized into two narratives that exemplify the contributions of restorative justice to conflicts in an intercultural setting.

The flags protest

On 3 December 2012, Belfast City Council voted to restrict the flying of the British flag on the City Hall. This decision was followed by four months of protests many of which became serious riots. This period of disorder was generally perceived by the media as another example of Loyalist sectarianism and propensity for violence. This 'thin' description obscures the complexity of what Loyalists consider to be an intercultural conflict.

For Loyalists the flags dispute was a struggle to protect the political and national culture of Unionism: 'People thought it was another erosion of our British identity and that it was a political move being orchestrated by Sinn Fein to gain control over certain aspects of the council and also to score an element of one-upmanship' (Mark Black, CARE Manager).

In two areas there were community activists trained by Ulster University in restorative practices. In both areas they attempted to reduce the violence restoratively but with very different results.

Mark Black of the CARE project tells his story of the flags protests:

> I can only speak for the area around here and there was a conscious movement to ensure there would be no violence because of the fact that community relations with the police had been quite good for a number of years and there was regular liaison with the police.... There were times at the beginning where it was quite tight and I think senior PSNI [Police Service Northern Ireland] figures made a conscious decision that community relations that had been built up weren't going to be destroyed by young people hell bent on wreck and ruin and that also came from the leadership of paramilitary organisations that young people were not going to be allowed to wreck their own area.

This quotation emphasizes a key element of restorative justice: the importance given to relationship.

However, there were also differences within the Loyalist community: 'There were sinister elements that used young people to go out and cause violence on the streets and that caused so many young people to become involved with the criminal justice system.' The protests reinforced negative stereotypes of the Loyalist working class:

> The protestors were stigmatized by a lot of the media whether it be social media whether it be the normal media for their own political gain and those people suffered ... I think the looking down on protestors by the media ... was controlled by certain members of the business community that are more interested in making money for their own gain than they are in cultural expression and their cultural identity.

These statements begin to articulate a 'thicker' story: the conflict had an intercultural element in which young people were being manipulated by adults to engage in violent disorder and which in turn stimulated conflict between Loyalist communities and the state represented by the police. Finally, economic interests were in conflict with the interests of the protesters.

Yet in South Belfast the protests did not descend into violence and rioting: 'The one good thing is that people within this area have been able to maintain their protests in a dignified and productive manner.' This was due in part to the efforts of Mark and others who mediated between the protesters and the police:

> We were hearing from the police that technically the people who were protesting were breaking the law; we advised that if that was the case that any movement made against these people would destroy community relations for the next number of years and have adverse effects relating to further protests in and around this area.... The inspector on the ground made a conscious decision when he was under pressure from his bosses and decided to take a chance and hold off on deploying TSGs[2].... He gave the protests five more minutes to get the situation finished and dispersed peacefully. There was elements of shuttle mediation in between the factions concerned to try and ensure there would be a peaceful outcome.

This shows how communicative action, which is critical to the restorative process, rather than the strategic use of force can maintain peace even when the conflict is intense.

In the final analysis, Mark Black believes that the anger felt by Loyalists over the flags issue represents the sense that his community feels about being marginalized politically so that the social and economic concerns of the Protestant working class are ignored:

> There was a simplistic connection made between protests and the flag coming down but it wasn't just the issue of the flag coming down; it was connected to a whole myriad of problems, issues and tensions that have arisen over the years.

South Belfast experienced the period of protests over the flying of the flags without any serious damage to property or community life. Mark Black by using a basic restorative practice, mediation, was able to allow people to protest without causing violence. In this way local people experienced both enhanced justice and security, exercising their right to protest without serious disorder. The same could not be said in the case of East Belfast, which was the site of the most disorder, the most violence, the most conflict with the police and the most arrests.

In this area, there were also community activists trained in restorative practices striving to reduce the violence and arguing for democratic values. What was different? The short answer is: politics. East Belfast was the parliamentary constituency that the Democratic Unionist Party desperately wanted to regain from the Alliance party. It was in its interest to blame Alliance rather than the traditional enemy, Sinn Fein, for the flags being taken down from the City Hall. The party at first supported the protest. Then when the protests became unpopular with the business community, they condemned the protesters.

Activists within the UDA who had been trained in restorative processes participated in round table dialogues whose ostensible purpose was to find a peaceful solution. But it was clear to them that other community representatives, while they seemed to subscribe to the same purpose, could not be trusted in their commitments. They had another agenda that depended upon sustaining the conflict to achieve their political objectives.

This can be understood in the context of Habermas's (1990) validity claims. The purpose of communicative action is to reach a mutual understanding about something. For this process to be effective the speech must be subject to three claims to validity: truth, normative rightness and sincerity. In South Belfast, the mediations between the protesters and the police were truthful, undertaken in the right way and commitments to action were sincere. In other words, they were conducted through communicative action. In East Belfast, the meetings may have been set up with the right intention and conducted in a reasonable way. But the participants were not committed to speaking the truth or to being sincere in their future actions. In other words, some parties were acting strategically to achieve their own political ends.

We can conclude that a restorative process can only be effective if based upon communicative action. Strategic action involves predetermined objectives aligned to the conflicting interests of different parties and depends upon the exercise of power to win a conflict rather than resolve it.

The neighbours' dispute[3]

In another Loyalist community two neighbours were in dispute. One was a local female resident and the other was an Eastern European family. The dispute arose in July when many local people would have parties in their gardens and when Protestants celebrate their cultural and political identity through flying flags and bunting.[4] The Eastern European family complained about rubbish falling into their garden and some bunting blowing in the wind and falling over the fence into their property. The local woman complained that they were not respecting her flag and her culture. Other residents in the street supported the local woman. Compatriots of the foreign family were supportive and claimed that this dispute was racially motivated.

There was a risk of an escalation into violence. The house and the car of the Eastern European family were damaged maliciously and a house in the street occupied by another foreign family had been attacked. Local people were angry as outsiders assumed that the foreign nationals were the victims and that the local woman was at fault.

The worker from a local community organization, who had been trained at Ulster University through the ALTERNATIVE project, was asked by a representative of the Eastern European community to intervene. The worker visited the foreign family first to listen to their story. He said that he just wanted to understand their perspective and was not taking responsibility for dealing with the complaints. Neighbours saw him visit and waited outside to give their version of events. Most supported the local woman though one said privately that she had contributed to the problem. She had allowed weed killer to leak across the fence affecting the neighbours' garden. The other family had called the police but the police could not take action.

Having listened to both sides of the story the worker called a meeting inviting a local politician, another community activist (trained by the University), two police officers, neighbourhood wardens, the local woman and her supporters, the Eastern European family, another family from the same country to support and a family from another country who lived in the same street. Unfortunately the original foreign family were unable to attend the meeting at the last moment.

During the meeting everyone had the opportunity to tell their story and question each other. It was agreed that there were faults on both sides and that, although it had an ethnic dimension, it was not an intercultural conflict. It was a dispute between two neighbours. The local people invited the foreign families to a local celebration and they in turn offered to bring their food to the barbecue to share with the others. People shook hands and committed to being better neighbours in future. When the original family returned, the local woman went to them, shook hands and invited them to the street party. All parties agreed that it had been a just process, which succeeded in avoiding violence and improving the security of the street.

This story illustrates that a restorative process can be very effective in not only resolving conflict but also improving community relations. The key was a reliance on communicative action. The police could only take action if a crime was committed. Both the local community and the foreign nationals were inclined to define the conflict as cultural or racist. This would have both politicized and escalated the conflict and would probably have resulted in violence. The communicative action focused on the real issues of a specific situation rather than the general political discourse regarding foreign immigrants.

The growth of community-based restorative justice in Loyalist areas

One significant outcome from the work of the Ulster ALTERNATIVE team with CARE is that other Loyalist community activists heard about it and asked for the same support. As a consequence since the ALTERNATIVE project began community-based restorative justice projects have been established in working-class areas in East Belfast, the Shankill area of West Belfast, Ballymoney and Coleraine and the Clooney area of Derry/Londonderry. It is anticipated that they will play a significant part in resolving conflict in local areas and in reducing incidents of violence.

Conclusions

The research in South Belfast and in other Loyalist areas has demonstrated that the principles of restorative justice can contribute to the security and justice experienced by local communities affected by conflicts in intercultural settings. On the basis of this research the Ulster University team was stimulated to critically re-examine its model of practice and revise it. Manuals on how to implement these new restorative processes are now available for other initiatiaves and will become part of the University teaching curriculum.

However, these initiatives are in a precarious situation. They are funded by a non-governmental organization for temporary periods. They need to gain credibility and the trust of statutory bodies and funders if they are to survive. The next section examines more closely the frontier between state and community and how this has an impact on the sustainability of community-based restorative justice.

West Belfast

Context

The Review of the Criminal Justice System (2000) in Northern Ireland stated that community-based restorative justice should be enabled to address low-level crime committed in local communities. However, because community restorative justice had its origins in the provision of an alternative to paramilitary punishments and because ex-prisoners were taking a lead in the schemes, the government would not fund the schemes or permit its agencies to cooperate with them. Concerns were also raised regarding the coercion of parties to a restorative process, the lack of due process and the possible abuse of human rights.

Discussions between the schemes and the government were initiated to resolve these issues. The sticking point was the unwillingness of Community Restorative Justice Ireland to work with the Police Service. This was resolved by a change in Sinn Fein policy: in 2007, protocols (Northern Ireland Office, 2007) for community-based restorative justice schemes were finally agreed. The principles underpinning the protocols were designed to conform to the Human

Rights Act 1998, the UN Convention on the Rights of the Child, equality legislation and the UN Basic Principles on the use of Restorative Justice in Criminal Matters. To ensure that these principles were observed, the schemes would have to agree to be subject to regular inspections by the criminal justice inspectorate, to participate in an independent, external complaints mechanism and to undertake appropriate training.

The impact of state regulation

These were all reasonable safeguards to require of any community organization involved in work with people responsible for crimes and with people harmed by crime. However, the critical provision related to referrals: community schemes had up to that point taken referrals directly from members of the community. In 2006, the Community Restorative Justice Ireland (CRJI) scheme in West Belfast dealt with just over 1,000 cases. The schemes could take direct referrals and respond quickly, flexibly and informally. The new arrangements required all crimes to be reported directly to the PSNI: referrals to community restorative justice schemes would have to come through the PSNI and Public Prosecution Service (PPS) after they had completed their investigation and assessment of each case.

The table[5] below shows how many cases were referred to the Public Prosecution Service by the Police Service for consideration of their appropriateness for facilitation by a community-based restorative justice (CBRJ) project. The second column shows how many cases were actually referred to a CBRJ project. Over a period of five years only nine cases were considered suitable for community-based restorative justice. In the last two years there were no cases even though CRJI has complied with the protocols and worked closely with the police. The implication of this is that a large proportion of cases are being reported to the police and dealt with through the criminal justice system and another large proportion are reported to neither the police nor CRJI.

We also found indications that community-based restorative justice projects have been co-opted by the criminal justice system. In two meetings observed by the researchers, leading members of community-based restorative projects have

Table 7.1 Numbers of suspects referred

Year	*Number of suspects referred from the police to the PPS*	*Number of suspects referred from the PPS to CBRJ projects*
2010/2011	10	6
2011/2012	6	2
2012/2013	4	1
2013/2014	0	0
2014/2015	2	0
Total	22	9

made statements signifying a shift in identity and role. One senior manager said: 'We are now part of the criminal justice system.' In the other meeting the person said: 'We don't want to deal with crime; better to leave that to the police.' The first statement signifies that this organization is working so closely with the state's agencies that it sees itself as much as part of the system as representing its local communities. The second statement acknowledges a belief that crime is best left to the professionals. In part this may be due to an unwillingness to take responsibility for processes of justice, for which projects may be criticized by their own communities. In seeking funding support from statutory agencies these projects are increasingly involved in youth work, social work and prisoner resettlement. Each of these tasks is important for both crime prevention and the well-being of individuals but they are not core restorative justice tasks.

The potential of community-based restorative justice

Even under these conditions we have evidence of the quality of restorative work that CRJI can accomplish in collaboration with the state. This is one of many examples. A young man who was well known and popular in his community was murdered by another young man from a minority ethnic community. It was not racially motivated but it was over a young woman who had previously been in a relationship with the person responsible for the killing. The police quickly arrested the accused person and he was remanded in custody. However, the anger in the community was expressed through social media and rumours about the complicity of other members of the minority ethnic group circulated. A car was rammed into the window of a barber's shop owned by a relative of the accused and his life was threatened. CRJI asked the police to offer the minority community more protection and then opened up communication with the relatives of the victim. Having spoken to the family of the accused they were able to correct the rumours with the truth. This prevented the violence from escalating.

In this case CRJI was able to perform tasks that the formal criminal justice system could not do. Restorative justice organizations understand that harm ripples out from the incident and affects families and communities. Holding the offender in custody does not address this hidden harm. In such cases the discovery of the truth and its communication to all parties can help to restore both justice and security.

Conclusions

This study has found that the restorative justice work of CRJI is gradually being eroded by the state in spite of the credibility that CRJI has earned through conforming scrupulously to the protocols imposed by the state. Community-based restorative justice is being shifted gradually from its role of restoring justice towards working with the state to rehabilitate offenders. This does not mean that the project is not continuing to do valuable work in relation to conflicts in intercultural settings. But it does mean that this type of work is increasingly marginalized and not fully funded.

Ulster University has been involved in dialogues with a range of stakeholders within the criminal justice system including the Police Service, the Probation Board, the Public Prosecution Service and the Department of Justice with a view to encouraging the state system to open up more space for community-based restorative justice. There are some promising signs of progress on this front. The Probation Board has undertaken a new pilot initiative, which includes restorative interventions in two areas of Northern Ireland in partnership with CRJI and Northern Ireland Alternatives.[6] The Department of Justice is preparing a government strategy on restorative justice with adults, which should include a role for community-based restorative justice. The Police Service has been advocating collaborative decision making involving other parties in civil society and this may offer an opportunity to develop truly effective partnerships with community-based restorative justice projects.

New understandings and applications

The conflicts that we studied; the problem of drugs in Derry, the protests over the flying of flags over Belfast City Hall, and tensions between migrants and local residents in Loyalist communities; exposed the limitations of a strategic security response through the criminal justice system. Unless an individual admits to a criminal offence there is little that the criminal justice system can do. Even when an individual is prosecuted for an offence as many were in the flag protests, the underlying political, cultural and social issues are not addressed. These conflicts concerned groups of people rather than individuals and these groups did not assume or accept the identity of either victim or offender even when they felt victimized.

These findings challenged us to re-imagine a restorative justice that was appropriate and effective in intercultural contexts. Following Habermas (1987), the world in which people live their daily lives together, the lifeworld, is construed as having three elements: culture – the shared beliefs and values which offer people purpose and meaning; society – a fabric of relationships and norms; and personality – the capabilities which enable individuals to communicate and act. The restorative practices that Ulster University has developed for intercultural contexts:

- provide space for people to meet and communicate;
- enhance a culture of respect;
- strengthen just social relations;
- and address directly harmful behaviour.

A diagram of the model is displayed in Figure 7.1.

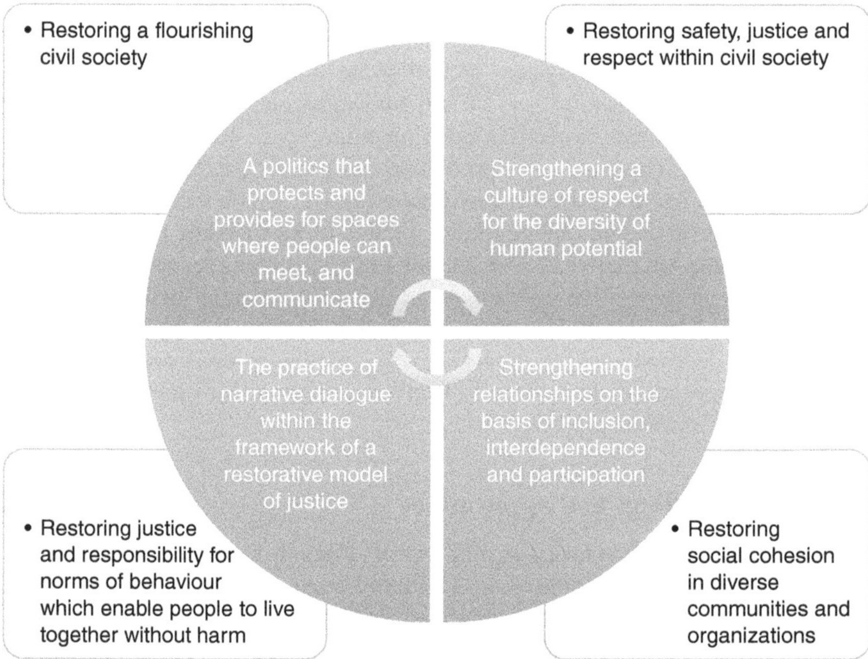

Figure 7.1 Model of restorative practices.

A politics that protects and provides for spaces where people can meet and communicate

While we argue that restorative processes must be based upon communicative action to be effective, creating the opportunity to facilitate restorative processes depends upon the strategic action. Community-based restorative justice projects need the state system to legitimize their work and support it with funding. A flourishing intercultural society needs civil spaces in which people can meet, communicate and erase the frontiers that keep them apart.

Community-based restorative justice has demonstrated in our view that it is capable of resolving conflicts in intercultural settings which the criminal justice system either cannot engage in or may even exacerbate through a coercive approach to restoring order. Rather than protecting people by strengthening frontiers and building walls, a restorative process invites people to move towards what they fear and supports them to interact and recognize their interdependence.

In Derry, the ALTERNATIVE project opened up a space free of political domination or threat for local people and representatives of community-based organizations to speak freely about an issue that concerns them greatly. Such a space can engage civil society in generating fresh understandings and responses to contentious issues such as drug dealing. These processes have also proved effective in keeping the peace in conflicts in sectarian or ethnic contexts. When they work, local people do experience an improved sense of both security and justice. Restorative justice processes facilitated in the community are not only effective but produce outcomes more quickly and at a higher level of satisfaction expressed by the participants. Furthermore these processes facilitated by community activists almost certainly cost much less than statutory responses which rely upon professionals and complex bureaucratic systems.

Community-based restorative justice projects require the support, the respect and the trust of the state system if they are to facilitate these restorative processes effectively. The need to reduce the cost of public services due to austerity offers an opportunity to transfer funds and authority from the state to the community sector in this field.

To close the gap between the potential of community-based restorative justice and the reality, several steps need to be taken. The first step is the responsibility of the state: the protocols, which were described in the West Belfast section of this chapter, should be revised to include definitions of:

1 the tasks that community-based restorative justice can in general perform more effectively and efficiently than statutory agencies;
2 the tasks that community-based restorative justice could work with the statutory agencies as partners; and
3 the tasks that are appropriate only for statutory agencies.

The second objective is the responsibility of the community projects. We have come to the conclusion that community-based restorative projects will never achieve real credibility with the public and the state until they completely distance themselves from their association with paramilitary organizations. This cannot happen immediately but these organizations need to be seen to be progressing in this direction.

We have observed how community-based restorative justice projects have cooperated and supported each other across the sectarian frontier in both Belfast and Derry. The community restorative justice sector needs to be coordinated so that it can deliver throughout Northern Ireland and not just in areas that are associated with paramilitary organizations. Perhaps a network should be coordinated centrally but continue to be delivered locally by people who are in tune with the local communities. This may involve the engagement of new organizations where there is no current service provision.

Strengthening a culture of respect for the diversity of human potential

Eriksson (2009), describing the history of community-based restorative justice in Northern Ireland, emphasized the important role of local projects performed in contributing to a transition from a culture of violence that emanated from the civil conflict. This was undertaken through a process of community education.

Through the ALTERNATIVE research project in Northern Ireland Ulster University has enabled CARE:

1 to develop a strategic plan for the development of restorative justice in Loyalist working-class areas in South Belfast;
2 to design and deliver training programmes for awareness raising and for training including: a community education presentation; volunteer training in restorative justice; and Restoring Respect, a programme to engage young people.

This work has attracted the attention of community organizations in other Loyalist areas. Ulster University are now actively supporting the development of four new community-based restorative justice projects. This has been extended to Republican areas in Strabane and Derry/Londonderry.

Strengthening relationships on the basis of inclusion, interdependence and participation

It is important that more 'shared space' is created where people from different communities can meet, communicate and resolve their differences. The two community projects, CARE (Protestant area) and CRJI (Catholic area), planned to open a community justice house in an area on the 'frontier' between the two communities. Unfortunately there has been little progress on this vision. This was due to the plans being disrupted by major political issues, such as the flags dispute, within the Loyalist communities.

Justice houses could still be established so that the community restorative justice projects could work across frontiers with their statutory partners. Regular meetings could then determine which agency should engage in specific cases.

Conflicts in intercultural settings tend to involve groups of people rather than individual 'offenders' and 'victims'. We realized that we needed to adopt a process that reflected this reality. Restorative circles (Pranis, 2005) rather than conferences are the appropriate process. We have designed such a process and written a manual to guide the practice of facilitators in community restorative processes (Chapman, Campbell and Wilson, 2014). This was the process that worked so well in the case of the neighbours' dispute.

Restoring the future

Our analysis of conflicts in intercultural settings is based upon the premise that they are the product of the internal frontiers of society. These frontiers, demarcating communities based upon identity, generate a politics that directs people's attention towards the grievances of the past and the perceived threats of the present. What can restore the future for ordinary people who are struggling to find a way of living at peace within an increasingly interdependent and diverse society? By restoring the future we mean that people's daily concerns and actions are no longer driven by the past but by moving on with their lives and striving for an imagined better future.

We have concluded that restorative justice applied to conflicts in intercultural settings is more effectively delivered in the community rather than in the criminal justice system. Restorative justice creates a space where members of society can encounter each other and communicate without fear of domination or exploitation. They must speak truthfully, follow a fair process of dialogue and be sincere in their mutual understanding and commitments to action. We have seen, for example in the case of the flags protests, how political strategy distorts this process and leads to power struggles rather than rational decision making.

Security is then achieved by moving towards those whom one fears rather than seeking protection from them. In this encounter, differences may be respected and common needs recognized. Knowing the other through communication reduces the processes that lead to many conflicts and creates a community at ease with diversity. Through the restorative process, people can explore the reality of what they fear and they are enabled to reclaim definitional power over what is and is not a risk to them. By reaching mutual understanding and making commitments on how they should act towards each other in the future, a measure of trust is restored. In this discourse, justice is no longer a thing that is granted by an institution through the expertise of professionals by following procedures: justice is an activity in which one participates.

Community and identity are simply concepts, which mean very little in the daily lives of people unless they are activated. We have seen in Northern Ireland that if these concepts are used to mobilize a form of politics based upon shared identity, they can sustain frontiers in society, which divide people and may result in violent conflict. Sennett (2012, p. 39) distinguishes two versions of solidarity. One emphasizes the unity of the group. The other values inclusion of difference. The first relates to politics, the second to society. The ALTERNATIVE research has observed (as in the neighbours' dispute) how the communicative action of restorative justice can activate a sense of community, which enables people in conflict to respect each other's identities and resolve conflict to their mutual satisfaction. We see community as something people do. So for us: community is an active and reflexive communicative practice, which enables people to live equitably in interdependence with an increasingly diverse range of others. In conclusion, we believe that this action research has found evidence that restorative justice can contribute to building a pluralist society at peace with itself and in which identity is not a source of harmful conflict.

Notes

1 Activists are people from the local area who are either paid or volunteer to work for their community.

2 Tactical Support Group – police officers trained to manage public disorder.

3 During the research period, there were several interventions by community-based restorative justice projects in cases of neighbour disputes, many with an ethnic dimension.

This case is discussed in depth as it illustrates the effectiveness of restorative circles in such cases.

4 Small flags connected by a rope as a form of outdoor decoration.

5 This table has been provided with the permission of Lauren Hogg of Queens University Belfast from her PhD research: 'The Impact of State intervention on the work of Community-based Restorative Justice Projects in Northern Ireland' (2016).

6 A community-based restorative justice project, which operates in Loyalist areas.

References

Agamben, G., 1993. *The coming community*. Translator Michael Hardt. Minneapolis: University of Minnesota Press.

Atran, S., 2010. *Talking to the enemy: faith, brotherhood and the (un)making of terrorists*. New York: Harper Collins.

Bauman, Z., 2001. *Community: Seeking safety in an insecure world*. Cambridge: Polity Press.

Chapman, T., Campbell, H. and Wilson, D., 2014. *Appropriate restorative justice interventions tailored to each site designed in the form of a practice manual*. Belfast: University of Ulster. Public deliverable 7.5 of the ALTERNATIVE project. Available at: www.alternativeproject.eu/assets/upload/Deliverable_7_5_Appropriate_restorative_justice_interventions_manual.pdf [accessed 14 July 2015].

Christie, N., 1977. Conflict as property. *British Journal of Criminology*, 17, pp. 1–26.

Cohen, S., 1972. *Folk devils and moral panics: the creation of the mods and rockers*. London: McGibbon and Kee.

Criminal Justice Review Group, 2000. *Review of the criminal justice system in Northern Ireland*. Belfast: HMSO.

Eriksson, A.M., 2009. *Justice in transition: community restorative justice in Northern Ireland*. Abingdon: Willan Publishing.

Esposito, R., 2013. *Terms of the political: community, immunity, biopolitics*. New York: Fordham University Press.

Eyben, K., Morrow, D. and Wilson, D., 1997. *A worthwhile venture? Practically investing in equity, diversity, and interdependence in Northern Ireland*. Belfast. University of Ulster.

Geertz, C., 1973. *The interpretation of cultures*. New York: Basic Books.

Girard, R., 1986. *The scapegoat*. Baltimore: The Johns Hopkins University Press.

Habermas, J., 1987. *The theory of communicative action, Vol. 2: lifeworld and system: a critique of functionalist reason*. Boston: Beacon Press.

Habermas, J., 1990. *Moral consciousness and communicative action*. Cambridge, MA: MIT Press.

hooks, b., 1990. Choosing the margin as a space of radical openness. In: b. hooks, ed. *Yearning: race, gender, and cultural politics*. Boston: South End, pp. 145–153.

Isaacs, W., 1999. *Dialogue and the art of thinking together*. New York: Random.

Kennedy, D., 2011. *Don't shoot: one man, a street fellowship and the end of the violence in inner-city America*. London: Bloomsbury.

Lorey, I., 2012. *State of insecurity: government of the precarious*. London: Verso.

Northern Ireland Office, 1998. *The agreement*. Available at: www.gov.uk/government/publications/the-belfast-agreement [accessed 15 June 2016].

Northern Ireland Office, 2007. *Protocol for community-based restorative justice schemes*. Belfast: Criminal Justice.

Pavlich, G., 2004. Restorative justice's community: promise and peril. In: B. Toews and H. Zehr, eds. *Critical issues in restorative justice*. Monsey, NY: Criminal Justice Press, pp. 173–190.

Pranis, K., 2005. *The little book of circle processes: a new/old approach to peacemaking*. Intercourse: Good Books.

Reason, P. and Bradbury, H., 2006. *Handbook of action research*. London: Sage Publications.

Sennett, R., 2012. *Together: the rituals, pleasures and politics of cooperation*. London: Allen Lane.

Shapland, J., Robinson, G. and Sorsby, A., 2012. *Restorative justice in practice: evaluating what works for victims and offenders*. Abingdon, Oxon: Routledge.

Shriver, D., 2007. Truths for reconciliation – an American perspective. NI Community Relations Council. Available at: www.community-relations.org.uk/about-us/news/item/125/an-ethic-for-enemies/?keywords=Donald+Shriver [accessed 2 January 2013].

Staub, E., 2001. Individual and group identities in genocide and mass killing. In: R.D. Ashmore, L. Jussim and D. Wilder, eds. *Social identity, intergroup conflict and conflict reduction*. Oxford: Oxford University Press, pp. 159–184.

United Nations Office on Drugs and Crime, 2006. *Handbook on restorative justice programmes*. New York: United Nations.

Walgrave, L., 2002. From community to dominion; in search of social values for restorative justice. In: E.G. Weitekamp and H.J. Kerner, eds. *Restorative justice: theoretical foundations*. Portland, OR: Willan Publishing, pp. 71–89.

Walgrave, L., 2008. *Restorative justice, self-interest and responsible citizenship*. Cullompton: Willan Publishing.

White, M., 2000. *Reflections on narrative practice: essays and interviews*. Adelaide, Australia: Dulwich Centre.

Wright, F., 1987. *Northern Ireland: a comparative analysis*. Dublin: Gill and Macmillan.

Young, J., 1999. *The exclusive society*. London: Sage.

Zinsstag, E. and Chapman, T., 2012. Conferencing in Northern Ireland: implementing restorative justice at the core of the criminal justice system. In: E. Zinsstag and I. Vanfraechem, eds. *Conferencing and restorative justice*. Oxford: Oxford University Press, pp. 173–188.

8 Qualitative comparative analysis

Mario Ragazzi

Introduction

The ALTERNATIVE project could be imagined as an exploratory venture. It pushes the established methods and practices of restorative justice out of their applicability comfort zone, towards social conflicts in intercultural settings where many of the discipline's assumptions dither. Following an initial conceptual mapping study, detailed plans of operation were drafted and action research started rolling in four countries. Alas, as forewarned by some Prussian general, there is no plan that survives the impact with the battlefield and things got much more complicated. To start with, as it often turns out in overseas explorations, the new territories were far from being empty spaces. In fact a variety of social workers, alternative dispute resolution practitioners, community workers and related academic fields were already thriving there. This spurred some soul-searching about whether the discipline had something relevant to say or novel practices to offer. But this was the easy part. The main structural difficulty faced by the project lay in the goal itself. Restorative justice – at least the enhanced form being explored here – resorts to open dialogue and non-violent communication in order to (re)build trust among those affected by a conflict and often bitterly harmed by it. Once mutual trust is restored, participants can address their oppositions, or at least manage the conflict in a non-destructive way, eventually cooperating towards achieving some common goal in the spheres of justice and security. Unfortunately, after Robert Putnam's findings (Putnam, 2007), there are some reasons to think that communication, trust and cooperation are precisely what is *not* going to happen in intercultural settings, those with high ethnic or racial diversity at least, where people 'hunker down'. How to get out of the impasse? Acknowledging it, dissecting it are but the beginning of an answer.

The first section introduces the Qualitative Comparative Analysis methodology and the dataset. The second section realigns the vocabulary of concepts articulated in the theoretical studies enriching them with the vernaculars emerging from the case studies, with a particular regard for the conflict dynamics, ideas of justice, perceptions of security and how the different mechanisms of participation, dialogue and trust building unfolded in each case. The final section discusses the evaluation criteria and main outcomes for the restorative justice approaches to conflicts in intercultural settings experimented with during the research and proposes a novel approach based on the restoration of communication, restoration of trust, and restoration of cooperative action for justice.

Methods and data

This chapter focuses on data collected from the research partners in four countries (social housing estates in Vienna; Kisváros, a small town in rural Hungary; three border towns in Serbia; Belfast and Londonderry/Derry in Northern Ireland) during the course of the project.

During its first phase, the comparative exercise focused mainly on recasting and honing the project's conceptual tools. The comparison happened on two dimensions. A 'vertical' one, following the ethnographic method of continuous dialogue between the etic and emic understandings of a concept in each site (roughly speaking, contrasting and enriching the researchers' understanding of a concept with its local understanding by participants). The 'horizontal' gaze compared the findings in the different research sites among themselves. The researchers met regularly during the first three years to identify and discuss extensively the key concepts that were more relevant for the research and adapt them to take account of empirical observations. In order to unfold and feed this rather dense and articulated communication process the researchers had to develop methodological communication protocols and a suitable infrastructure to support them.

The main tool used by the researchers to turn their logbook observations and field notes into comparable data took the shape of 'evaluation grids' (Ragazzi, 2015a; Vanfraechem, 2013). The evaluation grids are the first approximation of the emic towards the etic understanding of a concept, a collection of empirically rich and thickly described observations and reflections. The grids include a thorough analysis of the 'societal ecology', a framework to interpret events that arise from 'multiple causes and in multiple institutions and multiple dimensions' tracing and understanding how social systems change (Vanfraechem, 2013, p. 6; Bolivar Fernández, Pelikan and Lemonne, 2015) and a 'thick description' of the situation in all its aspects, understanding the context, learning about intentions, thoughts and feelings of participants and beginning to interpret them (Ponterotto, 2006; Vanfraechem, 2013, pp. 17–18), being explicit about what is understood locally when referring to a certain concept. The use of language is important in this regard and the researchers note which words, expressions and idioms are used by participants to refer to the central concepts. The researchers use the common evaluation grids to keep track – and communicate to each other – how their empirical work has been informing their understanding of the key concepts in the project.

In order to allow the partners to follow the developments of the comparative analysis and as a tool for qualitative analysis, I designed and implemented a remotely accessible database to store, code and analyse the grids, making it accessible to partners on the web and through a dedicated solution for the iPad tablet. As part of the data-processing protocol, the grids themselves are uploaded to the online database that allows for structured queries by keyword or properties across all the fields of the grid itself, e.g. key concepts, action research site, thick description, local language, societal ecology, etc.

Each evaluation grid analyses a concept starting from the thick description of a 'situation' and its societal ecology. These thickly described situations are suitable to be thematized and analysed as 'cases'. Switching to the 'case' as the unit of analysis allows us to focus on tracing processes within it, participatory ones in particular, and analyse the action research's outcomes. The case formalization, linked to the evaluation grids, together with visual analysis tools were implemented in the shared database as well. The remotely accessible database at the centre of the collaborative data management infrastructure (illustrated in Figure 8.1) implements the following main functions:

1 Data entry and validation.
2 Linking the grids with formalized 'cases' or observed situations that they thickly describe and that can be considered units of analysis.
3 Characterizing each 'case' along a set of formally defined conditions (or variables, see section below).
4 Conceptual analysis and feedback to the action research sites for conceptual realignment based on the grids.
5 Set-theoretical, visual analysis tools of the cases for synoptical overviews and quick hypothesis testing.
6 The database feeds the Qualitative Comparative Analysis system coded in R, a free software environment for statistical computing and graphics.[1]

The discussion on the concepts had started early in the project and it developed further during various phases until a final, annotated list of key concepts was decided upon. Some concepts that are clearly central to the project have been included since the beginning, namely active participation, civil society and community, conflict and crime, identity, interculturality, justice, restoration and restorative principles, security (safety). Besides these key concepts, the researchers re-assessed the relevance of trust during the last year of the project when discussing issues of trust building as an instrumental condition for carrying out action research. By the end of the field research phase, the researchers in the different action research sites drafted a total of 65 evaluation grids covering the key concepts. The complete set of annotated grids were collected in one of the project reports (Ragazzi, 2015a) as well as making them available on the shared database for further analysis.

While the quantity of grids is of little overall relevance in itself, a minimum methodological condition to be fulfilled in order to be able to compare the four research sites is to have at least one grid from each that covers the same concept, at least for those concepts that are at the core of the project. This has been achieved almost across the board, especially when taking into consideration that some concepts were less relevant in some research sites. The core concepts of *justice*, *security* and *restorativeness* are sufficiently covered by all research

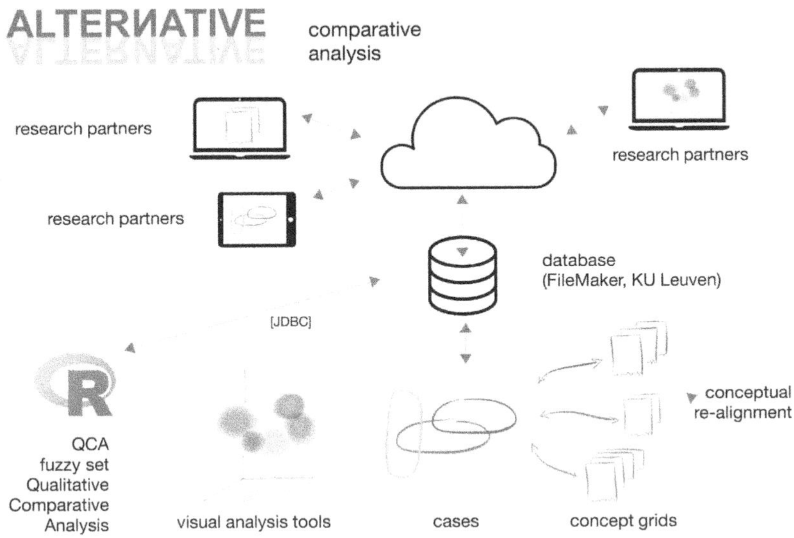

Figure 8.1 Comparative analysis information management infrastructure.

teams and allow for fruitful comparison. *Conflict* is broadly covered by almost all research groups, with a particular intensity in Hungary where a well-defined case-based methodology took precisely local conflicts as the main unit of analysis. *Community* was not uniformly relevant and was mainly treated in Northern Ireland and Hungary, with an original angle on it as *togetherness* from Vienna.

Comparing empirical findings

The empirical findings are analysed and compared introducing a case-based approach and applying the methods of Qualitative Comparative Analysis (QCA) of the 'cases' so formalized, thus shifting the unit of analysis from the action research site, as a whole, to smaller situations formalized as 'cases' that can be compared between themselves and, with some caveats, across the research sites. After this move, how to treat the 'context' that surrounds the cases in a comparative analysis: should it be considered as a black box external to the units of analysis, or as a set of variables at a higher level of analysis (Schench 1990, Table 2.1)? Also taking into account the purpose of the comparison itself, in our case we will treat the intercultural context as a set of variables in itself, a space where cases tend to cluster according to their societal ecology features, that should enable us to specify the coordinates of certain observed phenomena.

Concepts, grids and cases

As we have already seen, the concept-centred evaluation grids emerge from a particular 'situation' that they thickly describe and, reflexively, look back at from a specific conceptual angle.

'situation' → grids → concepts: emic ↻ etic

These 'situations' are themselves part of a broader social and methodological dynamic at the research site. While retaining the comparative grids for the conceptual alignment within the project, adopting a conveniently broad definition of 'case' as unit of analysis would help the 'action/process' and 'evaluation/outcome' sections of the comparative analysis.

'case' ⇄ 'situation' → grids → concepts: emic ↻ etic

However, given the overall project's methodological heterogeneity across the action research sites, it was difficult to adopt a definition of 'case' sufficiently capacious and flexible to apply to all and at the same time retain some analytical edge. For example, in the Hungarian small town, the researchers applied a case-based methodology from the very beginning. They explicitly structured their methodology around a definition of case taken from RJ practice with many important details about the referral phase, signalling, the receiving party, clients definition etc. But in Northern Ireland they prefer to work around broader issues rather than individual cases.

So if a case is defined around a conflict/harm situation which was handled by someone it can offer us insights about cultural framing, modes of handling, participation, etc. but would still be rather blunt in shedding light on assumptions about restorative justice, security, and so on. Vice versa, if the case definition includes discussion workshops, it can offer insights about communication, understanding of justice and security, but not about actual reparation of harm and other restorative outcomes.

For the purposes of the comparative analysis the definition of case will have to be quite broad and thus include also situations where the 'intervention intensity' of the action research itself is in fact limited to interviews and participant observation.

Stylized model of 'case' development:

1 During a communication process with the researchers, some participants refer to a conflictual social dynamic on the site of the action research (signalling).
2 The researchers assess the 'conflict' situation based on certain criteria.
3 Some kind of 'action' is agreed upon, planned and carried out to address the conflict.
4 The action and its outcomes are evaluated.

Even if the action research does not reach stage three, for the purposes of the comparative analysis we will still consider the 'case' as valid, just assigning to it a lower level of 'intervention intensity'.

In between there are situations where the case did involve an action, but this was not organized and carried out by the ALTERNATIVE researchers directly. For example, in Vienna the researchers observed mediation sessions between neighbours carried out by wohnpartner (the agency of the Municipality of Vienna providing mediation services in the social housing estates). In Belfast, an ad hoc restorative conference between locals and immigrants was organized by a restorative practitioner trained by the researchers and later referred to them. Whatever the actual role of the researchers in these cases, ranging from participant observers to conveners, considering that, first, the case happened during the research; second, those who handled it are working in partnership with the ALTERNATIVE researchers; and, third, the case forms part of the empirical material on the project (e.g. through the grids), we considered it as a case where an intervention has taken place. But it will be important to qualify the role played by the researchers in the action.

The resulting definition of 'case' is an inevitable trade-off, broad enough to encompass the methodological diversity within the project and sufficiently formalized to be operational.

Case conditions

The term 'variable' is attuned to the jargon of statistical analysis, while causal 'condition' refers to the language of case-based Qualitative Comparative Analysis (QCA). A variable by definition can assume numeric values to express varying degrees of intensity of a certain property while a condition represents a categorical feature originally expressed in a dichotomous way thus defining a set of cases that verify that property. In fuzzy-set QCA (fsQCA), conditions are not restricted to a dichotomous semantic and can assume continuously varying numeric values. The calibration process (Rihoux and Ragin, 2009, pp. 93–94) takes care of transforming these values in set membership scores (see section 'Comparing empirical findings', above).

If the set membership relation is not defined in terms of the intermediate values of the condition's range, the treatment of intermediate values is critical and it is a good practice to use a calibration function that filters them out in a non-linear way. If the initial data do not contain values in the central range in the first place, the calibration is easier and more straightforward. In order to achieve this, the researchers in their assessment of the degree of intensity of a condition have to make two successive dichotomous choices: first between 'high' and 'low'; then, respectively, between 'very high' (assigning the value 5) and 'intermediate high' (4) or between 'very low' (1) and 'intermediate low' (2). Following this procedure in the construction and assessment of the conditions makes them ready for a fuzzy-set analysis.

QCA-based methods should start from the desired outcome and then proceed to the theoretically informed selection of the conditions that are likely to contribute to explain it. However, in ALTERNATIVE there is no easy or univocal choice of a single outcome that lends itself to a reasonably simple formalization and assessment. This is because of the fundamental methodological and theoretical openness of the project. In order to address this difficulty, we opted to mirror this openness in the choice of possible outcomes and selection of relevant conditions, keeping as guiding principle of course the overarching questions that the project asks about justice and security and the organic relationship to and path dependence from restorative justice. This openness and interpretive latitude is implemented in software that allows the choosing of one possible output at a time and its theoretically related, adjustable constellations of conditions and then carry out various rounds of fsQCA on them.

The conditions that describe each case cover various categorical properties of the *intercultural context*, the *type of conflict* (including how the participants morally frame the conflict; whether there are explicit harm claims and how severe they are; whether the participants activate the 'justice' signifier and how); the *type of action* (the type of practice involved in the action, its level of formalization and the implicit intensity of the intervention; the level of the researchers' involvement in the action); *participation* in the action (whether all relevant stakeholders were involved and took part or there were omissions and refusals; whether the participants assume the roles of victims, offender and community – as in standard RJ practices – or these are not applicable; whether there are public institutions involved) and perceptions of *security* (whether and how participants activate the 'security' signifier and how, its scope from personal safety to threats to a collective identity). These conditions are briefly described in the annex to this chapter.

Case outcomes

Based on the project's objectives and the theoretical results of the earlier phases we identify here some outcomes at the case level that alone or in combination with each other are relevant in operationalizing the overall project outcomes. Some aspects of the action research *process* can be considered as outcomes in themselves and will be presented first.

Intervention as outcome. The action research intervention as an outcome in itself (considering that not all cases saw a significant intervention for various reasons), assessed according to its intensity.

Justice formalization. Main criterion: the action research's distance from, or degree of interpenetration with the law and court system (criminal and civil justice system: State Law System: SLS, including police and public order agencies) and thus ultimately a measure of the legally enforceable coercive potential underlying the action research.

Considering that the desired outcome for restorative justice process is whether the 'system' of formal justice has not played a relevant role, the 'lifeworld' (Pelikan, 2003) condition semantic is by definition the opposite of justice formalization.

Participation as outcome. The researchers assess participation as outcome based on the completeness of stakeholders representation in either the three-stakeholders VOC model or a broader model where stakeholders are not assigned to predefined roles. Reference hypothesis: *participation vs delegation* in RJ.

Restorative outcomes. The researchers assess the following outcomes as dichotomous conditions (i.e. absence or presence, yes or no) based on the established evaluation criteria of restorative outcomes.[2]

Restored Communication: assessment of the quality of communication among participants during and after the intervention.

Taking responsibility: the participants accept responsibility for their actions in the conflict.

Changing positions: the participants change their initial positions towards a more open and cooperating attitude.

Agreement reached: the parties in the conflict reach an agreement about how to manage it and move ahead.

Change in security (safety) perceptions: when the intervention led to observed changes in the security (safety) perceptions of the participants. An important condition, but not systematically monitored and difficult to operationalize.

Repaired Harm: when the practice facilitated by the intervention led to some kind of reparation of the harm claimed by some participants. Considering the RJ specificities, this is particularly relevant.

Ongoing Conflict: when the conflict is premised on structural conditions and has a continuous character, although with varying intensity.

Ongoing Treatment: the intervention is still ongoing at the moment of the final assessment, normally because it is carried out by partner agencies with a degree of independence from the research project.

Case-based comparative methodology steps

Starting from this admittedly non-fully rigorous definition of a case, the researchers in the four sites, in close communication and coordination with the comparative team in Leuven, followed these methodological steps:

1 In each site the researchers identified and selected a certain number of cases, broadly defined as above. The criteria for selection varied across the action research sites and will be discussed later.

2 The cases were linked with the existing evaluation grids (and therefore with the thick descriptions of the situation, analysis of societal ecology, conceptual development, etc.).
3 The comparative team in Leuven assessed each case and – using the tools of the shared database – assigned values to the various conditions for each case, including the outcomes, briefly commenting on them explaining the rationale of their choices. The initial formal assessment of the cases was done centrally in Leuven in order to ensure a more homogeneous interpretation of the meaning of the conditions and application of the assessment criteria.
4 The researchers in the four sites logged into the online database, reviewed the initial assessment of the cases, discussed them thoroughly with the comparative team in Leuven, amended wherever necessary and eventually validated the data.
5 The Leuven team carried out a fuzzy-set QCA on the validated data and reported the findings (Ragazzi, 2015a) together with the conceptual realignment and the results of other analytical methods.

For this methodological protocol to work, it is important to have as clear definitions as possible of the conditions that describe each case and of the underlying theoretical hypothesis that justify their inclusion in the characterization. During the course of the project the researchers extensively discussed the key concepts among themselves during periodic meetings. The local meanings and understandings of concepts emerging from the field were shared through the online database and further discussed, thus creating a reasonably common knowledge base across the research sites, making the assessment of the various conditions less idiosyncratic. It goes without saying that the analysis will be as good as the initial data.

Qualitative Comparative Analysis

Qualitative Comparative Analysis (QCA) was introduced and developed by Ragin (1987). A more recent overview of the state of the methodology taking stock of past experience, criticism and new development, can be found in book-length form in Rihoux and Ragin (2009) and Schneider and Wagemann (2012) or, in a shorter format, in Marx, Rihoux and Ragin (2014).

The application of QCA in ALTERNATIVE is methodologically problematic. The original research design foresaw a Qualitative Comparative Analysis of the four action research sites, but it did not contemplate QCA as such. However, switching the unit of analysis to the expanded 'case' definition as presented above, with a multiplicity of them in each action research site, it is possible to apply QCA on a sufficient number of cases and this has been implemented in particular as fuzzy-set QCA in R.

The database interface allows the researcher to select which cases, conditions and outcomes are to be made available for the fuzzy-set Qualitative Comparative

Analysis implemented with a script written by me for the R environment and using the QCA libraries (Thiem and Duşa, 2013; Duşa and Thiem, 2014).

The last methodological node to untie is the problem of how to treat the context within QCA, taking into account that, as discussed earlier, we are modelling the 'intercultural context' as a set of conditions and that cases from the same research sites are non-independent from each other relatively to cases in other research sites where the context changes significantly. The debate among QCA researchers is interesting. Some propose using a multilevel approach; in our case this would entail subdividing cases by action research site (Denk, 2010; Denk and Lehtinen, 2013). Others argue for just adding the context conditions and run a single analysis (Thiem, 2014). Interesting but moot for ALTERNATIVE because of the limited diversity problem: there are not enough cases in each action research site for a first-level QCA run and adding the context conditions to the whole dataset would likewise expand too much the combinatorial space. Taking into account these limitations we will apply QCA cautiously to all the cases available without over-stretching its explanatory remit.

Dataset and main descriptive findings

The 28 cases analysed here have been selected by the researchers in each site because they are particularly informative of the kind of processes and dilemmas involved in researching new understandings of justice and security in situations of conflicts in intercultural contexts. They do not exhaust the range of research activities carried out by the ALTERNATIVE partners because certain activities were not amenable to being analysed as cases even under the very broad definition adopted here. *Failures* vis-à-vis some kind of baseline restorative justice metric, that itself will need re-assessment, are as important as *successes* in this kind of qualitative analysis and they have been included regardless of their statistic prevalence. The cases analysed here are therefore representative of the action research activities carried out in each site, although not in a statistical way.

A brief description of each case can be found in the annex and in a more detailed version in project documents (Ragazzi, 2015a; Ragazzi, 2015b, pp. 43–47). Based on the case formalization outlined earlier and the data validated by the researchers, the full dataset can be found in Ragazzi (2015b, pp. 47–48).

For dichotomous conditions, the *No* value (absence) is mapped to 1 and the *Yes* value (presence) is mapped to 5 in the [1, 2; 4, 5] scale used for the other conditions.

Some cases are (almost) 'identical' in the current formalization, but we have to consider also the outcomes before making a final decision about the cases that could be omitted from the analysis.

Subset inclusion relationships

The data corresponding to the various conditions is plotted using bubble diagrams where three variables can be represented at the same time: horizontal axis, vertical axis and bubble radius. Each chart shows a fourth colour-coded variable representing the research site: light blue for Vienna (WP4), light yellow for Hungary (WP5), light green for Serbia (WP6), light orange for Northern Ireland (WP7). The chart space is normalized for the values assumed by the variables on the scale from 1 to 5. Binary variables are mapped to 1.5 (No, 0) and 4.5 (Yes, 1). To take into account that there are both a margin of ambiguity in the definition of the variables and a subjective element in the researcher assessment, at the time of charting a white noise random error in the interval from −0.5 to +0.5 is added to each data point. Apart from acknowledging the qualitative and constructed origin of the data, the random noise has the added benefit of scattering data points around within the limits of their semantic portion of space, thus allowing for a more readable chart. While each chart rendering is different from the other in the minutes details, its qualitative properties – it goes without saying – do not change.

The database system where these data are stored can easily generate charts representing two or three variables (conditions or outcomes) at a time. Considering that all conditions assume either dichotomous (binary) values or are the result of a double dichotomy (e.g. first between low and high and later between very high or intermediate high), representing the cases as a scatter plot in the space of two (double) dichotomous conditions allows for quick inspection of logical relationships between them. With the increase of the number of conditions and the size of the combinatorial space, the visual inspection can easily be supplemented with semi-automated procedures that explore the subset inclusion relationships between conditions.

A subset inclusion relationship between conditions A and B ($A \subset B$) does not imply in itself a causal relationship between them ($A \Rightarrow B$), although it is a good candidate for further analysis considering that this relationship was observed in *all* cases in the current dataset. We will use the subset inclusion notation $\subset$ as a shorthand to express these kinds of findings and the implied tentative causal relationship within the chosen methodology. As a first step we analyse the cases so formalized looking for subset inclusion relations between conditions without looking at the outcomes for the nonce. This preliminary phase bears some similarity with the vector autoregression analysis of quantitative methods and yields the following main descriptive findings.

$II \subset HC$ High intervention intensity practices happened only in cases with explicit and serious harm claims (see Figure 8.2)

$VOC \subset HC$ and $VOC \subset PUB$ A ‘standard’ RJ participation model where the roles of victims, offenders and community are well identified applied only in cases with explicit and serious harm claims and where there were public institutions’ representatives among the participants (see Figure 8.3).

$SI \subset PUB$ When security, regardless of the scope of its definition, was more of a concern (high security intensity) there was always a public stakeholder present (see Figure 8.4).

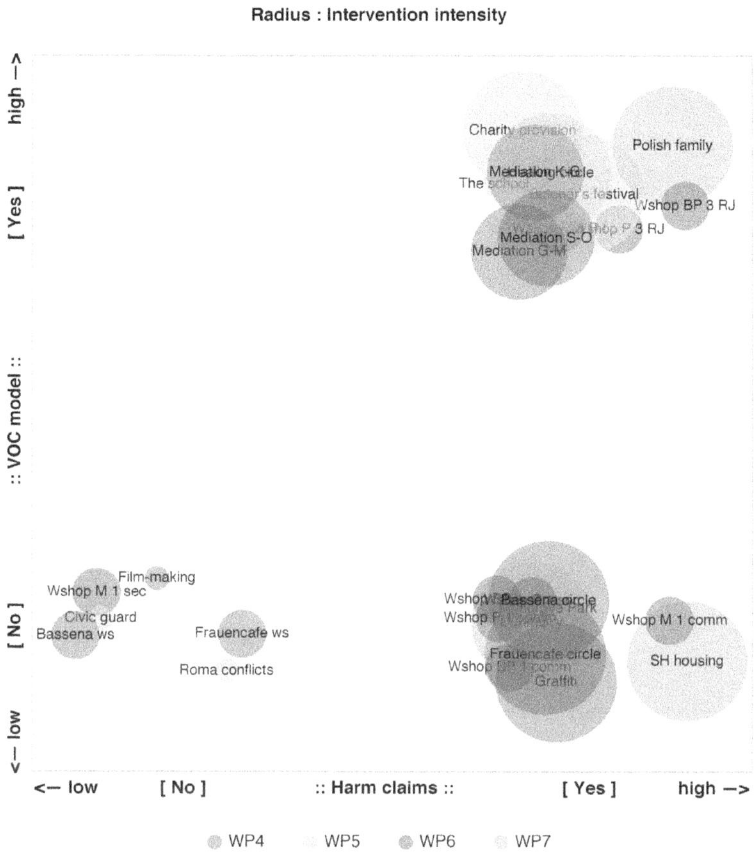

Figure 8.2 Harm claims, VOC participation model, intervention intensity.

$MF \subset PF$ The cases that were morally framed as 'wrongdoing' (as opposed to misbehaviour or the morally neutral conflict of interest) were dealt with by more formal practices following a standard Victim-Offender-Community participation model; besides, these cases were associated with a wider security scope, but not necessarily a high security intensity (see Figures 8.5 and 8.6).

Conceptual realignment

Following the ethnographic method of continuous dialogue between the etic and emic understandings of concepts, a second, 'vertical' comparative gaze aims at honing and realigning the understandings of key concepts like conflict, justice, security, community, participation, trust and cooperation across the sites.

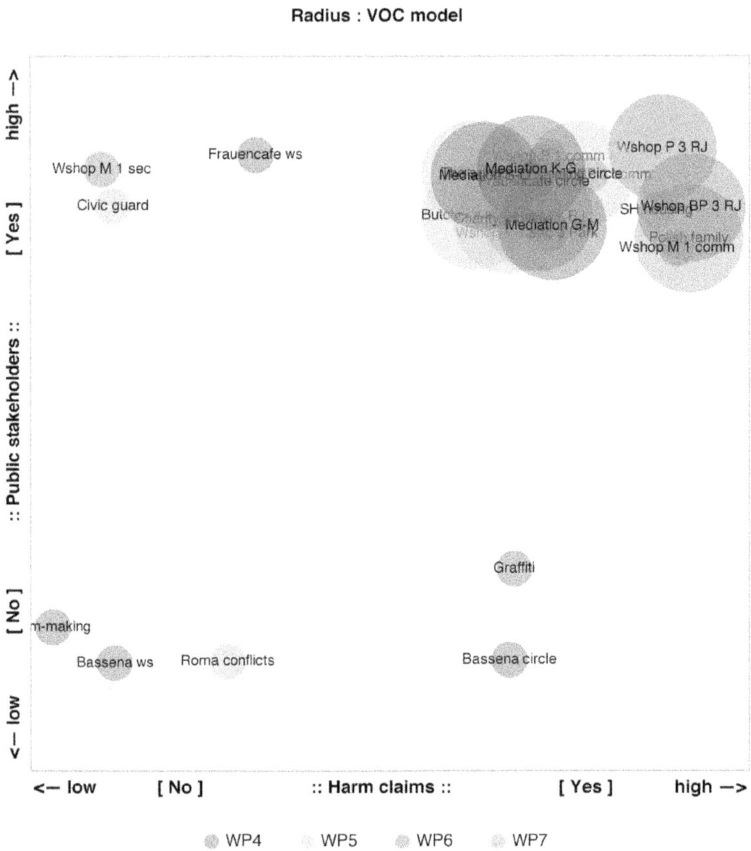

Figure 8.3 Harm claims, public stakeholders, VOC participation model.

Conflict

The methodological move towards choosing the 'cases' as units of analysis cannot be complete without its epistemological counterpoint about a constructivist understanding of the conflicts themselves. Constructivist because the referral system for the identification of cases is based on participants – including the researchers – signalling that some situations are affecting them and it is based on their perceptions and subsequent inter-subjective deliberation that these situations should be considered as conflicts.

Denial of conflict. To start with, there are many situations of 'denial of conflict' or, put more reflexively, there is no conflict that participants – again, including researchers – can agree about without reservations. In Vienna a group of teenagers refuses to let outsiders define and frame the inhabitants of the housing estates as marginal and disadvantaged. They constitute and defend the pride of place as

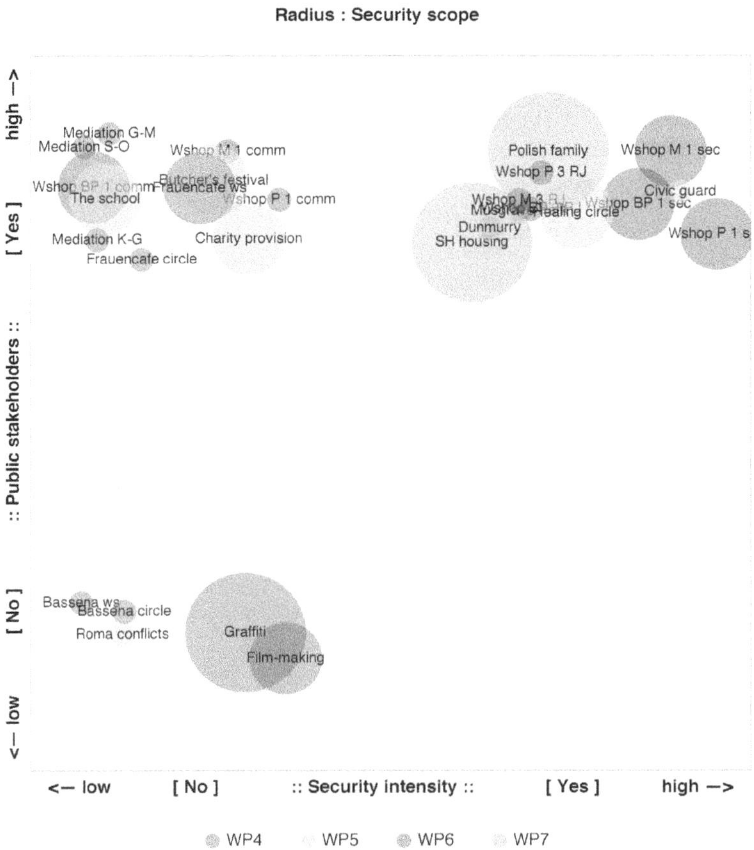

Figure 8.4 Security intensity, public stakeholders, security scope.

identity instead of acknowledging a higher-level social conflict (WP4 #38). Still in Vienna, in the Graffiti case[3] as well the researchers noted that the residents and participants to the circle were in denial about considering the ‘anti-islamic’ graffiti as a particularly serious slur, or perhaps it was a conscious refusal to let the collective existential threat framing get out of hand. In Kisváros the ‘culture of silence’ is precisely about the denial of acknowledging conflicts or at least to talk about them openly and publicly once they have indeed been signalled by some resident: ‘conflicts came up in different waves reflecting on the dynamic of their relationships’ (WP5 #59). Sometimes, more than denial, it seems a matter of suspension. There are few open conflicts in the post-conflict societies of the three towns researched in Serbia, but also little contact and communication between people. People live next to each other while keeping some social distance (e.g. in disapproving of mixed marriages, where the religious and ethnic dimensions overlap, WP6 #8).

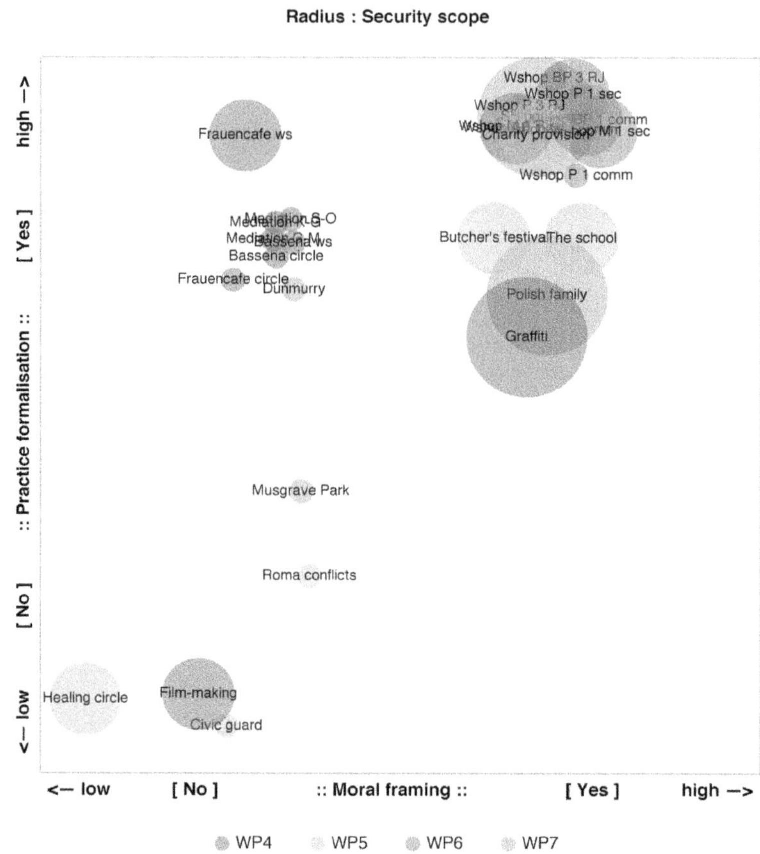

Figure 8.5 Moral framing, practice formalization, security scope.

Continuous conflicts. A second general observation is that, contrary to certain conflict lifecycle models, there are many conflicts that just refuse to peter out or burst, they look more like steady states, with varying and generally not cyclical levels of intensity, because the underlying structural conditions (e.g. the way the housing estates were built, the thickness of the walls, the lack of sound barriers etc., WP4 #41) do not change.

Varying levels of symbolic activation. The conflicts in the different research sites are situated at various levels on the micro-meso-macro scale. In fact, some incidents thickly described in the evaluation grids are rather similar: disputes between neighbours. Disputes between neighbours figure prominently in Vienna, by construction. But they appear also in Kisváros and South Belfast (the keyword 'neighbour' or 'neighbourhood' appears in the same context as 'conflict' or 'dispute' in a subset of grids from all research sites, in particular grids

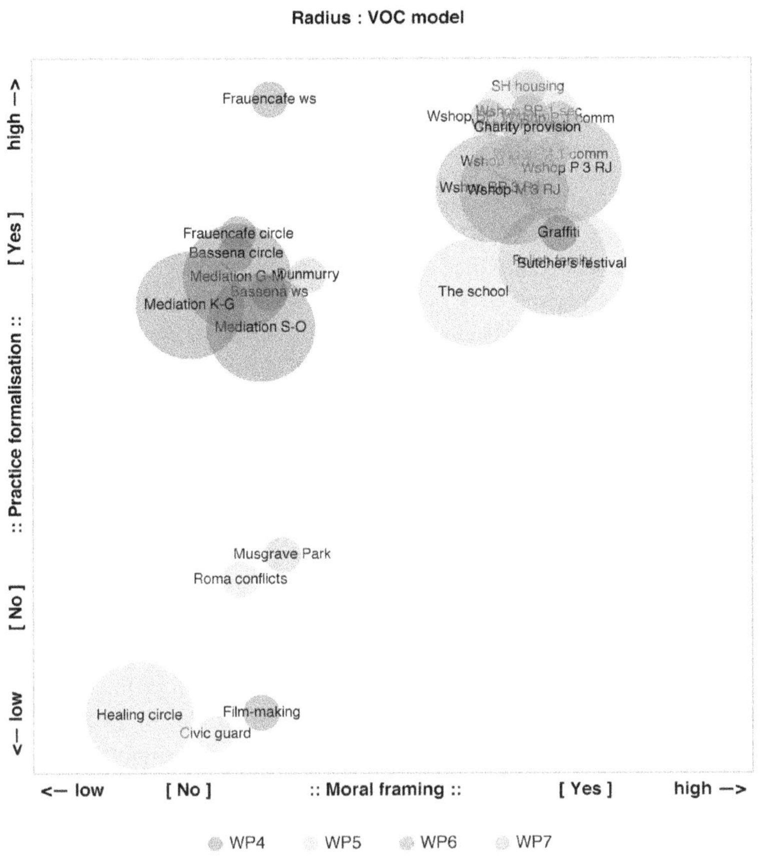

Figure 8.6 Moral framing, practice formalization, VOC participation model.

#17 and #41 from Vienna; grids #11 and #14 from Hungary; grids #9, #16, #18 and #23 from Serbia; grids #29 and #52 from Northern Ireland).

However, conflicts that are apparently similar (issues about unpleasant noises, smells etc.) are narratively framed at different levels both in space – in the various sites – and in time. The same dispute can have a history with various phases, switching level and with it the narrative frame of symbolic activation, moving 'up' from interpersonal to communal or ethnic or religious framing, and possibly vice versa.

At the basic level, sort of ground zero of the disputes between neighbours, there is a semiotic of visual, olfactory, auditive or pressure signals exchanged between one private (e.g. apartment) or public space (e.g. street, yard) with another private or public space. The intensity, nature, duration and pattern of these signals are perceived as highly unpleasant and disturbing by the receiver.

So much so that 'life becomes impossible' (WP4 #41). The receiver is not passive, but engages with the source at various levels in what could be analysed as a 'semiotic of reception'. A warped instance of aggressive, reversed semiotic of reception happens when the actual source of the disturbing sensorial signals blames the receiver for bothering him/her. In one case from Belfast (WP7 #29) there is a similar situation: a Polish family complains first about rubbish falling in their garden and some flags falling over their fence during the traditional July celebrations of Loyalist/Protestant identity. Reacting to this complaint, the source of the rubbish herself, a local resident, rallies the neighbours against the 'foreigners' for not respecting the local traditions and flags.

In almost all instances of such conflicts the source of the signals belongs to a 'minority' group (immigrant background, ethnic, religious etc.) while the receiving party belongs to the majority in the local societal ecology. In all cases described there is a third party engaging in practices that range from mediation (institutionalized or ad hoc) or good offices to simple communication link/enabler (e.g. translator).

The symbolic level of framing of the disputes depends on what the participants, researchers included, make of it. At the interpersonal level the dispute is inter-subjectively framed by those involved, including the researchers, as between two families or persons that happen to live door to door. Ascriptions of race, ethnicity, religion etc., however potentially present in the subjective representations of the 'other', are not part of the common narrative of the parties about the issue. At the meso–communal level the issue is inter-subjectively framed in terms of e.g. newcomers vs locals, different social classes, immigration background vs old resident, ethnic-cultural minority vs majority (e.g. Roma) but without a national dimension. A third level would be the macro or ethnic-national framing.

A difference in *level* is independent from the *intensity* of the dispute; this is rather crucial. An interpersonal quarrel can reach a very high intensity – perhaps including violence and aggression – while a higher-level framing could simmer for a long time at a relatively low level of animosity.

A sketchy ideal-typic representation of the patterns of dispute dynamics in the various locations would be something like the following. In Vienna the overall institutional framework, system of mediation and shared norms keep the disputes within the interpersonal level. The partners not only try to find pragmatic solutions, but also – deliberately or simply by normative default – to prevent the dispute from escalating to a communal-ethnic level. What seem to be an underlying unspoken framing in ethnic-cultural terms of the disputes occasionally manifests itself, but is immediately withdrawn through either normative pressure or mediator's intervention. Occasionally a latent framing at a higher level (e.g. social class prejudice) by one of the parties, although not fully acted out, makes it more difficult to find a pragmatic solution that can work for both.

In Kisváros, the framing seems relatively stable at the ethnic-cultural level even if the intensity of the disputes themselves appears to be relatively low. Rather, the cases emerging from the grids have more to do with the porous boundary between private and public space. The disturbing sensory signals originating from the private space (e.g. burned plastic smell, unkempt garden views) are construed more as a confirmation of a difference, a hiatus in civilized behaviour, rather than a personally and directly felt discomfort.

In one case from South Belfast, as already hinted at above, there is an apparently sudden 'escalation' towards a higher-level framing of the complaints on the part of the native, old residents that almost as quickly de-escalates after the intervention of a restorative practitioner with a prompt extension of recognition to the minority party (direct, personal invitation to a street party).

In the four locations in Serbia, there are no reported cases of this kind of conflict between neighbours that bend themselves to such a simplified model. Nevertheless, there are references to different levels of symbolic activation of conflicts between the 'political-personal' and 'ethno-national' levels. An NGO activist in Bačka tells of intimidations and occasional attacks to his property that happened to him in the post-war period. When asked ('do you think that such behaviour was motivated by the differences in ethnicity?'), he specifies that in this case he was probably targeted not because of his ethnicity but because of his activity with the NGO, thus for 'personal' or 'political' reasons.

The different levels of activation or narrative framing of a conflict are interconnected and in fact a 'political' actor can be instrumental in escalating an interpersonal dispute, framing it at a higher level in order to leverage the associated reverberation of the case to further his political project. It is therefore an important aspect to analyse in order to design restorative practices that are able to change the frame and preventing a personal or neighbourhood conflict to escalate being framed as ethnically motivated, thus increasing its potential for politicization.

Both respondents in Bačka seem to agree that the cases of conflict (harassment, tensions) experienced after 2000 were not ethnically motivated, but rather linked to local politics or other reasons. Based on field observations and respondents' opinions it seems that the public attitude in Bačka at the moment are averse to frame conflicts in ethnic terms for many reasons (e.g. the experience of recent war, a more open society where a plurality of voices can be heard, bridge-building grass-roots activities etc.).

The dynamic variability of the level of symbolic framing of conflicts is perhaps one of the variables to take into account when attempting a comparative reflection on what kind of institutionalization, if any, and what kind of public participation to restorative practices would be more effective for enhancing people's safety and demands for justice, taking into account the political environment, public attitudes and expectations, etc.

Justice

Participants in the four action research sites speak rather sparingly about justice. When directly prompted to do so in a reflective way – as in a discussion group in one of Vienna's *Gemeindebau* (WP4 #10) – or from other, more contingent, observations, a wide array of ideas about justice emerges, almost covering the whole theoretical spectrum. Here are some offerings on (social) justice as:

- *Impossibility*: 'something communism tried to reach, but it went wrong about trying to realise it'; 'justice does not exist, for everyone has an opinion' (WP4 #10).
- An *impartial* political arrangement, a regulating system where some authority (the EU, the municipality, a mother figure) has the power to keep conflicting interests and excessive competition in check, as well as the human tendency to exclude and oppress the weak and the diverse ('when children are in a group the many turn against one, the weakest one, or the only one with red hair') (WP4 #10).
- As *legitimization* of the dominant group's interests: 'Only one "justice" exists, the justice of the majority.' All the groups that are involved have their own idea of 'justice' that can legitimate processes and decisions. The native villagers do not want to have a common wreath and memorial ceremony with other organizations and they overrule the informal decision of a group of people that had approved the joint celebration (WP5 #01).
- Mutual *recognition* among adults 'capable of seeing for ourselves what is right in a given moment', without the need of third supra-entity (WP4 #10). In grid WP5 #13 reciprocity is an important factor in building relationships with the neighbours, especially if they are Roma as seen from an influential member of the majority: 'He offered me … if here are any duties I should just call him and he will come. In fact, I will call him. This is what we call "fair." There and back.'
- *Equality*, equal shares: 'it was easy for me to share with my brother, when there was a chocolate, each one would get half of it' or 'when we'd all earn the same, that would be just' (WP4 #10).
- *Distribution* according to *needs* and *capabilities* (e.g. a bigger flat for a disabled person in a wheelchair) (WP4 #10).
- A normative framework to *handle differences.* 'Mine' would not like to cooperate with 'yours' and in case of conflict the priority is not to find agreement and solution (WP5 #01).
- Fuelled by *envy* and *resentment*: 'people who saw my flat envied me, because they thought it was so big what they found unjust. They'd ask "why do you have such a big flat, I also want one" – They would not recognise my initial disadvantage, my disability to walk, my wheel chair' (WP4 #10).[4]
- *Injustice as capitalist system*: 'capitalism, which builds on inequality, implies that some have more and others less. Is that just, that one has millions and I don't? Or is that given by nature? Should we change this? Is that just, when I drink wine and you only get water?' (WP4 #10).
- *Self-determination*: 'Well, but what if I want to drink water and not wine?' (WP4 #10).
- The quintessential *social feeling*: 'the feeling of being treated unjustly or justly, only comes when I compare myself with somebody else, when I am

> alone, that doesn't matter, only when a second person joins, this becomes important. When I am alone in the wood, I am fine and I am free, justice does not play a role' (WP4 #10).

Last but not least, justice emerges also as the place where the longing for justice and the institutionalized legal system of criminal justice awkwardly try to meet. The shortcomings of formal, procedural justice (slow, does not repair the damage that is caused by crime etc.) are no secret: 'I asked a villager why he did not denounce [a theft]: "Will I get back my ham and bacon? No, I will not"' (WP5 #15). But the formal, procedural, impartial criminal justice system is also seen as the place to seek justice in case of serious crimes. Referring to a heinous war crime that occurred in the 1990s in Bosnia (WP6 #21), the interviewees spoke about justice in terms of prosecution and punishment. The recourse to criminal justice as a system of legal norms protected by the state (*pravo*) is seen as the correct (just, fair) way to achieve justice as *pravda*, the feeling of justice, justice of the people (WP6 #23).

> Therefore, justice in this case is linked to the legal justice – the need to establish the responsibility of those involved in this crime, to punish the perpetrators, but also organizers of the crime, while non-punishment of perpetrators is seen not just as unjust but also as a way of maintaining tensions and conflicts. In addition, some of them spoke about the need to find out what has happened, where the bodies are buried, for the family members of those killed to be recognized as civilian victims of war and to get reparation. This speaks in favour that justice in the post-conflict societies, i.e. transitional justice is linked to the judicial (criminal) justice, but it also requires some other mechanisms of dealing with crimes from the 1990s, including truth-seeking processes and reparation.
>
> (WP6 #21)

One of the rare emphatic, rhetorical references to 'justice' as both 'fairness' and avoidance of suspected racist exclusion happened during the discussion at Kisváros's City Council on the issue of the Butcher's festival. As the mayor put it: 'It is unfair that Roma residents of [our town] mustn't visit the festival', something total contrary to everything he had been fighting for during the last 10 years, and he was determined to prevent it (WP5 #36).

However, according to the researcher who observed the meeting, the emotional elements are so prominent that they may obscure other dimensions of 'justice':

> The representatives of the city council do not speak about justice. They are 'only' outraged, angry and sad because of the suspected anti-Roma sentiments of [the organizer of the Festival]. What do these emotions mean? Do they feel lack of justice? Is the city council fighting for something? What is it? Is it equality? Is it the local residents? Is it justice? Is it moral justice? Is it an agreement which was done previously?
>
> (WP5 #36)

Justice as dialogical process, even allowing for the limits to consensus building in matters of justice, is contrasted with justice as spoils of the political struggle, a justice of the majority that is a recurring feature of the societal ecology in Kisváros:

> Dialogue, agreement and reconciliation are not typical in Hungary. This is the characteristic of the whole society but the government that has been in power since 2010 made this 'habitus' stronger. Consensus building is not the basic idea of the ruling party. Opposition parties found themselves in the position of the 'enemy'. Not wide consensus but the idea of 'decision made by us' is the ruling one. Only one 'justice' exists – the justice of the majority.
>
> (WP5 #36, #01)

Justice is thus understood in the research sites as an essentially and literally contested ground. All groups involved in the various issues emerged during the action research in Kisváros 'have their own idea of "justice" that can legitimate processes and decisions'. These diverging understandings are thoroughly analysed in the charity provision case (grids WP5 #3, 4, 33). Even if direct open dialogue and cooperation between 'us' and 'them' is normally eschewed, groups do have norms to handle their differences and conflicts (WP5 #01) and prevent them from escalating in a destructive way, but without open communication of the kind the researchers intended to champion. As a terrain characteristically open to epistemological struggle even at the micro-level, understandings of justice are themselves part of the conflict and as such subject to possible inter-subjective construction through restorative processes of open communication.

Cases analysis: moral framing, harm and justice claims

The majority of the cases were reported by the researchers to be morally framed at a sufficiently high level as 'wrongdoing' by one of the parties involved, though short of outright 'crime'. In certain cases[5] though, some kind of 'criminal activity' forms part of the conflict background, even if not as the main issue that the action research tried to address. Another major group of cases are framed as the morally toned down 'misbehaviour' and only one as a neutral conflict of interests (see Table 8.1).

Trying to map the moral and justice framing of the conflict addressed during the action research in the various sites shows that when participants claim that they have been harmed in a conflictual situation, they do not necessarily activate the 'justice' signifier at the same time (bottom right sector of the chart, see Figure 8.7).

This disjunction still holds if we restrict the set of cases to those where the conflict was explicitly addressed through a more intensive intervention (conference, public assembly, circle, mediation) (see Table 8.2).

Table 8.1 Moral framing

Moral framing	*All cases*	*Cases with high intervention intensity only*	
Crime	–	–	
Wrongdoing	15	5	Vienna: graffiti Hungary: Butcher's festival, charity provision Northern Ireland: Polish family, SH housing
Misbehaviour	12	6	Vienna: mediations (G-M, S-O, K-G), Bassena circle, Frauencafé circle Northern Ireland: Dunmurry
Conflict of interests	1	1	Hungary: healing circle
Totals	28	12	

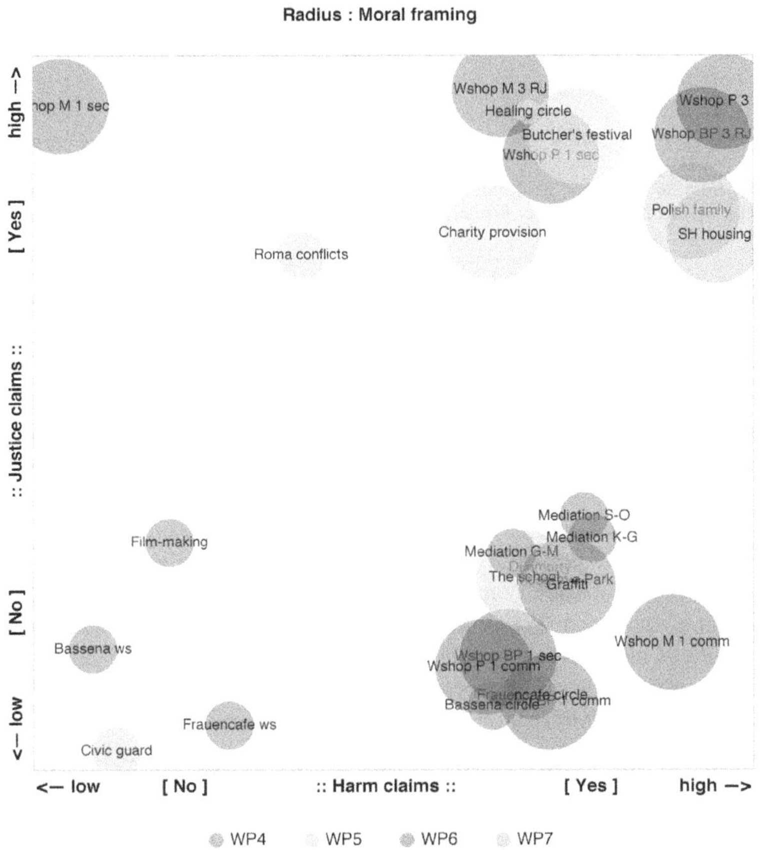

Figure 8.7 Harm claims, justice claims, moral framing.

Table 8.2 Justice formalization

Justice formalization	*All cases*	*Details*
High	–	All situations and cases in the research sites do not get even close to court, in fact none of them is morally framed as 'crime' and criminal activities figure in the background of three cases only
Intermediate high	5	Vienna: Mediation K-G Northern Ireland: Polish family, SH housing, Dunmurry, Musgrave Park
Intermediate low	6	Vienna: mediations (G-M, S-O), graffiti Hungary: Butcher's festival, charity provision, school
Low	8	Vienna: Frauencafé workshop, Frauencafé circle, Bassena circle, Bassena workshop, film-making Hungary: Civic Guard, Roma conflicts, healing circle
Total	19	

Note
The cases from Serbia are all workshops that did not deal with actual conflict situations and did not report an assessment of the 'justice formalization' condition.

The cases are assessed in terms of the formalization of the justice practices and ideas that emerged in their development. The ideal continuum of formal to informal justice is defined according to the relative distance from the coercive shadow of the justice system and its related institutions. The cases where the level or justice formalization is intermediate high are for the most part those where police officers were among the participants (see Figure 8.8). This is not to say that there cannot be 'restorative justice' in the presence of police officers, as it is widely practised around the world. The contention here is circumscribed to mapping the relative presence and influence, if any, of the latent threat of legal coercion among many other factors that condition the cases' development.

As soon as one zooms in to the individual cases, the role of police officers in these practices acquire interesting nuances. For example in one of the Serbian locations a programme titled *Development of the police in the community*, initiated by the Serbian Ministry of Interior, benefited from the ideas and knowledge that two police officers acquired participating in one of the seminars organized by ALTERNATIVE in 2014 and is now being implemented by the local police in partnership with a variety of statutory agencies, local NGOs and schools. Likewise, in Bačka Palanka a police officer who attended the ALTERNATIVE seminars initiated meetings of the local restorative team to discuss further cooperation (Nikolić-Ristanović, Ćopić and Srna, 2015).

If enhancing communication with crime victims, in particular the vulnerable ones, may 'contribute to regain and enhance trust in the police' (Nikolić-Ristanović,

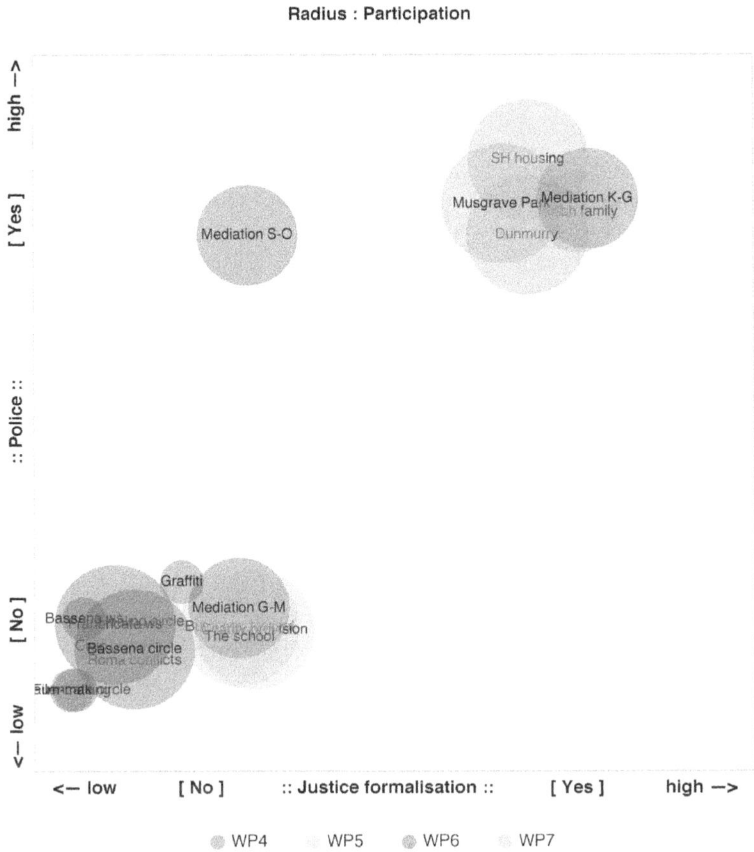

Figure 8.8 Justice formalization, police forces, participation.

Ćopić and Srna, 2015), the relationship between community and police forces are often non-linear, as in Northern Ireland where the establishment of a reformed force, the new Police Service of Northern Ireland (PSNI), was central to the Good Friday Agreements. Despite the undertaking of a radical organizational change programme, a peculiar form of *devolution* of duties that was common before the reforms – when the communities policed themselves – has left a legacy that is only slowly fading out.

> Some loyalists are critical of the police: ‘we are trying to establish a new culture of going to police and they (the police) are letting us down by not punishing people who commit crimes, they are too reliant on us to deal with it … there is no fear of punishment in young people nowadays, back in my day you’d have been dealt with … police are scared of community reaction

> … the whole process takes too long, there will be people in court this month (June 2013) for trouble that happened in Ardoyne last July (2012), they should arrest them and put them through due process to send a message'.
> (Internal project document analysing the social context in Northern Ireland)

In many cases there is a significant association between moral framing and practice formalization. Or, conversely, there are no cases where an informal practice is used in the presence of 'high' moral framing (crime or wrongdoing). Incidentally, we can also observe how the cases with high moral framing and formal practices tend to be also those where the security scope is wider, i.e. involving also the socio-economic dimensions and possibly threatened collective identities beyond personal safety concerns (see Figure 8.5).

Security (safety)

Security has been conceptualized throughout the project as personal safety, therefore most observations refer to this field and in particular to (the absence of) crimes against property (theft, burglary etc.) or serious violations of physical personal integrity (assault, murder, rape, kidnapping, etc.). There is a strong conceptual overlap with the narrower meaning of 'human security' as *freedom from fear*.

While personal safety perceptions are good in the small town in Hungary (the statement 'I feel safe in Kisváros' scored 4.2 out of 5 on a Likert scale), crime is still a concern for many. There are already some security solutions in place that involve the Civic Guard – a voluntary organization expression of civil society – as security provider:

> I remember when the alert started to work in my neighbourhood and I called the Civic Guard. And within a few minutes they were there. You can feel that our members are attentive. It makes me stronger to know that they are taking care of us.
> (WP5 #15)

The importance of neighbourhood solidarity stressed by some participants ('We should not be selfish. If I hear that the dog at my neighbour is barking all night … I also switch on the light, go out and ask if everything is all right. We, neighbours support each other. The whole street …') complements and strengthens this participatory, civil-society-based approach to security. In Hungarian security-as-safety is called *biztonság*, a word that suggests a linguistic link with *bíz-ik*, trust. If solidarity, trust and a voluntary, do-it-yourself approach to security can be alternatives to the techno-institutionalization of security, they are also potentially open to exclusionary practices. In fact, Kisváros citizens of Roma background have quite a hard time to be accepted in the Civic Guard.

Societal securitization processes of existential threats to collective identities are at work in the background in Kisváros and Belfast, and are part of the societal ecology of the action research. For example in Northern Ireland

> From the Loyalist point of view the biggest threat to their security is the perceived strategy of republicans to deprive them of their British identity. [...] 'Our culture is being attacked. There is no fear of a Sinn Fein bombing campaign now we fear a loss of identity.'
>
> (Chapman *et al.*, 2013, p. 164)

However, the 'securitization' analytical framework, in particular the sector of societal security concerned with threats to collective identities (Buzan, Wæver and de Wilde, 1998), was discussed but not adopted by the project and therefore it is not possible to apply it here ex post for a fully fledged analysis. The conceptual identification of security and safety, and the operationalization of safety as – by and large – the absence of crime against property and personal integrity has the advantage of bringing the concept closer to the 'human' dimension, as already mentioned. At the same time, this methodological approach is analytically blunt if one were interested in analysing the political consequences ('what security does') of the securitization of crime and – by extension – of conflict. In one case from Hungary there is an incipient threat construction where the referent object for security is ... security itself, although there is no consensus about it:

> Here, the participants turned back to the 'Roma crime' issue. According to Laci and Anna, the Roma are the ones – besides strangers – who endanger security. Peter did not agree with them: 'It is not an issue that has to be linked solely to the Roma. I know non-Romas who are burglars. There is a disadvantaged group and they have to commit crime.'
>
> (WP5 #15)

Although in this case it is clear from the thick description that security/safety means absence of crime, there is no identification of a threat to a collective identity (as in the discursive activity of right-wing political groups) and therefore it is not part of a societal securitization process.

The reification of security, or even its personification as a source of normative behaviour[6] is in itself interesting, but cannot be analysed here. More concretely, in Medvedja members of the Albanian minority identify the 'police' as a security threat itself. Participants are keen not to generalize and specify that only 'some' individual officers did mistreat or disrespect them. At the same time they make clear that these are not just random offenders or lunatics, but the legacy of a policy of institutionalized harassment against the Albanian minority during the 1990s. Officers that were trained and 'socialized' at the time were never vetted afterwards and continue to constitute a threat to the minority.

> The Albanian male student explained this best: 'We feel safe with regard to our neighbours, but many policemen did bad things and they are still policemen. Now, when someone sees the policeman that did such things to him or his family, of course he will not feel safe.' The Albanian male NGO activist

> also said that he cannot feel 100% secure because: 'There are still policemen, that were active during the times of conflict in the Presevo valley in the 1990s and that were harassing Albanian citizens. Some of these men committed crimes and they were not punished. And they continue to act badly like the war is still going on.' [...] He added: 'Many who were harassed during the war feel badly because of it ... The policemen can recognize those who are not from around here and when you are an Albanian they tend to question you.... It all reminds me of the 1990s.'
>
> (WP6 #18)

The Roma inhabitants of the Hungarian small town – or at least the former leader of their minority self-government – have identified in the de facto exclusion of Roma inhabitants from the local Civic Guard a conflictual issue. The attempt to establish a new Civic Guard, open to Roma volunteers as well, however, failed, but not because of direct exclusion or discrimination (as described in WP5 #34 and Benedek *et al.* (2015)).

A departure from the 'security as personal physical safety' frame occurs in a couple of occasions when the understanding of personal safety is expanded to economic security. For example, respondents in Bačka link the economic insecurity and lack of jobs to the poor performance of the government (WP6 #20). In Kisváros the members of a focus group agree that more jobs would contribute to personal economic safety and, crucially, to stem criminality (reminding how the collective farms of the previous regime kept many people busy and away from crime). Interestingly, they place job creation within provision of 'social security' connecting the contribution of 'local entrepreneurs [who] should hire local employees and thus support the village' to that of charities (WP5 #15).

There is hardly any use of the language of security in Vienna at the time of the research, although there had been attempts at securitizing the conflicts in the *Gemeindebau* by the right-wing Freedom Party (FPÖ) during a previous political contest. It seems that the enveloping institutional embrace of the Municipality based in a mix of corporatist welfare paternalism, pragmatic approach to conflict mediation and community service provision through NGOs have created conditions for the apparently stable de- or non-securitization of neighbourhood disputes.

> There is not so much evidence of the respondents' participation in local networks and associations. Anyway we would suggest, and have argued elsewhere, that according to the empirical evidence from some Viennese residential quarters urban residents' sense of security is based on their trust in 'the system' (=local welfare state and the urban infrastructure) rather than on regular involvement in activities and patterns of association and participation operating on a local level.
>
> (Sessar, 2004, p. 105, quoted in an internal project document analysing the social context in Vienna)

Cases analysis: security scope and intensity

The case formalization tries to capture the security dimension using two conditions, one for the security scope (narrowly conceptualized as personal safety, or widened as to construe some kind of threat to a collective identity, or mainly focused on socio-economic concerns) and the other for the security 'intensity' or how important is security – however locally defined – for the participants (see Table 8.3).

The overall picture is mixed as shown in the chart (see Figure 8.9). There is of course a relative prevalence of the narrow scope – inevitably confirming a research design since it was a deliberate choice by the researchers to focus on security as personal safety. The deviations from this general direction are highly informative though, especially the emergence of a rather strong signal about the socio-economic dimension of security, in particular from the discussions in the workshops held in Serbia where the worries for lack of jobs and opportunities are sharper.

There are no obvious inclusion relationships between security scope and its intensity across all the cases, but there are some simple regularities within each research site, confirming that there is no language of security – i.e. low intensity – in Vienna even if the scope varies. The fact that the usually more 'combustible' threat to a collective identity is not construed as a security emergency hints at a socio-institutional ecology where pragmatism and 'normality' tend to prevail. The top-left corner could be seen as the space for those cases where putative de-securitization or better, the prevention of securitization is effective. The cases from the small town in Hungary cover almost all the available spectrum, testament to their careful choice in order to add detail and various facets to the analysis. There are only three cases where the security scope widens to include threats to a collective identity. In two of them – both in Northern Ireland – this is combined with a higher intensity of security concerns.

As already seen in the section about the main descriptive findings (see Figure 8.4) there is a subset inclusion relation (or tentative 'causal' implication)

Table 8.3 Security scope and intensity

Security scope	*All cases*	*Cases where security issues are more important*	
Personal safety	15	6	Hungary: Civic Guard Serbia: workshops on RJ in three locations Northern Ireland: Dunmurry, Musgrave Park
Socio-economic security	10	4	Hungary: healing circle Serbia: workshops on security in three locations
Collective identities threatened	3	2	Northern Ireland: Polish family, SH housing
Totals	28	12	

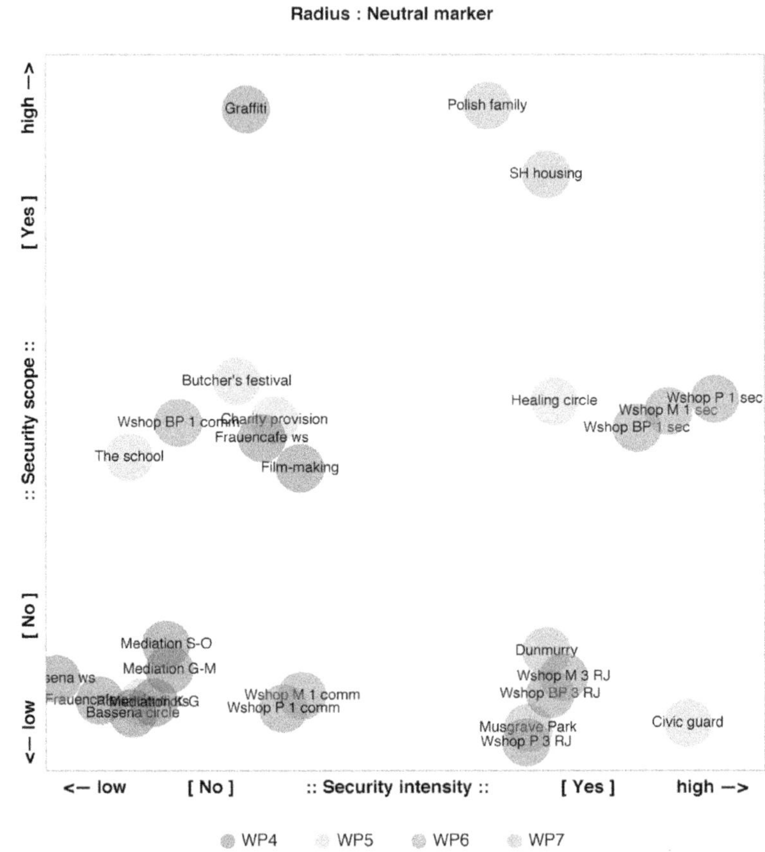

Figure 8.9 Security scope, security intensity.

between security intensity and the presence of public stakeholders. When security – regardless of the scope of the definition – is more of a concern, there is always a public stakeholder present.

Community

The concept of community is a very difficult terrain for a comparative exercise since some research sites, Northern Ireland in particular, rely heavily on it, even making a specific, communicative understanding of community and its restoration into a goal in itself. On the contrary, the idea of community is almost totally absent, despite their name, from fieldwork in Vienna's *Gemeindebau*.

Still, community matters a great deal, especially in certain contexts and societal ecologies, and it would be unwise to wipe it out only because a single, neat conceptual definition cannot be found by researchers. Just to give an example among many about the effects of the simple utterance of the 'community,' signifier, research in behavioural economics and experimental psychology has shown that

> minor changes in the (experimental) context can affect behaviour. For example, there is evidence that subjects [in the United States] contribute more in a one-shot PD [Prisoner's Dilemma game] if it is called 'community game' than if it is called 'Wall Street game'. Under the plausible assumption that the community frame triggers more optimistic beliefs about other subjects' inequity aversion our model is consistent with this observation.
>
> (Fehr and Schmidt, 1999, p. 852)

The following sparse observations resulted from realigning the material emerging from the comparative grids with the theoretical output of other action research sites. Within ALTERNATIVE, the concept of community is particularly relevant – by design – in the Northern Ireland site (WP7) and, to a lesser degree, in the small town in Hungary (WP5). The working definition adopted by the researchers in Northern Ireland of community as a communication process, both object and means of a widened restorative approach to justice, is original and fecund of further developments. For example along the lines of the admittedly more abstracts suggestions sketched by George Pavlich in a series of seminal contributions (Pavlich, 2004). However, the way 'community' is still treated conceptually in most of the comparative grids is still a rather static, personified entity, more a noun than a verb to use Pavlich's language in a recent seminar (Pavlich, 2014).

Researches in Hungary observed how the various civic groups or NGOs acted as 'organized' loci of formal solidarity often in opposition to, or simply not representing the interests of more 'organic' communities. This was particularly the case of EU-funded NGOs parachuted on Kisváros with the purpose of mobilizing the Roma community for the European Parliament elections of 2014.

Adopting the insights of Esposito (1998 and 2002), Sloterdijk (2014) and others on the inextricable link between community and immunity one can start a fruitful work on the implications of security and securitization in contexts where 'community' is an important conceptual reference. Sometimes co-obligations, internal policing of mores and customs, are legally sanctioned in new governance agreements between the 'community' and state agencies. For example, community-based policing is of interest in Northern Ireland (regional workshop, autumn 2014), while a grass-roots, self-help 'Civic Guard' is important in Kisváros (grids WP5 #15 & #34) although it is also a point of friction in the majority-minority relations.

While in Vienna the concept of community seems much less relevant, the researchers have reflected on 'togetherness' (WP4 #54) as a substitute or proximate concept and asked 'what is the relationship between "othering" and boundary making?', such as the expressions of *maternalism* from the 'Austrian' majority women towards women of immigrant background, speculating that 'it could be interpreted as a manifestation of dominance of the Austrian majority taking a condescending, protecting and controlling attitude towards the members of the minority'. But it could also be interpreted as 'concealing helplessness and the longing for contact. It reminds us once again that the analysis of power-relations must not proceed too hastily.'

Active participation

In order to achieve active participation that goes beyond a token of bodily presence, it is crucial to analyse exhaustively who are the stakeholders affected by the conflict and what are their interests. The key insight is to define participation itself in terms of the stakeholders' actual decision-making powers and the resources they can invest or claim in the process, thus owning it. For an analysis of 'participation with power and property' see (Pelikan and Ragazzi, 2018). A promising line of inquiry, suggested by research findings on cooperation in institutional economics (Ostrom, Walker and Gardner, 1992; Gürerk, Irlenbusch and Rockenbach, 2006), hints at the importance of devolution of certain constituent powers to the participants, i.e. not only decision-making powers within the rules of the practice, but a deliberative voice in setting the rules themselves.

The analysis of the cases tried to capture to what extent the standard restorative justice Victim-Offender-Community participation model was relevant and to what extent the various stakeholders groups were actually represented. The researchers assessed that in less than one third of the cases the stakeholders could be represented by the standard categories, and among these, only in five cases victims and offenders were both present. In most cases the conflict situation was such that the categories of victim and offender were not relevant and could not be applied. In this subset of cases it is still important to assess whether participation was complete, i.e. if all relevant stakeholders did take part in the action (11 cases out of 17) or if some stakeholders were left out (six out of 17 cases), either because of their refusal to join, or because of other reasons (see Table 8.4).

The VOC participation model and higher intensity of intervention are both closely associated with explicit harm claims, as can be seen in Figure 8.2 above.

The few interventions that result in significant reparation of harm all unfold under standard RJ approaches (formal mediations, but also an ad hoc informal restorative conference) where the roles of 'victim' and 'offender', with the addition of 'community' are well delineated and identified, as shown in the following chart (Figure 8.10).

The ideal justice formalization and practice formalization continuum is well represented in the ALTERNATIVE field research, although there's only one case where an informal practice is combined with a relatively formal approach to justice. A more complete participation seems to be facilitated by more formal practices, while it seems not affected by the degree for justice formalization.

Table 8.4 Participation models

Participation model	*All cases*	*Subsets*		
VOC: standard RJ with 'Victims', 'Offenders' and 'Community' stakeholder groups	11	2	V+O+C *all* present	Hungary: Butcher's festival, charity provision
		2	V+C (no offender)	Hungary: school, healing circle
		3	V+O (no comm.)	Vienna: mediations (×3)
		1	O+C (no victim)	Northern Ireland: Polish family
		3	no V no O no C*	Serbia: workshops on RJ (×3)
Stakeholder groups are not characterized in terms of victims and offenders	17	11	Participation 'complete'	Vienna: Frauencafé workshop, Bassena circle Serbia: workshops on comm. and security (×6) Northern Ireland: SH housing, Dunmurry, Musgrave Park
		6	Participation *not* complete	Vienna: Graffiti, Frauencafé circle, Bassena workshop, film-making Hungary: Civic Guard, Roma conflicts
Total	28			

Note

* The VOC participation model applies theoretically in these cases, but the roles were not played by the persons actually affected.

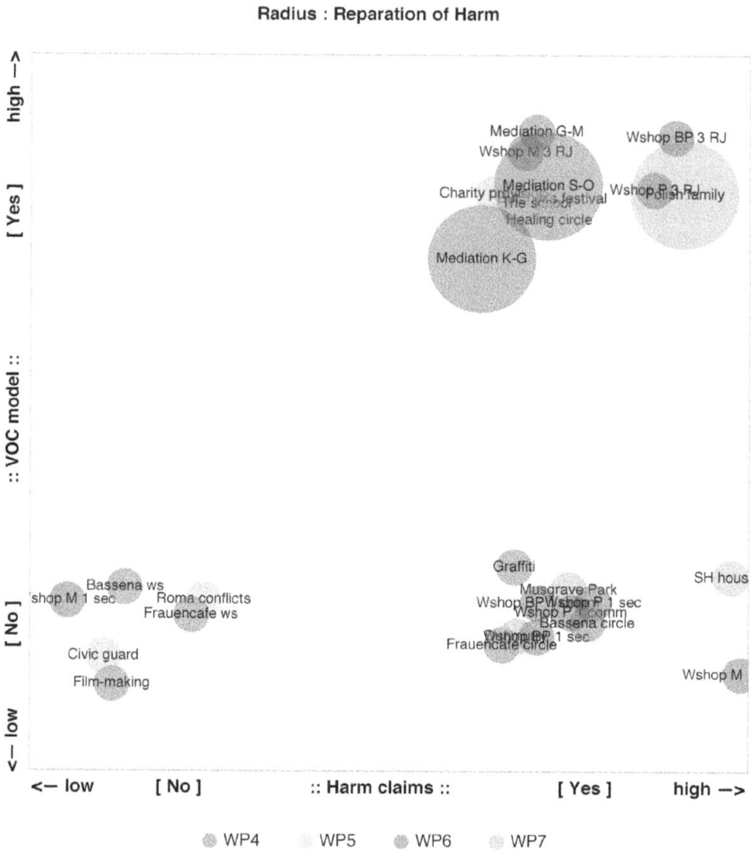

Figure 8.10 Harm claims, VOC participation model, reparation of harm.

Trust and cooperation

The heuristic relevance of the concept of 'trust' became apparent during the last year of the project when researchers across all sites discussed issues of trust building as a condition that is instrumental to carrying out action research and to prepare the ground to implement restorative justice in intercultural contexts.

Most references to 'trust' in ALTERNATIVE are found in the problem analysis in the small town in Hungary (Benedek *et al.*, 2014) and in the analysis of interethnic conflicts in Serbia (Nikolić-Ristanović *et al.*, 2014), as well as in the Restorative Justice practices manual (Chapman, Wilson and Campbell, 2014) and RJ contributions to peace building (Chapman, Wilson and Campbell, 2013) developed by the team in Northern Ireland. In Vienna there are few explicit references to 'trust' although it could be argued that trust and solidarity are already embedded in an impersonal institutionalized form in welfare institutions. When analysing the importance of trust building and its connection to restorative justice there are important differences among the research sites: from meta-level dialogue to handling concrete conflicts and the related questions of legitimacy/authority like whether to challenge or not the 'culture of silence' and how.

In Vienna trust building is not referred to explicitly and it is touched as a lateral concern linked to the general question of the legitimacy to intervene ('who are we to ...?', 'did people ask for our help?'). Working with already-established institutions and programmes, there isn't an issue of 'greenfield' trust building. During the attempted circles in Vienna (Kremmel and Pelikan, 2015), when presented with RJ or dialogical principles, participants showed: 'resistance, avoidance, falling back, dwelling on experiences of fear and xenophobia'.

In Hungary the researchers have identified in the so-called 'culture of silence' – the reluctance of the inhabitants in talking openly about conflicts – a central interpretation key that generates several questions: What does it mean to want people to talk openly about their conflicts?; Is silence a strategic tool?; When is it OK to challenge and when is it better to leave things as they are?; When does breaking the silence make people vulnerable?; Who benefits from the silence?; How far can you go as a practitioner and how far must you go?

After the restorative interventions, participants showed more readiness to face conflicts and tensions, to listen to 'the other', to engage in dialogue. Considering the initial low trust of the general setting, these are arguably trust-building activities that have some potential.

During the participatory workshops in Serbia, working with experts, creating a safe space, capacity building, education, raising awareness, sharing knowledge are all seen as preparatory work laying the ground for future restorative interventions. The ALTERNATIVE researchers in Serbia explicitly posit the importance of the restoration of open dialogue and non-violent communication in order to leverage the contact theory in post-conflict societies:

> Thus, the main factors that contribute to establishing and maintaining communication and dialogue include: optimal contact, readiness for communication, and gradual setting of conditions for constructive communication (dialogue). This provides a basis for cooperation, trust-building and moving conflicting parties closer to each other. The research of the 'Third way' model development confirmed the relevance of the contact hypothesis, and of the communication and dialogue as a means of changing attitudes, behaviours and relationships in post-conflict societies. It also suggested the importance of coordination of activities and cooperation that offers a good basis for the development of trustful relationships towards reconciliation.
>
> (Nikolić-Ristanović, Ćopić and Srna, 2015, p. 16)

They articulate the potential of restorative circles as trust-building methods through 'storytelling, which is important for both self reflection and for understanding others, and focusing on (re)building relationships, trust and mutual understanding' and focused on experiences of mutual trust during the second workshop in all three locations, highlighting among the main findings the mutual character of trust and the impact of different life experiences and differences among individuals in their attitude and practices of trust (Nikolić-Ristanović, Ćopić and Srna, 2015, pp. 17–18).

But in the light of the literature on trust and social capital (Stolle, 2003) there are serious assumptions to be made in order for the contact hypothesis to work: if the participants in the putative dialogue are deeply unequal in terms of socio-economic conditions and education, and diverse in 'race' (at least in the US context) there are few chances for a constructive communication to flow and this leading to increased trust. Rather, evidence points in the direction that it is more likely that the opposite may happen (Alesina and La Ferrara, 2002; Putnam, 2007). Attempts at reproducing Putnam's findings in Europe have admittedly yielded mixed results (Gesthuizen, Van Der Meer and Scheepers, 2009; Hooghe *et al.*, 2009).

In fact, in post-conflict context like the societies that emerged from the 1990s wars in the former Yugoslavia, and in particular in controlled environments like the seminars organized and conducted by the researchers in Serbia, if 'ethnicity' is the main factor of diversity dividing participants that are otherwise quite similar in socio-economic outlook and education (middle class working in government agencies, NGOs, education etc.), the contact hypothesis and related communication methods have a much higher chance to work, as in fact they do.

Unlike the other action research sites, the researchers in Northern Ireland have actually been invited to intervene and their local partners (CARE, CRJI, Northlands Centre) have strong roots in the communities. The working relationship with some of the partners in Belfast started before ALTERNATIVE. As a consequence there is no need for trust building in this site, and no legitimacy/authority questions as in some of the other sites. While working on issues of drugs, new social housing and hate crime they challenge the idea that trust building should be associated with neutrality and stand for all-partiality, transparency, a clear stance against violence and commitment to restorative-based communities (personal communication to the author).

When community is a relevant concept, one of the possible answers to the research questions of 'what do we mean by restorative practices' and 'what to restore?' could head in the direction of trust in particular and social capital in general, adopting Putnam's classic definition (Putnam, 1995) that sees the former as part of the latter, together with norms, networks and other features of social organization that facilitate coordinated action.

Trust is based on the 'esteem' kind of recognition, to use the Hegelian semantic, and as such – unlike respect – it is not mandatory, it cannot be the object of legal sanction and thus it is not universal. Economists are extremely interested in how this kind of social capital is reproduced or depleted because there are good reasons to think that it is a very important ingredient of economic success and growth in market economies. Should RJ and ALTERNATIVE set 'trust' and its restoration as a goal in itself or just as an instrumental intermediate stage towards other ends?

If past experiences do have an impact on the participants' initial negative attitude, considering that the inverse association with trust tends to fade relatively fast (after one year Alesina and La Ferrara, 2002, pp. 219–220, could not find any significant impact) it is important to, first, engage participants at least in the medium term; second, to prevent as much as possible re-occurrences of the trauma, which is not easy in situations of continuous conflict where the structural determinants of the conflict are not likely to change. The traumatic experiences of the wars of the 1990s loom large in the memory of participants from Serbia; there are little doubts about how serious they are. But an important qualifying point emerging from the field research is how the 'small' harassments in everyday life and repeated episodes of corrupt or predatory behaviour by local authorities keep bringing back the past traumas, (re)generating mistrust and making participants feel unsafe (Nikolić-Ristanović, Ćopić and Srna, 2015).

The restorative practitioner who facilitated the circles in Vienna gives a remarkably compact and comprehensive formulation of what could be taken as a blueprint for an 'expanded RJ' approach (Kremmel and Pelikan, 2015, pp. 24–25):

- Raise the participants' awareness of the structures they are living into and reproducing.
- Sharpen their senses for the interconnectedness with others.
- Provide a space for learning about the dynamics of conflict and dialogue in general and very specifically about conflicts in the communities the participants were part of, as well as the participants' roles in these conflict situations with their possibilities of creating or impeding dialogue.
- Raise their ability to become co-creators of conditions for conflict and dialogue (restoration of communication) that strengthen the relationships within the community creating understanding, trust, cooperation, engagement.

The last part implies the active participation in the production, reproduction and restoration of public goods that are all components of *bridging* social capital.

Outcomes

An expanded evaluation space for a new approach

Preliminary to the definition and assessment of outcomes, a discussion is in order about which evaluation space – and relative metrics – is better suited to alternative understandings of restorative justice and security. The ALTERNATIVE project has prodded the boundaries of established RJ practices, trying to expand and test its field of application in several directions: the cultural context; the level of analysis; the scope of the action research; the participation model. The intercultural features of the societal context are problematized by design and brought to methodological centre stage. Crucially, the scope of the research is widened to deal with more complex 'conflict' situations in society, where responsibilities and harm claims are more blurred than the 'crime' situations of established restorative justice where the identification of a 'victim' and an 'offender' are normally a given. We will call these restorative justice approaches to conflicts in intercultural settings explored by the project as RJCIS for short.

There are obvious similarities between RJCIS and both the 'standard' RJ and the 'Restorative Practices' (RP) approaches (Wachtel and McCold, 2004), but also significant differences that qualify the new approach experimented in this project:

- RJCIS focuses on conflicts instead of criminal wrongdoing or offences or harm, without considering conflict as a necessarily negative manifestation of social life. Within each conflict, justice claims, harm claims and moral framing of the issues are as central as they are contested.
- RJCIS critically problematizes the importance of the intercultural context as a central variable, rather than a background concern to be taken into account with secondary degree adaptations. This is especially relevant for the design and implementation of open communication approaches to restorative dialogue: communication as restorative outcome (see infra).
- The proponents of Restorative Practices seem to consider the restorative methods as sort of generic formats – like 'circle', 'conference', 'mediation' – whose application and instantiation in specific fields (from education to RJ to office management) are the actual restorative practices. ALTERNATIVE's action research may also deploy and adapt certain restorative practices, but one of its key insights is that practices-as-techniques are not neutral, do not translate seamlessly into different socio-institutional arrangements, and it is important to analyse critically their implications as *restorative governmentalities* (Pali, 2015).
- Adding depth to the informal-to-formal continuum of practices format, ALTERNATIVE thematizes also an informal-to-formal continuum of justice: from the highest formalization in the criminal justice system to the most informal ideas (expectations, practices etc.) of justice that each participant holds and are acted upon in the various case studies.
- RJCIS critically problematizes the implications of new governance models on participation and proposes a radical approach to active participation as full process ownership (participation with power and property).
- RJCIS builds upon open communication and repeated interaction that contribute to reduce uncertainty for the restoration of localized trust, as well as improving perceptions of personal safety.
- At the same time, with a parallel problematization of the structural conditions that lead to lower generalized trust, namely socio-economic inequality in itself and especially when combined with ethnic diversity.
- Hence, the new approach has a renewed focus on justice (as opposed to the technicalization and neutralization of restorative practices) as the original multilevel, multi-dimensional *raison d'ètre* of the field. Multi-dimensional but with a relative hierarchy of priorities: distributive justice has a direct

implication on the conditions of possibility of the restoration of communication and trust in highly diverse intercultural settings.

One major underlying assumption for this new approach is to treat restorative justice processes in intercultural settings as essentially public goods provision problems where trust and cooperation are of paramount importance. From this point of view, as an example of how the new approach includes the standard RJ methods, let us consider the agreement that the parties eventually reach through mediations, circles and conferences and its implementation. It can be considered as a form of cooperative solution to a public goods problem – 'making' justice by reparation, reintegration and reconciliation – with varying degrees of negative (latent) and positive sanctions, 'costs' (emotional, social if not necessarily financial) borne by participants, possibility of free-riding, institutional check etc.

Since restorative justice makes a clear normative and methodological option for voluntary and non-coercive participation, there is a reasonable case for introducing some elements of economic analysis of cooperation dilemmas. The working definition adopted by ALTERNATIVE researchers in Northern Ireland of community as a communication process, both object and means of a widened restorative approach to justice, also falls in this generalization and already beckons it. Restoring communication while restoring community and vice versa implies (re)building both the in-group 'bonding' trust, and intergroup 'bridging' kind of trust. This can be assessed from successful inter-community cooperation on justice and security matters.

Based on this expanded understanding of restorative practices in intercultural settings, the following sections will assess first the outcomes that are closer to the standard approach to restorative justice, namely the reparation of harm. The following sections will look at the 'extended' outcomes as restoration of communication, trust and cooperative action for justice.

Reparation of harm

The new approach moves beyond the established field of application of restorative justice, without departing from it completely though. Ideally, it encompasses the original RJ domain while at the same time extending beyond it. Thus, starting from the established RJ outcomes such as reparation of victims' harms, the offenders taking responsibility, their reintegration in a reconciled community and so on, but as the main restorative outcomes.

The main finding within the restorative justice outcomes field more narrowly understood is that the tried and tested practices of restorative justice like mediations, circles and conferences, can be effective also to address well-defined conflicts arising in intercultural contexts. Or at least this has been observed (for a synopsis of the fsQCA results about the reparation of harm as main outcome, see Figure 8.10), provided that harms are claimed explicitly and are dealt with through formal practices facilitated by trained practitioners with the involvement of public institutions, including police officers. The latter may contribute to the practice's formality and 'seriousness', perhaps even adding some latent negative incentive to sustain cooperation in implementing the agreement reached by participants, provided that they are considered sufficiently 'neutral' relative to the parties involved. This could be a critical factor in certain social contexts where institutions tend to be weak and captured by dominant groups.

Restoration of communication

Those conflict situations where there were no direct RJ outcomes in terms of the participants taking responsibility and reparation of harm can still be assessed in restorative terms looking at the quality of communication.

The clearest signal coming from the research sites is about the centrality of open, non-confrontational communication in restorative justice approaches to conflicts in intercultural settings. The main features of a 'restorative dialogue' are that it is (1) inclusive (it involves all the parties directly affected by the conflict, at least both victim and offender, in some settings also the community); (2) grounded in restorative principles and values and (3) hosted by a facilitator. Restorative dialogues are used to identify the needs and interests of the participating parties and tend to favour reparation of harm rather than retribution (WP4 #50 quoting Barbara Raye and Ann Warner Roberts from the *Handbook of Restorative Justice*, 2006). This is rather well known and it is perhaps the 'killer app' that the ALTERNATIVE researchers brought in the rucksack from their RJ mainland.

Communication and open dialogue are more than 'techniques'. For example, the ALTERNATIVE researchers in Northern Ireland adopted a working definition of community as a communication process itself, both object and means to a widened restorative approach to justice, i.e. restoring communication while restoring community and vice versa, a non-referential and inter-subjective communication that accepts and assumes 'otherness'.

In the Vienna's circles – or workshops preparing for actual restorative circles – communication was (partially) restored by slowing it down, asking a participant to repeat what her interlocutor had just said to her, until the person who made the utterance in the first place was satisfied that her message had reached the intended recipient and there were no misunderstandings. This redundancy is standard practice in communication protocols, to be sure (Cerf, Dalal and Sunshine, 1974, p. 35), but its specific significance here goes beyond a technical requirement of bitwise message reproduction: it is meant to tune up attention, listening attitude and respect (and, why not, given the effective bandwidth limitation imposed by the protocol with its retransmission overload, it may also act as an incentive for self-restraint on the more effusive participants).

The specificities of restorative dialogue as a space for storytelling (Kremmel and Pelikan, 2015, p. 35; Nikolić-Ristanović, Ćopić and Srna, 2015, p. 17), are amplified by the deliberate choice of participatory film-making as an action research method throughout the project. The combination of storytelling and a certain formalization of communication creates a performative atmosphere that echoes the dramatic character of the criminal trial in court, but with the key difference that the circle is egalitarian, participation is active and free, there is no coercion and so on.

ALTERNATIVE researchers in Serbia leveraged existing findings based on the 'Third way' model, 'a non-conflict, inclusive, two-way communication of people with different experiences of war and other conflicts about the past, which implicates dealing with all crimes, victims and perpetrators regardless of their ethnic or other belonging, affiliation or personal features' (Nikolić-Ristanović, Ćopić and Srna, 2015, p. 7). Participants in the workshops organized in three localities in Serbia reacted positively to this kind of restorative dialogue, as a communication framework that can contribute towards handling of conflicts between people in their local communities.

These results, similar to others from the various research sites in which participants 'sharpen senses and acknowledge interconnectedness', highlight the link between restoration of communication and restoration of trust. Or, from another conceptual angle, when communication is restored in this or similar ways, the counteracting effect on 'othering' could be seen as a potential for the production of raw 'bridging' social capital.

It all sounds very good and promising, but there's a catch. The communication – in the sense of techniques, processes and tools – that RJCIS wants to restore should be a communication that participants *can understand* and be reasonably comfortable with. In fact, it should be a 'restoration', not an implant that is not recognized, a 'communication that cannot communicate' because external to the (localized) social system.

Conclusion: restoring cooperative action for justice

Combining the main findings from field work on the essentially contested, intersubjective and performative character of justice and security (see the sections on 'Justice' and 'Security (safety)' above respectively) with a radical understanding of participation in terms of decision-making powers and ownership of resources by the participants (see the section 'Active Participation' above) the ALTERNATIVE project proposes a new approach for research and practice of restorative justice to conflicts in intercultural settings.

In the absence of, or limited role for a central authority, the provision of justice and security in conflict situations are public goods problems that require cooperative solutions. These are articulated in three phases or interlinked dimensions: restoration of communication, restoration of trust, restoration of cooperative action for justice. RJ methods and practices have proved themselves apt at restoring respectful, non-violent communication in almost all conflict situations explored during field research. Besides, restorative justice methods in general, as experienced during ALTERNATIVE's action research in particular, have a significant *pistipoïetic* potential in generating, producing and reproducing localized 'bridging' trust (intergroup). This can be instrumental for the small-scale cooperation involved in certain methods or techniques. There are already some theoretical proposals that identify the breach of trust as the fundamental harm implied by crime and seek to redefine the goal of justice in terms of 'restoration of trust' (London, 2003, 2011). However, the new approach has to focus also on generalized trust and its determinants.

Social class cleavages are the second most relevant dimension – after ethnic diversity – in the definition of the intercultural setting in all sites, just as issues of socio-economic inequality are substantially present in the definitions of the types of conflict studied in the cases. The combination of socio-economic and ethnic inequalities are the strongest social determinants of low generalized trust: this finding is perhaps the single most significant one in the literature on social capital (Alesina and La Ferrara, 2002; Uslaner, 2003; Putnam, 2007; Gesthuizen, Van Der Meer and Scheepers, 2009; Portes and Vickstrom, 2011). We can therefore sketch a tripartite field of tensions between various behavioural outcomes in intercultural contexts. First, *destructive* open conflict, bad race relations, hostility. Second, *isolation*, 'hunkering down', withdrawal from collective life along with the securitization of social conflict in general (from petty criminality to migrations). Third, *cooperation*, where higher levels of socio-economic equality, and hence of trust, allow to address conflicts. Considering the central importance of trust building – at least localized trust among the participants – in restorative practices this poses a big question mark on the possibility of developing meaningful restorative methods in such contexts. Therefore, especially when dealing with conflicts in intercultural settings, restorative justice should strengthen its unique approach to justice as disjointed from penal punishment. But if restorative justice really wants to redefine the goal of justice in terms of 'restoration of trust' it should focus especially on redistributive justice as the deep equalizing factor, beyond ripples of cultural diversity. Far from expecting that at some point a perfected institutional arrangement could be found thus 'resolving' most conflicts, restorative justice embraces conflicts as the locus where, through restoration of communication, people learn to trust each other so that they may engage in a cooperative action for justice.

Appendix A: annexes to Chapter 8

A.1 cases

A brief description of the cases that are referred to throughout the chapter, whose details can be found in the project documents.

Cases in Vienna's **Gemeindebau,** *Austria*

Mediation G–M – Observation of the mediation session between two neighbours living one upstairs of the other in one of the housing estates, about issues of noise.

Mediation S–O – Observation of the mediation session between two neighbours living one upstairs of the other in one of the housing estates, about issues of noise.

Mediation K–G – Observation of the mediation session between two neighbours living one upstairs of the other in one of the housing estates, about issues of noise.

Graffiti – An 'Anti-Islamic' graffiti is found on the wall of one of the social housing estates and it triggers some anxiety and uneasiness. A circle is organized to reflect on it.

Frauencafé workshop – Communication capacity-building workshop at the Women's Café, a meeting place for women in one of the housing estates.

Frauencafé circle – Attempted circle at the Women's Café trying to address the issue of a group of 'Turkish' women who left the room during a lecture on Christmas traditions organized by other community workers.

Bassena workshop – Communication workshop at one of the social housing estates focusing on Anna's story and the difficulties of an elderly woman dealing with groups of lively children playing loudly on her doorstep.

Film-making – Participatory film-making with the teenagers of one of the housing estates. The adolescents referred to themselves as foreigners, although they had been born in Austria. They talked of the stigmatization of their housing estate due to class and ethnic issues. The adult they interview speaks of the problems dealing with youth in the estate.

Bassena circle – A restorative circle about issues of noise and misbehaviour in the housing estate. One of the participants referred to a 'real' situation of noise in the neighbourhood that affected her and 'played' herself, while the others' roles (children and their parents) were played by other participants and not by the actual parties involved in the case.

Cases in Kisváros, Hungary

Butcher's festival – Several sessions of the Municipal council discussing the organization of and participation in the traditional Butcher's festival, trying to address the complaints of the Roma inhabitants who maintained that in the previous edition they could not afford the entrance ticket and felt excluded.

Charity provision – Conflict around the distribution of aid packages by the Red Cross where a Roma woman questions the eligibility criteria of potential recipients.

Civic Guard – Discussions around the 'Civic Guard' (volunteer night watch patrols) and failed attempt to establish a new one open to the Roma minority.

Roma conflicts – Conflicts within the Roma community where an unemployed woman (who once held some governmental position though) accuses the incumbent leader of the Roma minority self-government of favouring only certain families (related to him) in the distribution of the resources he has access to through his public office.

The school – In the local school some Roma children are accused of theft by teachers and principal. Their parents complain that they have been singled out unfairly and mistreated and in turn accuse the teachers of racism. An attempted circle trying to address this conflict does not take off despite preparatory interviews.

Healing circle – Psychological support, post-electoral debriefing and restoring morale with the former mayor after his defeat in the local elections.

Cases in Bačka Palanka, Prijepolje and Medvedja, Serbia

Workshop BP1 communication – Seminar in Bačka Palanka, Workshop 1 on communication about conflicts, victimization and security: small groups discussion on the empirical research findings on victimization, gender and ethnicity.

Workshop BP1 security – Seminar in Bačka Palanka, Workshop 1 on communication about conflicts, victimization and security: small groups discussion on survey findings about feeling of safety, similarities and differences.

Workshop BP3 RJ – Seminar in Bačka Palanka, Workshop 3 on restorative justice and conflict resolution: testing restorative circle model.

Workshop M1 communication – Seminar in Medvedja, Workshop 1 on communication about conflicts, victimization and security: small groups discussion on the empirical research findings on victimization, gender and ethnicity.

Workshop M1 security – Seminar in Medvedja, Workshop 1 on communication about conflicts, victimization and security: small groups discussion on survey findings about feeling of safety, similarities and differences.

Workshop M3 RJ – Seminar in Medvedja, Workshop 3 on restorative justice and conflict resolution: testing restorative circle model.

Workshop P1 communication – Seminar in Prijepolje, Workshop 1 on communication about conflicts, victimization and security: small groups discussion on the empirical research findings on victimization, gender and ethnicity.

Workshop P1 security – Seminar in Prijepolje, Workshop 1 on communication about conflicts, victimization and security: small groups discussion on survey findings about feeling of safety, similarities and differences.

Workshop P3 RJ – Seminar in Prijepolje, Workshop 3 on restorative justice and conflict resolution: testing restorative circle model.

Cases in Belfast, Northern Ireland

Polish family – Two neighbours in dispute in South Belfast in July (parade season); one is a local resident and the other is a Polish family. The Polish family complained about rubbish falling into their garden and some flags falling over the fence. The local woman complained that they were not respecting her flag and her culture. The house and car of the Polish family had been damaged maliciously and another house in the street occupied by a foreign family had been attacked. Having listened to both sides of the story an RJ practitioner organized a conference inviting a wide set of stakeholders.

SH housing – Tensions and procedures around the announced construction of 100 new apartments of social housing in Seymour Hill (South Belfast). The conflict has several dimensions: local working-class protestant-unionist-loyalist (PUL) residents feel entitled to the new social housing after many years of neglect but fear that they might be assigned to families from other neighbourhoods thus altering the composition of the community. The housing agency, developers and local politicians do a poor job of informing the residents.

Dunmurry – Anti-social behaviour and generational conflict in Dunmurry (South Belfast). Committee meeting of the Greater Dunmurry Positive Relations Partnership (GDPRP) to discuss issues affecting the local Dunmurry village which is considered a frontier as it lies equidistant between Loyalist and nationalist areas.

Musgrave Park – Conflict between young people and the local residents in South Belfast resulting from anti-social behaviour of young people who are gathering in local parks on weekends.

A.2 conditions

A brief description of the categorical properties that characterize the cases studies in the field research.

Intercultural context. What are the prevailing dimensions that define the intercultural context in the case at hand? Not the conflict in itself but its context. Not the context of the action research on the site in general, but its more specific facets that emerge and are relevant in the case. Assessment: based on how the intercultural dimension is identified and analysed in the grids' combination of emic and etic conceptual understandings. Some dimensions, possibly overlapping: Age; Ethnicity; Gender; Historical memory; Migration (international); Migration (domestic); Profession; Race; Religion; Social class; etc.

Conflict type. What kind of conflict is it? Some types of conflict, taken from the empirical evidence from ALTERNATIVE, possibly overlapping, are: Anti-social behaviour; Armed; Communal; Criminal activity (prejudice included); Discrimination (institutional); Economic (misdistribution); Ethnic; Gender based; Generational; Identity (mis-recognition); IHL violations; Interpersonal; Neighbourhood; Old-time residents vs Newcomers; Police or public security involved; Political–politicization; Public vs Private space; Racially motivated; Religious; etc.

A further feature that that the researchers assessed is *how relevant* is the intercultural context, characterized as above, in the specific conflict at hand in each case? This assessment takes into account the views expressed by the participants and is based on how the intercultural context of the conflict is identified and analysed in the grids as a combination of emic and etic understandings: highly relevant (5); somehow relevant (4); barely relevant (2); not relevant (1).

Moral framing of the conflict issue. How participants, or at least some of them acting as initiators or referrers of the case, present the conflict issue on an ideal scale of moral framing, from highest (*crime* or criminal wrongdoing) to intermediate (*wrongdoing*) to low (*misbehaviour*) or even to the absence of a moral dimension at all (assuming that this is actually possible) in cases of 'simple' conflict of *interests* between two or more parties.

Harm claims. Even if the existence of some kind of harm could be considered a defining feature of the conflict, it is important to register whether and how the participants talk about harm, if at all. The underlying hypothesis here would be that if there isn't an explicit 'harm claim', a restorative justice intervention aiming at the reparation of harm would found itself on a precarious ground.

Justice claims. This is about the discursive framing of the conflict in terms of a 'question of justice' and is linked to the moral framing of the issue. It is also an operationalization of the participants' ideas and understanding of justice that emerge from the case through the grids.

The underlying hypothesis here would be to probe whether there is a 'justice continuum' (in both framing and formalization, see below) and whether it is independent from the 'practice formalization' *à la* Wachtel and McCold (2004) in order to assess if there can be such a thing as a 'restorative practice' without a 'justice' dimension.

The assessment of this condition ranges from low, when participants *do not* talk about the issue in terms of justice/injustice and rather frame it in an interest-based, pragmatic way; to *high*, when participants strongly frame the issue in terms of justice/injustice: 'It is a question of justice!', 'It's not fair!', etc. And, as usual, the intermediate low and intermediate high values according to the double dichotomy assessment.

Practice type. In the case abstraction defined above for this methodology, we consider all research practices as action research, although at different levels of activity. Those practices that are more closely linked with standard – non-explicitly active – social science research methodology, like interviews, focus groups etc. will cluster towards the lower half of the activity scale, while practices explicitly aimed at dealing with situations arising from the cases will score higher. The type of practice is implicitly, the level of activity or 'intervention intensity' in action research.

Practice formalization. According to the restorative practices approach there is a continuum of practices from informal to formal. We look at the practice in itself, regardless of its specific content in terms of 'justice' or 'moral claims'.

Note that according to this definition the practice's type and its level of formalization are not fully independent variables. Some types of practice have a more restricted range of formalization: conferences will vary between intermediate to highly formal; interviews will swing in the lower half of formalization values.

Researchers' involvement in the action. The role of the researchers in the practices reported in the grids varies a great deal and with this condition we try to capture it. In a way it is the assessment of the level of *participation* of the researchers themselves in the case and related practice looking at decision making and resources invested. In fact, with this single condition we are trying to map three distinct levels of involvement: initiative (who makes the first move towards the action), planning and actual implementation. In order to limit the space of combinations to those that arguably are more empirically relevant, these conditions are amalgamated in codified levels of participation.

Participation. Does the standard RJ categorization and related discursive framing identifying clear roles for those affected by conflict or crime as victims, offenders and community members apply to the case? If so, which of the main stakeholders' groups (VOC) did actually participate?

Even if the VOC model does not apply to the case, for example because the participants do not identify themselves as victims or perpetrators, it is important to assess if participation was *complete*, that is whether all relevant stakeholders were included or, conversely, whether no important stakeholder was left out of the process, based on the stakeholder analysis identifying interests, power distribution, etc.

Admittedly, this operationalization and formalization of participation is still anchored to the standard restorativeness criterion of stakeholders groups presence (VOC). It does not reflect key ownership variables whose importance have been outlined during the last year of the project. We will take into account this limitation when analysing the data about active participation.

Refusal. With these dichotomous conditions we map those cases where there is a substantial mismatch between planning and implementation of an action. In particular, there is a 'refusal' condition in a case when as a consequence of an explicit or implicit denial by some key stakeholders to participate, the organizers of the practice have to change its *type*, namely from a higher intensity of intervention (e.g. a circle or assembly) to a lower one.

Public stakeholders. The participation of public stakeholders – public institutions at all levels of government, elected or appointed – is considered relevant to test various hypotheses on the relationship between RJ processes and governance models and is therefore included as a dichotomous condition on its own. In particular, because of its influence on the formalization of justice and relevance to the kind of 'lifeworld' approach to justice that is specific to RJ (Pelikan, 2003), it is important to map whether representatives of the police or other law enforcement agencies have been involved in the process.

Security scope. The researchers in ALTERNATIVE have discussed the concept of security at some length and have eventually settled on considering mainly security as personal safety. But how do participants understand security first and foremost? Three possible options, from a narrow personal scope to a wider, societal one:

> *Personal safety*: physical safety of self and close family and related property.
>
> *Socio-economic*: an understanding of security that starts from the personal level but includes also the economic/financial dimensions (e.g. job security) and the safety net of public assistance and social security.
>
> *Collective identity*: the main referent object of security is collective identities (e.g. 'our culture', 'our religion', 'our nation', 'our welfare state', etc.) that are perceived as threatened.

Security intensity. Regardless of the prevailing understanding of security in the case (security scope, see above), how relevant is the 'security' dimension for the case, how important is the 'security' signifier for the participants?

A.3 dataset

Based on the case formalization outlined earlier and the data validated by the researchers, the fuzzy-set Qualitative Comparative Analysis was carried out on the dataset illustrated in Table 8.A.1.

Table 8.A.1 QCA dataset

Case	*Conditions*										
	JC	*PF*	*HC*	*SI*	*II*	*PUB*	*RI*	*MF*	*SS*	*VOC*	*P*
WP4-c01 Mediation G–M	2	4	4	1	4	5	1	2	1	5	1
WP4-c02 Graffiti	2	4	4	2	5	1	4	4	5	1	1
WP4-c03 Frauencafé ws	1	5	2	2	2	5	5	2	3	1	1
WP4-c04 Frauencafé circle	1	4	4	1	5	5	4	2	1	1	1
WP4-c05 Bassena ws	1	4	1	1	2	1	5	2	1	1	1
WP4-c06 Film-making	2	1	1	2	1	1	5	2	3	1	1
WP4-c07 Bassena circle	1	4	4	1	5	1	5	2	1	1	1
WP4-c08 Mediation S–O	2	4	4	1	4	5	1	2	1	5	5
WP4-c09 Mediation K–G	2	4	4	1	4	5	1	2	1	5	5
WP5-c01 Butcher's festival	5	4	4	2	5	5	2	4	3	5	1
WP5-c02 Charity provision	4	5	4	2	5	5	5	4	3	5	1
WP5-c03 Civic Guard	1	1	1	5	1	5	5	2	1	1	1
WP5-c04 Roma conflicts	4	2	2	1	1	1	5	2	1	1	1
WP5-c05 The school	2	4	4	1	1	5	4	4	3	5	1
WP5-c06 Healing circle	5	1	4	4	5	5	4	1	3	5	1
WP6-c01 Wshop BP1 comm.	1	5	4	1	2	5	5	4	3	1	5
WP6-c02 Wshop BP1 sec	1	5	4	5	2	5	5	4	3	1	5
WP6-c03 Wshop BP3 RJ	5	5	5	4	2	5	5	4	1	5	5
WP6-c04 Wshop M1 comm.	1	5	5	2	2	5	5	4	1	1	5
WP6-c05 Wshop M1 sec	5	5	1	5	2	5	5	4	3	1	5
WP6-c06 Wshop M3 RJ	5	5	4	4	2	5	5	4	1	5	5
WP6-c07 Wshop P1 comm.	1	5	4	2	2	5	5	4	1	1	5
WP6-c08 Wshop P1 sec	5	5	4	5	2	5	5	4	3	1	5
WP6-c09 Wshop P3 RJ	5	5	5	4	2	5	5	4	1	5	5
WP7-c01 Polish family	4	4	5	4	5	5	2	4	5	5	5
WP7-c02 SH housing	4	5	5	4	5	5	2	4	5	1	5
WP7-c03 Dunmurry	2	4	4	4	5	5	1	2	1	1	5
WP7-c04 Musgrave Park	2	2	4	4	1	5	5	2	1	1	5

Notes

Key	Condition.
MF	Moral framing.
HC	Harm claims.
JC	Justice claims.
PF	Practice formalization.
II	Intervention intensity.
RI	Researchers involvement.
SS	Security scope.
SI	Security intensity.
PUB	Public stakeholders participating.
P	Police officers participating.
VOC	Victims, Offenders, Community participation model.

Notes

1 Details about R on the project's website www.r-project.org. For further details about QCA please refer to the section 'Comparing empirical findings'. The R script developed by the author is reproduced in Ragazzi (2015b, annex A).

2 RJ manuals often include also the apology as a desirable outcome, however, a preliminary study of the project documents drafted by the different action research sites showed that the notion of apology figured significantly only in the conceptual framework and field work conducted in Serbia, while it was hardly mentioned elsewhere. Considering that the action research in Serbia itself did not deploy restorative practices on actual cases, this specific outcome has been omitted from the case formalization.

3 An 'Anti-Islamic' graffiti was found on the wall of a social housing estate in Vienna and it triggered some anxiety and uneasiness. A circle was organized to reflect on it (case WP4-c02).

4 The element of 'resentment' and 'envy' in justice, as the dark side of the emotion of 'anger' or 'moral indignation' (for example in Talcott Parsons), triggers mobilization. While Žižek makes the sweeping statement that 'Lacan shares with Nietzsche and Freud the idea that justice as equality is founded on envy: our envy of the other who has what we do not have, and who enjoys it' (Žižek, 2006, p. 37), according to Sloterdijk one has to distinguish 'anger' from 'resentment', '*gamme d'émotions qui appartiennent au régime du thymos, c'est-à-dire au régime de la fierté. [...] la fierté de soi*' (Truong, Sloterdijk and Žižek, 2011). Hence, with self-pride, self-esteem and self-respect as inter-subjectively constructed and developed we go back to 'recognition' as a struggle (Honneth, 1995).

5 In the case of the 'Civic Guard' in Kisváros a background of burglaries in town is the main reason for the existence of a voluntary night watch, but the issue that sparked the case was not crime itself, but the de facto exclusion of Roma inhabitants from the Civic Guard (on suspicions that they would be associated with the burglaries) and the ultimately failed attempt of the leader of the Roma minority self-government to establish a new Civic Guard. In the cases of anti-social behaviour by youth in South Belfast ('Dunmurry' and 'Musgrave Park') this involved also some minor criminal offences (damages to public property).

6 'Security does not allow it!' – personal observation from fieldwork in Afghanistan.

References

Alesina, A. and La Ferrara, E. 2002. Who trusts others? *Journal of public economics*, 85(2), 207–34. Available at: www.sciencedirect.com/science/article/pii/S0047272701000846 [accessed 5 August 2015].

Benedek, G., Héra, G., Kelemen, K., Győrfi, É., Balla, L., and Szegő, D. 2014. *Community problem analysis: building the bridges of trust with and within the communities* (No. D5.2, January). The ALTERNATIVE project. Budapest.

Benedek, G., Héra, G., Kelemen, K., Győrfi, É., Balla, L., and Szegő, D. 2015. *Implementation report on the application of restorative justice in the community: grasping action and research* (No. D5.3, September). The ALTERNATIVE project. Budapest.

Bolivar Fernández, D., Pelikan, C. and Lemonne, A. 2015. Comparison of the main results: variations and similarities. In: I. Vanfraechem, D. Bolivar Fernández and I. Aertsen, eds. *Victims and restorative justice*. London: Routledge, pp. 172–200.

Buzan, B., Wæver, Ø. and de Wilde, J. 1998. *Security: a new framework for analysis*. Boulder, CO: Lynne Rienner Publishers.

Cerf, V., Dalal, Y. and Sunshine, C. 1974. *Specification of internet transmission control program* (No. RFC0675, December). The Internet Engineering Task Force, Network

Working Group. Fremont, California. Available at: www.ietf.org/rfc/rfc0675.txt [accessed 18 March 2017].

Chapman, T., Campbell, H., McCord, J. and McCready, P. 2013. *A baseline research report into issues and needs in three sites where the community is experiencing conflict* (No. D7.4, July). The ALTERNATIVE project. Belfast. Available at: www.alternative-project.eu/publications/public-deliverables/ [accessed 15 March 2017].

Chapman, T., Wilson, D. and Campbell, H. 2013. *Report on the contribution of RJ to peace building* (No. D7.2, February). The ALTERNATIVE project. Belfast. Available at: www.alternativeproject.eu/publications/public-deliverables/ [accessed 15 March 2017].

Chapman, T., Wilson, D. and Campbell, H. 2014. *Crossing frontiers: community-based restorative justice practices manual* (No. D7.5, February). The ALTERNATIVE project. Belfast. Available at: www.alternativeproject.eu/publications/public-deliverables/ [accessed 15 March 2017].

Denk, T. 2010. Comparative multilevel analysis: proposal for a methodology. *International Journal of Social Research Methodology*, 13(1), 29–39. doi:10.1080/13645570802583779.

Denk, T. and Lehtinen, S. 2013. Contextual analyses with QCA-methods. *Quality & Quantity*, 48(6), 3475–3487. doi:10.1007/s11135-013-9968-4.

Duşa, A. and Thiem, A. 2014. Qualitative comparative analysis: R package (Version 1.1–4). Available at: http://cran.r-project.org/package=QCA [accessed 19 June 2015].

Esposito, R. 1998. *Communitas*. Torino: Einaudi.

Esposito, R. 2002. *Immunitas. protezione e negazione della vita*. Torino: Einaudi.

Fehr, E. and Schmidt, K.M. 1999. A theory of fairness, competition, and cooperation. *Quarterly Journal of Economics*, 114(3), 817–868. doi:10.1162/003355399556151.

Gesthuizen, M., Van Der Meer, T. and Scheepers, P. 2009. Ethnic diversity and social capital in Europe: tests of Putnam's thesis in European countries. *Scandinavian Political Studies*, 32(2), 121–142. doi:10.1111/j.1467-9477.2008.00217.x.

Gürerk, Ö., Irlenbusch, B. and Rockenbach, B. 2006. The competitive advantage of sanctioning institutions. *Science*, 312(5770), 108–111. doi:10.1126/science.1123633.

Honneth, A. 1995. *The struggle for recognition: the moral grammar of social conflicts*. Trans. J. Anderson. Cambridge: Polity Press.

Hooghe, M., Reeskens, T., Stolle, D. and Trappers, A. 2009. Ethnic diversity and generalized trust in Europe a cross-national multilevel study. *Comparative Political Studies*, 42(2), 198–223. doi:10.1177/0010414008325286.

Kremmel, K. and Pelikan, C. 2015. *Towards restorative circles: action research interventions in Vienna's social housing estates* (No. D4.4, July). The ALTERNATIVE project. Vienna.

London, R. 2003. The restoration of trust: bringing restorative justice from the margins to the mainstream. *Criminal Justice Studies*, 16(3), 175–195. doi:10.1080/0888431032000151844.

London, R. 2011. *Crime, punishment, and restorative justice: from the margins to the mainstream*. Boulder, CO: Lynne Rienner Publishers.

Marx, A., Rihoux, B. and Ragin, C. 2014. The origins, development, and application of Qualitative Comparative Analysis: the first 25 years. *European Political Science Review*, 6(1), 115–142. doi:10.1017/S1755773912000318.

Nikolić-Ristanović, V., Ćopić, S., Petrović, N. and Šaćiri, B. 2014. *Conflicts, security and justice in intercultural context of Serbia* (No. D6.2, January). The ALTERNATIVE project. Belgrade. Available at: www.alternativeproject.eu/publications/public-deliverables/ [accessed 15 March 2017].

Nikolić-Ristanović, V., Ćopić, S. and Srna, J. 2015. *Action research report on the applicability of restorative justice in interethnic settings* (No. D6.3, September). The ALTERNATIVE project. Belgrade.

Ostrom, E., Walker, J. and Gardner, R. 1992. Covenants with and without a sword: self-governance is possible. *The American Political Science Review*, 86(2), 404–417. doi:10. 2307/1964229.

Pali, B. 2015. *Final research report on RJ and security* (No. D1.3, November). The ALTERNATIVE project. Leuven. Available at: www.alternativeproject.eu/publications/public-deliverables/ [accessed 15 March 2017].

Pavlich, G.C. 2004. Restorative justice's community: promise and peril. In: B. Toews and H. Zehr, eds. *Critical issues in restorative justice*. New York: Criminal Justice Press, pp. 173–190.

Pavlich, G.C. 2014. *Promising common justice.* Leuven (Belgium). Available at: www.esf.org/ [accessed 23 June 2016].

Pelikan, C. 2003. Different systems, different rationales: restorative justice and criminal justice. In: F. Moyano Marques, ed. *Project DIKÊ: protection and promotion of victim's rights in Europe*. Lisbon: APAV, pp. 223–227.

Pelikan, C. and Ragazzi, M. 2018. Critical reflections on active participation under new governance models. In: B. Pali and I. Aertsen, eds. *Restoring Justice and Security in Intercultural Europe*. London: Routledge, pp. 164–181.

Ponterotto, J. 2006. Brief note on the origins, evolution, and meaning of the qualitative research concept thick description. *The Qualitative Report*, 11(3), 538–549. Available at: http://nsuworks.nova.edu/tqr/vol. 11/iss3/6 [accessed 15 March 2017].

Portes, A. and Vickstrom, E. 2011. Diversity, social capital, and cohesion. *Annual Review of Sociology*, 37(1), 461–479. doi:10.1146/annurev-soc-081309-150022.

Putnam, R.D. 1995. Bowling alone: America's declining social capital. *Journal of Democracy*, 6(1), 65–78. doi:10.1353/jod.1995.0002.

Putnam, R.D. (2007). E pluribus unum: diversity and community in the twenty-first century. The 2006 Johan Skytte prize lecture. *Scandinavian political studies*, 30(2), 137–174. Available at: http://onlinelibrary.wiley.com/doi/10.1111/j.1467-9477.2007.00176.x/pdf [accessed 22 June 2015].

Ragazzi, M. 2015a. *Analysis of empirical developments in the action research sites* (No. D8.4, July). The ALTERNATIVE project. Leuven.

Ragazzi, M. 2015b. *Comparative analysis in the action research sites* (No. D8.5, November). The ALTERNATIVE project. Leuven. Available at: www.alternativeproject.eu/publications/public-deliverables/ [accessed 15 March 2017].

Ragin, C.C. 1987. *The comparative method: moving beyond qualitative and quantitative strategies.* Berkeley–Los Angeles–London: University of California Press.

Rihoux, B. and Ragin, C.C., eds. 2009. *Configurational comparative methods: Qualitative Comparative Analysis (QCA) and related techniques.* Los Angeles–London–New Delhi–Singapore: SAGE.

Schench, E.R. 1990. The development of comparative research. In: E. Øyen, ed. *Comparative methodology: theory and practice in international social research.* Studies in International Sociology. London: SAGE Publications, pp. 19–37.

Schneider, C.Q. and Wagemann, C. 2012. *Set-theoretic methods for the social sciences: a guide to Qualitative Comparative Analysis.* Cambridge: Cambridge University Press.

Sloterdijk, P. 2014. *You must change your life*. 1st edn. Cambridge: Polity.

Stolle, D. 2003. The sources of social capital. In M. Hooghe and D. Stolle, eds. *Generating social capital: civil society and institutions in comparative perspective*. New York and Basingstoke: Palgrave Macmillan, pp. 19–42.

Thiem, A. 2014. Analyzing multilevel data with QCA: yet another straightforward procedure. *Quality & Quantity*, 5 December. doi:10.1007/s11135-014-0140-6.

Thiem, A. and Duşa, A. 2013. *Qualitative Comparative Analysis with R.* SpringerBriefs in Political Science. New York: Springer New York. Available at: http://link. springer. com/10.1007/978-1-4614-4584-5 [accessed 21 May 2015].

Truong, N., Sloterdijk, P. and Žižek, S. 2011. Des idées-force pour éviter les impasses de la globalisation. 2 September. *Le Monde.fr.* Available at: www. lemonde.fr/idees/ article/2011/09/02/des-idees-force-pour-eviter-les-impasses-de-la-globalisation_1528141_3232.html [accessed 28 November 2014].

Uslaner, E.M. 2003. Trust, democracy and governance: can government policies influence generalized trust? In: M. Hooghe and D. Stolle, eds. *Generating social capital: civil society and institutions in comparative perspective*. New York and Basingstoke: Palgrave Macmillan, pp. 171–190.

Vanfraechem, I. 2013. *Comparative framework and data recording system* (No. D8.3, April). The ALTERNATIVE project. Leuven.

Wachtel, T. and McCold, P. 2004. From restorative justice to restorative practices: expanding the paradigm. In: *Building a global alliance for restorative practices and family empowerment, part 2.* 5th international conference on conferencing & circles. 5 August. Vancouver. Available at: www.iirp.edu/article_detail.php?article_id=Mzk5 [accessed 20 March 2015].

Žižek S., 2006. *How to read Lacan.* London: Granta.

Conclusion

Action research through restorative justice

Inge Vanfraechem and Ivo Aertsen

As spelled out in the Introduction and Chapter 1, the aim of this book was to offer and to discuss concrete examples of implementing action research in the criminological field in order to discern its potential and challenges, one of them being the intercultural context of the field of application. In this conclusion, we draw together some of the findings with regard to action research on the one hand and restorative justice on the other hand.

Conditions and challenges for action research

A comparative framework

Challenges were encountered both in the action fields in the four involved countries, as well as for the project as a whole. For ALTERNATIVE as a European project, a comparative research methodology had to be developed in order to integrate the data from the four different settings, dealing with conflicts on a micro-, meso- and macro-level. To this end, various methods were used, such as observations, interviews but also logbooks, evaluation grids and discussion on the local results both within the local team as well as with the Leuven team. From the start, it was clear that the intention was not to set up a similar research in the four settings, but rather to go with the local, societal ecology (see infra) and adapt the research to the changes on the field. This is exactly why the action research methodology was chosen.

The project partners met up twice a year in European steering committee meetings to discuss both the methodology and intermediary research results – these meetings proved to be not only fruitful, but necessary as well to develop ALTERNATIVE as one common project, rather than the different project partners working out their research on their own little island. For the Leuven team, responsible for the comparative research, these meetings provided the necessary input to get an insight in the different local realities, in order to come to a 'relativist' or 'interpretivist' (Pakes, 2004) view on the data. The advantage of this approach includes that the research is being carried out locally by 'natives' who can thus describe the situation as it 'really' (i.e. culturally defined) is, whereby these local experts should be reflexive about how they themselves are 'part of the context they are describing' (Nelken, 2010, p. 91). The comparative framework can then take the local habits and understandings into account to come to a realistic and holistic comparison.

Different steps in the project were outlined: theoretical conceptualization (through concept notes written by all partners); operationalization; application; feedback to theoretical concepts; and adaptation of theory where needed. For the operationalization and application, partners were asked to fully describe ('thick description', Geertz, 1973) the situation in all its aspects and be explicit about what is understood locally when referring to a certain concept, e.g. security or justice. An evaluation grid formed the basis to collect and analyse and thus apply the concepts (see Chapter 8, this volume). Through the local and cross-national discussions, the empirical data were linked to the concepts, adapting theory where needed (see infra).

Local action researches

As said, the local researches varied in their approach and methods used. In Austria, the researcher followed the practices as a kind of 'intern', while practitioners were involved in analysing practices. In Hungary, the research team included researchers as well as mediators, who each had their distinctive role. Local people were included in Local Support Groups as well as Local Learning Groups, both to learn about restorative justice and refer cases where appropriate, as well as to reflect with researchers on conditions and activities on the ground and to pave the way to further action by building trust among the local community. In Serbia, researchers worked together with local people to disseminate information on victim support if respondents needed it after participating in the research. In the seminars, a circle was tried out and a manual was co-created with local people. In Northern Ireland, the researchers set up activities with local organizations to reach out to the local community through group conferences and helped a local community-based organization to develop a strategy for further development.

Despite these different approaches, common themes came to the fore.

Community building for preparing the ground

When the project was set up, the aim was to implement restorative justice approaches such as mediation and circles in the various settings. This proved to be more complicated than expected: the settings differed in their extent to which the people on the ground were familiar with restorative justice. Ultimately, only the community-based organizations in Northern Ireland knew about and practised restorative justice. Since Ulster University has a long tradition of working in the field, the trust was in place before ALTERNATIVE started and the Ulster team set out to guide and follow up activities on the ground. In the other countries, researchers worked together with practitioners (as in Austria) or provided restorative justice approaches themselves, as in Hungary where they made a distinction between 'researchers' and 'dialoguers', or in Serbia where researchers organized a circle within the participatory seminars. To this end, researchers used the first year of the project to discover and describe the 'societal ecology' (Bolivar, Pelikan and Lemonne, 2015; APAV, 2016) of the field: what organizations and structures are available in the local community? Do restorative justice organizations exist to which cases can be referred? How can practitioners and researchers work together, e.g. through creating a Memorandum of Understanding? Aertsen in Chapter 1 referred to this as the 'preliminary phase' of the action research.

Next to the societal ecology, other questions were more related to the research: What is the baseline against which changes will be evaluated? What concepts underlie the research? All local research teams developed theoretical reports with regard to concepts central to ALTERNATIVE as a whole, but at the same time relevant to the local setting. These included concepts such as active participation, community and identity, restorative justice approaches, victimization and conflicts in intercultural settings. These concepts were then used in the evaluation grids in order to structure research findings (see Chapter 8, this volume and Ragazzi, 2015).

Throughout the project, it became clear that time was necessary to build relations with people on the ground and come to a common understanding of what was to be achieved. Community building and non-violent communication approaches were the broader practices to indeed lay a fertile ground in which restorative justice approaches could eventually be applied. At the same time, restorative principles provided an added value to existing community-building initiatives.

Local challenges changing the course of the action research

A typical element of action research is that the research needs to adapt continuously to changes in the field. In Austria for example, difficulties were encountered through a different understanding of what the women in the Women's Café needed: while the circle keeper had a (be it rather vague) plan in her head, wohnpartner thought the women needed more guidance throughout the circle. After some racist venting, the organization wanted to end the cooperation with the mediator and asked the researcher to step in. The researcher did not take over this role but kept reflecting with the practitioners on what the next step could be.

In Hungary, a Memorandum of Understanding was signed with the mayor in power at the beginning of the project. Towards the end, local elections were held and the new mayor proved to be rather sceptical about the whole research set-up. It was a challenge for the research team to keep the communication going, but through restorative thinking and particular practices including participatory filming, other views on the village came to the fore which enabled the researchers to include the differing opinions in their analysis.

In Serbia, the social and political context was still too sensitive to try out restorative justice approaches such as circles. Nevertheless, fictive cases were used to improvise and role-play a circle during the participatory seminars and the participants were receptive to it. Researchers concluded that circles could be tried out with real cases if there had been more time.

Time concerns were common: preparing the ground, getting local people involved and setting the scene for local people to trust restorative justice approaches generally took more time and resources than was expected, as was the case for the filming.

Using participatory filming

As was explained in Chapters 2 and 3, ALTERNATIVE set out to use participatory filming throughout the action researches. The idea was that the researchers would get an initial training so they would be able to use the camera and film the local settings, together with the local people. Although the initial filming training went well, technical skills were to be acquired and this required more time and energy from the researchers than expected. Again, different solutions were found.

In Austria, a movie was made together with the young people of the neighbourhood so they could portray their own view on the social housing estates. Projecting these movies offered a nice point of departure for a discussion with all inhabitants. With the Turkish women, the camera proved to be a handy tool to communicate when language barriers existed. In Hungary, a professional film-maker volunteered to help make the movies, which not only increased the quality of the footage, but also enabled the researchers to make contacts with local Roma because of the film-maker's own background.

For the whole ALTERNATIVE project, a final movie was conceptualized as integrating all the local footages into one movie. Although common screenplays were thought out, the local footages were too different and again language was an issue to be overcome. Therefore, the decision was made in the end to interview the partners on their opinion of the different concepts and findings.[1]

Being involved yet remaining distant

As was explicated in Chapters 1 and 4, a challenge within action research lies with the researcher's role of being involved in setting up the action and at the same time remaining distant enough to be able to evaluate the practices. In ALTERNATIVE, this was done through the common work in the project's steering committee, through which concepts were worked out and operationalized. The evaluation grids offered room to describe local findings in details but at the same time linking them back to concepts. Observations and interviews were used in order to gather as many data as possible.

In Hungary, researchers were challenged to think about their own position with the new mayor coming in: through signing a Memorandum of Understanding with the previous mayor, the researchers were labelled as 'leftist', while they tried to involve different voices in the field. In Austria, the researcher was asked to step into the role of mediator, while this was clearly not her role from the start. Nevertheless, by just being in the field, one raises expectations about what can be achieved. In Northern Ireland for example, the university was asked to organize the community conferences since this would offer a more neutral invitation. The ALTERNATIVE research shows it is important to communicate clearly about what can and cannot be achieved in the framework of the research, which is always limited in time and resources. This brings us to the last challenge, namely that of leaving the field, which Aertsen in Chapter 1 has referred to as 'the concluding phase'.

Leaving the field

All partners had 'trouble' leaving the field, or on a more positive note: they did not really leave the field, but had to a more or lesser extent some ongoing contacts with the field after ALTERNATIVE had officially ended. For some this meant giving advice, for others it meant showing the movies to the local community. When the researchers have spent some two to three years in the field, they have a specific role and, especially when it comes to conflicts, one can pose the question to what extent the researcher can really leave the field if issues remain unsolved? On the one hand, this needs to be clearly communicated from the beginning. On the other hand, some researchers stay in contact with the field or even take up an active and more permanent role, as is for example the case in Belgium where we, after having been involved in the action researches in the 1990s (see Chapter 1), are still active as chair of a local steering committee on restorative justice programmes, or as policy advisor. In ALTERNATIVE, VDS has shown interest in further developing restorative justice as part of their 'Third way', in Northern Ireland the university has a long-lasting relation with local community organizations and continues to offer training in restorative practices.

Lessons for restorative justice

Restorative justice approaches

From the start of the project, we opted for the term 'restorative justice approaches' to point out that we were dealing with social conflicts rather than criminal acts. Therefore, although classical definitions such as Marshall's (1999) and Walgrave's (2008) were considered (see Introduction, this volume), we did not want to enter the debate on a 'purist' or 'maximalist' approach to restorative justice (see the Symposium on Restorative Justice, Community, Justice, and Transformative Justice in the special issue of *Contemporary Justice Review*, 7(1), 2004). We also decided not to abolish the notion of 'justice' in restorative justice, since we expected to find also 'justice' elements even in the most informal practices. We then incorporated the core elements of restorative justice as defined by Pelikan (2003, 2007) and thus see the idea of restorative justice as being an internally complex and open concept that continues to develop (Johnstone and Van Ness, 2007). The important question to ask is then 'not what is and what is not restorative justice, but what is restorative justice *about*?' (Pali, 2015, p. 21). Pelikan (2003, 2007) identifies three core elements of restorative justice as lifeworld, participation and reparation. Pali (2015) to these adds the element of transformation.

Lifeworld

As Pali (2015, p. 23) explains:

> The notion lifeworld (Lebenswelt) has been coined by Husserl and it mainly refers to the every-day world of practical, lived experience. Currently an integral part of Habermas' theory of 'communicative action', the sphere of the lifeworld is 'the intuitively present, in the sense of familiar and transparent, and at the same time vast and incalculable web of presuppositions' (Habermas 1987, 131) and 'the background consensus of our everyday lives, the vast stock of taken-for-granted definitions and understandings of the world that give coherence and direction to our lives' (Habermas 1987, 133).

Rather than sticking to the legal definitions of crime in the criminal justice system, restorative justice aims to get to the 'real' stories of the people involved, their 'thick' stories rather than the thin story the justice system tends to create. Restorative justice puts a crime in its relational and social context and therefore in a certain sense[2] gives room to increasing the complexity of the phenomenon, rather than decreasing it as necessarily happens in a criminal justice procedure. Through the communication process, people are enabled to relate their personal stories and – when experiencing deep respect for their own lives – to come to listening and an understanding of one another's story (see also Chapter 7, this volume). As Pali (2015, p. 24) formulates it: 'restorative justice proposes to recognize the wrongdoer and the wronged both in their individuality and in their social context rather than subsuming crime in a general, abstract and reductionist legal category'. Furthermore, restorative justice enables a discussion on what crime is (not), rather than the fixed definition which the criminal justice system adheres to. In that sense, restorative justice can encompass a broader form of justice, more related to relational and social justice (see infra).

Participation

Since the lifeworld is an important element, participation of the people involved in the aftermath of crime or conflict becomes central to restorative justice process (Christie, 1977; Zehr, 1990). Activating people may help to build a grass-root democracy: 'disputing over daily injustices is where we learn to become democratic citizens', Braithwaite says (1999, p. 78). At the same time, we have to take care that people are given the tools to be able to actively participate, rather than being excluded – a risk that has prevailed for example in conferencing practices where youngsters with a more difficult background tended to be excluded by judges (Vanfraechem, 2007).

Reparation

Reparation of the harm done is the aim, rather than inflicting pain on the wrongdoer (Walgrave, 2008). What this reparation may entail, forms part of the discussion taking place in the communication process. In broader terms, restoration after the harm has done becomes crucial; Ragazzi (2015) sees three elements to be core when it comes to restorative justice for conflicts in intercultural settings (RJCIS), where restorative justice is stretched beyond criminal acts towards conflicts, but still related to matters of justice (as opposed to the even still broader concept of restorative practices, McCold and Wachtel, 2002): restoration of communication, restoration of trust and restoration of cooperative action for justice. In this conception, reparation does not offer a black and white picture, or an all-or-nothing story, but much more a dynamic process. This resonates with the different levels of 'relational restoration' that can be distinguished at the 'purpose level' of restorative justice practices as applied in cases of (collective) violent conflict: from 'redress' (e.g. material reparation) over 'working through the past' (e.g. mutual listening) to 'coexistence' (e.g. mutual empathy) and 'reconciliation' (e.g. mutual forgiveness) (Rohne, Arsovska and Aertsen, 2008, pp. 21–30). In these understandings, the concept of justice is then mainly related to social matters rather than criminal justice in the strict sense.

Transformation and social justice

Pali (2015, p. 33) points out that restorative justice 'must lead to the transformation of the elements within the social situation rather than simply a restoration to the status quo (…)', thus moving towards a more dynamic understanding of reparation. As the ALTERNATIVE project has shown, matters of social justice came to the fore within communication processes, where justice was portrayed as matter of social (in)equality, job security, education, health, etc. Restorative justice can in that sense start to address or at least bring to the fore structural dimensions of criminal conflict, rather than adhering to the individualized approach as taken by the criminal justice system (Pali, 2015; Ragazzi, 2015).

> Llewellyn and Howse (1999, 41) argue that restoration cannot be simply about rectifying a wrong by restoring the *status quo*, but rather about restoring the relationships between the parties involved to an ideal state of social equality, which implies in their opinion the orientation of restorative justice toward restoring the future and not just the past.
>
> (Pali, 2015, p. 35)

Culture of silence

A last element which came to the fore, especially in the Hungarian case, but in Serbia as well is the so-called 'culture of silence': in the Hungarian town, conflicts were silenced and not openly addressed, at least not between groups. Conflicts were talked about within one group, but it proved to be very hard to open the communication towards 'the other'. In Serbia, conflicts were not openly labelled as 'ethnic' in order to avoid new instances of violence. Since communication is so central to restorative justice, this raises interesting questions for both researchers and facilitators: to what extent can you address conflicts you have heard about which people are not ready to discuss? Should one push the participants to communicate in order to avoid future (bigger) problems? What mandate does one have to do so? Do we, as researchers and facilitators, have a moral duty to break the silence when we for example know social (in)justice matters lay at its foundation? Do we, in restorative justice programmes, have non-verbal ways of dealing with crime and conflict and to initiate communication through other types of social and cultural expression? Important questions that have, to our knowledge, not been addressed in action nor restorative justice research....

Similarities between action research and restorative justice

To end, we would like to point out some similarities between action research and restorative justice. A first theme relates to 'active participation'. As Aertsen explains in Chapter 1, active participation of both the researcher and subject is a prerequisite in action research. Both are involved in the process of change and have their own active input, since 'action research can be defined as a form of action'. A de-localization of the position of the researcher takes place: he is neither an external expert nor a group member, but becomes a kind of affiliated participant. Group members from their side become co-researchers, actively contributing to the process of research. This constellation is mirrored most consistently in the model of 'participatory action research', where members of the group play an important role throughout the consecutive phases of the process. They contribute to defining the initial problem and the research questions, drafting the research plan, implementing the research activities, collecting and interpreting data and reporting the results. Action research, then, becomes a common learning process. This process cannot be reduced to a number of evaluations at certain moments, but requires an ongoing alternation of analysis and action. This ideal-typical model of action research has inspired the ALTERNATIVE partners from the beginning of the project. The previous chapters show how this model has worked in various settings.

One of the similarities between action research and restorative justice lies in the important role of the 'facilitator' of the learning process. This is clear both from a research perspective and in restorative justice practices, where the participants with the help of a mediator or facilitator go through a learning process, defining and re-defining the problem, i.e. the offence or the injustice that happened, and finding possible solutions. Participants do so according to their own perceptions, and it is through a process of mutual exchange with the concerned stakeholders and in a kind of dialogical process with the legal system, that they finally arrive at a new understanding of 'justice'. Both action research and restorative justice endorse a basic attitude of (and a believe in) active and responsive citizenship. Active participation is a central and critical concept in restorative justice, where parties are given the chance to actively participate in the resolution of the harm caused by the crime, rather than professional actors taking over (Christie, 1977). Kremmel and Pelikan (2015, p. 66) point out that

> [t]he experience of togetherness rests on active participation as a core element of restorative justice. This participatory element, i.e. getting actively involved, culminating in the experience of togetherness makes security/safety emanate from the experience, the feeling of being held and supported, of being and ultimately 'doing' something together with others.

In Hungary, action researchers found that locals interpreted active participation and justice as two related phenomena (Szegő, Benedek and Győrfi, 2015): injustice was perceived in relation to the lack of participation in decision-making processes or the lack of gaining access to information, goods or services.

At a more practical level, ALTERNATIVE has shown us another similarity between action research and restorative justice, in particular related to the follow-up of the research on the one hand, and the action on the other. Follow-up is indeed equally a challenge for action research and restorative justice. We already discussed the challenge of leaving the field after an action research has ended: the importance of discussing beforehand how the project will be finalized is stressed, but also the need to take care of the people on the ground. We also discussed the issue of final evaluation, and whether this does not require a more distant position than what the action researcher and the involved practitioners can offer. In restorative justice approaches such as mediation and circles, a similar concern has been voiced: the coming together of the parties is (usually) a one-time event, in which often an agreement is reached in which the engagements of the parties are explicated. But such an engagement needs to be followed up in order to ensure that parties do as promised. At the same time, support is needed in order to be able to comply with their commitments. Moreover, we learned in ALTERNATIVE that the long-term effects of restorative interventions – certainly in intercultural settings and societies characterized by diversity – can only be understood and supported when we take into account a larger community dimension, and community support.

As sketched in this book, action research and restorative justice meet each other in the field of criminology (Walgrave *et al.*, 2013). Criminology as an emancipatory discourse on crime overarching the micro-, meso-, and macro-level becomes a field par excellence where action research can contribute in a special way in order to come to alternative, and better understandings of crime, harm and justice – understandings that relate more closely to the lifeworld of people and at the same time support the functioning and ongoing development of our democratic institutions.

Notes

1 All the movies can be found on the online platform available at: http://alternativefilms.euforumrj.org/.

2 The following and other theoretical approaches are elaborated more in depth in the 'theory' book resulting from ALTERNATIVE (Pali and Aertsen, 2018).

References

Apoio à Vitima (APAV) ed., 2016. *Implementing victim-oriented reform of the criminal justice systems in Europe*. Lisbon: APAV.

Bolivar, D., Pelikan, C. and Lemonne, A., 2015. Victims and restorative justice: towards a comparison. In: I. Vanfraechem, B. Bolivar and I. Aertsen, eds. *Victims and restorative justice*. London: Routledge, pp. 172–200.

Braithwaite, J., 1999. Restorative justice: assessing optimistic and pessimistic accounts. *Crime and Justice*, 25, 1–128.

Christie, N., 1977. Conflicts as property. *The British Journal of Criminology*, 17(1), 1–15.

Geertz, C., 1973. *The interpretation of cultures: selected essays*. New York: Basic Books.

Johnstone, G. and Van Ness, D. eds., 2007. *Handbook of restorative justice*. Cullompton: Willan Publishing.

Kremmel, K. and Pelikan, C., 2015. *Action research report on training and implementation*. Non-public deliverable 4.4 of the ALTERNATIVE project. Vienna: IRKS.

Marshall, T., 1999. *Restorative justice. An overview*. London: Home Office, Research Development and Statistics Directorate. Available at: www.homeoffice.gov.uk/rds/pdfs/occ_resjus.pdf [accessed 20 March 2006].

McCold, P. and Wachtel, T., 2002. Restorative justice theory validation. In: E. Weitekamp and H.-J. Kerner, eds. *Restorative justice. Theoretical foundations*. Cullompton: Willan Publishing, pp. 110–142.

Nelken, D., 2010. *Comparative criminal justice*. London: Sage.

Pakes, F., 2004. *Comparative criminal justice*. Cullompton: Willan Publishing.

Pali, B., 2015. *Final research report on restorative justice and security*. Deliverable 1.3 of the ALTERNATIVE project. Leuven: KU Leuven. Available at: www.alternative-project.eu/wp-content/uploads/2014/12/Deliverable-1.3-Final-research-report-on-restorative-justice-and-security.pdf [accessed 31 March 2017].

Pali, B. and Aertsen, I. eds., 2018. *Restoring Justice and Security in Intercultural Europe*. London: Routledge.

Pelikan, C., 2003. Different systems different rationales: restorative justice and criminal justice. In: F.M. Marques, ed. *Apoio à Vitima, project DIKÈ, seminar: protection and promotion of victim's rights in Europe*. Lisbon: APAV, pp. 223–229.

Pelikan, C., 2007. The place of restorative justice in society: making sense of developments in time and space. In: R. Mackay, M. Bosnjak, J. Deklerck, C. Pelikan, B. van Stokkom and M. Wright, eds. *Images of restorative justice theory*. Frankfurt/Main: Verlag für Polizeiwissenschaft, pp. 35–56.

Ragazzi, M., 2015. *Report on comparative analysis in the action research sites*. Public deliverable 8.5 of the ALTERNATIVE project. Leuven: KU Leuven. Available at:

www.alternativeproject.eu/wp-content/uploads/2014/12/Deliverable-8.5-Report-on-comparative-analysis.pdf [accessed 8 June 2016].

Rohne H., Arsovska J. and Aertsen I., 2008. Challenging restorative justice: state based conflict, mass victimisation and the changing nature of warfare. In: I. Aertsen, J. Arsovska, H. Rohne, M. Valiñas and K., Vanspauwen, eds. *Restoring justice after large-scale violent conflicts*. Kosovo, DR Congo and the Israeli-Palestinian case. Cullompton: Willan Publishing, pp. 3–45.

Szegő, D., Benedek, G. and Győrfi, E., 2015. *Evaluation and follow-up report*. Public deliverable 5.4 of the ALTERNATIVE project. Budapest: Foresee. Available at: www.alternativeproject.eu/wp-content/uploads/2014/12/Deliverable-5.4-Evaluation-and-follow-up-report_revised_201512_01.pdf [accessed 29 March 2017].

Vanfraechem, I., 2007. *Herstelgericht groepsoverleg*. Brugge: die keure.

Walgrave, L., 2008. *Restorative justice, self-interest and responsible citizenship*. Cullompton: Willan Publishing.

Walgrave L., Aertsen I., Parmentier S., Vanfraechem I. and Zinsstag E., 2013. Why restorative justice matters for criminology. *Restorative Justice: An International Journal*, 1(2), pp. 159–167.

Zehr, H., 1990. *Changing lenses: a new focus for crime and justice*. Scottdale, PA: Herald Press.

Index

Page numbers in *italics* denote tables, those in **bold** denote figures.

For Product Safety Concerns and Information please contact our EU representative GPSR@taylorandfrancis.com
Taylor & Francis Verlag GmbH, Kaufingerstraße 24, 80331 München, Germany

www.ingramcontent.com/pod-product-compliance
Ingram Content Group UK Ltd.
Pitfield, Milton Keynes, MK11 3LW, UK
UKHW011006180926
475701UK00004B/597

9780367227517